The above book should be returned on or before the date
last marked below. If a book is not wanted by another
reader the loan may be renewed for a further twenty-eight
days by bringing the book to the library to be re-dated, or
by written application, giving the above particulars, the last
date on the label, and the reader's name and address.

# Ethnic Segregation in Cities

Edited by
Ceri Peach, Vaughan Robinson and Susan Smith

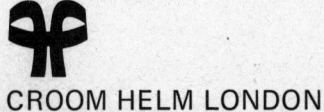
CROOM HELM LONDON

© 1981 C. Peach, V. Robinson and S. Smith
Croom Helm Ltd, 2-10 St John's Road, London SW11

British Library Cataloguing in Publication Data

Ethnic segregation in cities.
  1. Discrimination in housing
  2. Sociology, Urban
  I. Peach, Ceri
  II. Robinson, Vaughan   III. Smith, Susan
  307'.3      HD7287.5

ISBN 0-7099-2012-1

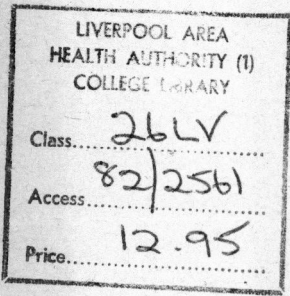
Printed and bound in Great Britain
 by Billing and Sons Limited
Guildford, London, Oxford, Worcester

# CONTENTS

# ACKNOWLEDGEMENT

The symposium from which this volume developed was held at
St Antony's College, Oxford, under the auspices of Professor Kenneth
Kirkwood, Rhodes Professor of Race Relations at the University of
Oxford. The contributors all wish to express their thanks to him for
his initiative and generosity.

# INTRODUCTION

Ceri Peach and Susan Smith

The symposium on ethnic residential segregation which gave rise to this volume marked a long overdue exchange between sociologists and geographers in the UK and USA. British academic interest in ethnicity quickened in the wake of black immigration to the country, which began in the post-war period and peaked in the early 1960s. With this interest came an avid reading of the American literature, an inter-disciplinary exchange of ideas, and a forum amongst sociologists of ethnicity interested in spatial relations, and geographers interested in race and ethnicity. The meeting was timely: sociologists now realise that ethnicity is not a spent force but a fissure displacing and perhaps replacing economic factors as a source of social differentiation; geographers demonstrate persisting patterns of segregation rather than the optimistically expected cycle of dispersal, desegregation and assimilation.

Contributions from both sides of the Atlantic illustrate the rich variety of material expected from culturally and politically diverse backgrounds. More surprising than the differences is the clear emergence of distinct and common themes. Concerns lie with assessing the conventional wisdom of public planning policies, given their unanticipated and often detrimental effects upon ethnic minority groups; with developing and applying more adequate methods to express patterns of segregation; with detailed empirical studies elucidating the roles of choice and constraint underlying these patterns; and with constructing theoretical tools able to explain the ethnic component of segregation in terms of its meaning for the groups involved.

Regrettably, during an era of 'radical' and 'critical' social science, none of the authors offers a marxist analysis or interpretation of segregation. Such a perspective is exemplified in the work of Harvey (1973), Castells (1977) and more recently Shah (1979). However, the analysis of social differentiation based on race, culture or ethnicity (or language or religion) sits uneasily in a marxist frame-work, subsumed by the fundamental societal division between capital and labour. Contributors to this volume confirm the persistence and consolidation rather than the dissolution of ethnic residential segregation. Theoretical inspiration is drawn from a tradition of Weberian sociology and a body of spatial concepts rooted in the work of Robert Park; a sound basis for empirical enquiry continues to centre on the graphic summary indices of the dissimilarist school.

## Spatial and Aspatial Analysis of Ethnic Segregation

Sociological interest in assimilation has been long standing, but it is possible to separate it into two main schools, the spatial and the aspatial. The aspatial school saw spatial segregation of groups as an incidental by-product of social attitudes and economic and social discrimination. Spatial sociologists, on the other hand, saw distributions as having a much more dynamic effect on process and not simply occurring as a result of process.

Perhaps the clearest exponent of the aspatial school is Milton Gordon. The main contribution of Gordon, from the point of view of the present discussion, was his view of the process of assimilation. Gordon defined seven stages: cultural, structural, marital, identificational, attitude receptional, behaviour receptional and civic (Gordon, 1964: 76). The critical divide in this scheme was between his cultural and his structural steps. Cultural assimilation or acculturation, according to Gordon, involved accommodating to the outward requirements of the host society, in dress, behaviour, civic law observations and so forth. Structural assimilation, on the other hand, involved social integration of the minority group with institutions, but more particularly the large-scale entry into friendship groups with the host society. If this occurred, according to Gordon, the other steps in this process of assimilation would proceed automatically (Gordon, 1964: 80–1). Although Gordon does not pay attention to the spatial aspects of assimilation, his theory of prime group membership fits in well with the arguments and findings of the spatial school.

If, instead of asking the question 'how does assimilation come about?' we were to ask 'how can a minority group preserve its ethnic identity in a foreign society?', the importance of spatial strategy becomes more apparent. The passing of cultural values from a group to an individual born into that group is through interaction between the individual and group members. Cultural values include language, accent, social values and religion. If a group is small, clustering is the most efficient spatial distribution to increase interaction. Clustering assists both the formal institutional arrangements of clubs, schools and churches, the crossing of commercial thresholds for specialised shops and the informal networks of friendships. Moreover, all of these personal and institutional networks are intertwined and mutually supportive. Dispersal would lead on the whole to increased interaction with non-ethnic group members and to a dilution of ethnic values. Patterns of dispersal and segregation and processes of assimilation or of perpetuation of ethnic identity are strongly interrelated. Gordon's view of the importance of structural assimilation is itself posited upon large-scale prime group membership. Large-scale prime group membership, in practice, requires high degrees of residential mixing. Residential mixing is a necessary, if not sufficient condition for prime group mixing.

A second pertinent question might be 'how is an ethnic minority group effectively excluded from full participation in a host society attempting to maximise and monopolise its scarce resources?'. Again the salience of spatial strategy is obvious. Enforced segregation precludes large-scale primary group mixing even if it is desired, and inhibits structural assimilation. Social and spatial exclusion are often synonymous, and both result from discrimination, institutionalised racism and an inherently disadvantaged position in the housing market.

Gordon's work can thus be seen as pivotal to the articulation of social and spatial traditions in the analysis of ethnic residential segregation. We leave the ethical question of whether segregation *per se* is a good or bad thing to the interpretations of the authors. In the following pages they disaggregate the fine balance of social, economic and political factors comprising the major dimensions of residential segregation. They attempt to demonstrate, understand and explain the role of ethnicity as a pervasive and persistent social basis for spatial separation. Such research illustrates that not only can the relationship between social and physical space be empirically verified and objectively explained, it can also be subjectively understood. In many ways an unexpected combination, the delicate interleaving of concepts derived from Park and Weber form a powerful theoretical substratum to the body of findings.

## Attacks on the Conventional Wisdom on Segregation

The first section of the book contains two outspoken attacks on the 'received wisdom' about segregation in the UK and the USA. It is a 'wisdom' inherited both by academics and planners, and neither group is excused for their unquestioning acceptance of it. Rex argues that successive British governments have attempted to deal with the problems of ethnic minorities by stealth; by treating their malaise as primarily geographical, contingent upon the physical deterioration of the country's inner cities. Rex points out that the inner-city location of coloured immigrants is a consequence of their structural position in British society. Their social and material needs are distinct from the requirements of a decaying environment, notwithstanding that the inner city *is* increasingly synonymous with residential concentrations of Asians and West Indians. In fact, Rex insists that, given the survival of the ethnic communities in spite of the tribulations of migration and the injustices of discrimination, dispersal would now be against their political interests. Continuing segregation *is* in the interests of Black Britons, and this should be facilitated without impinging upon their quality of life.

Kantrowitz's attack has a somewhat different thrust. His graphic awakening to continuing patterns of segregation in the United States leads him to argue that it is a fact of American life, and a fact which has been denied by the sociological establishment. He charts the persistence of European ethnic enclaves which, like the black ghettos, cannot be regarded as temporary or vestigial. Assimilation is not inevitable, but segregation need be neither bad nor lower class. Segregation can just 'be' — a spatial expression of collective identity.

**Methods and Applications**

Not all contributors to this volume adopt the polemic of Rex and Kantrowitz, or share their controversial positions. The second section of the collection is concerned primarily with the measurement of segregation, but even this is not the uncontroversial and objective technical subject that it may seem. In the late 1960s and during the 1970s, the 'index war' over the most appropriate measures of spatial segregation reappeared. The earlier exchange, apparently resolved first by Duncan and Duncan (1955) and then by Taeuber and Taeuber (1965) broke out in a new form in a paper by Cortese, Falk and Cohen (1976). Since the current war rages round the interpretation of the index of dissimilarity (ID), which is one of the central analytical tools of the literature, it is of particular interest to include in this collection the contribution of Stanley Lieberson. Lieberson is one of the most influential users of ID, but he now demonstrates the practical value of complementing it with a second index whose strengths comprise the very weaknesses ID was designed to overcome. The resulting ability to measure spatial isolation as well as spatial dissimilarity adds significantly to our repertoire of techniques describing and summarising segregation. More than this, Lieberson broadens our interpretative horizons alerting us to the ways in which researchers, apparently mesmerised by the properties of ID, have hitherto been limited.

Lieberson's paper thus marks an important development in the literature. To date, most argument has centred on manipulating ID, questioning whether it should be measured from a random base or from a zero (even) base, whether the finest possible areal scale should be used, and so on. Here, Lieberson looks less at the mathematical qualities of the indices, and more at their conceptual value, in the hope of capturing theoretically (as well as empirically) more sophisticated interpretations of spatial patterns. Observing that measures of dissimilarity represent situations which may appear very different to each of the groups concerned, Lieberson seizes upon one aspect of segregation which ID disregards, its asymmetry, and adopts a measure which highlights these non-reciprocal qualities.

The chapter by Taeuber, Wilson, James and Taeuber uses the same approach, complementing one measure with several others. For more than a decade following the 1954 US Supreme Court desegregation decision, public (state) schooling in the large cities of both North and South remained racially segregated. During the late 1960s and early 1970s, the federal government intervened in many school districts to alter the long-standing linkages among race, residence and school assignment. Because the intervention proceeded on a case-by-case basis, there was considerable variation in the timing and scope of desegregation actions. The study by Taeuber and his co-workers describes school segregation trends, 1968 to 1976, in the 87 districts which had more than 10,000 black students in the autumn of 1968. These large districts contained more than half of the US black students. Some of these districts experienced violent controversy over desegregation, some desegregated relatively peacefully and completely, and some have not yet taken any effective desegregation actions.

Three measures of desegregation are used to describe redistributive aspects of the desegregation experience: the index of dissimilarity, the exposure of blacks to whites, and the exposure of whites to blacks. In 1968, none of these districts was substantially desegregated; in 1976, they varied over the full range of segregation indices. The amount of desegregation between 1968 and 1976 was not related to the level of segregation in 1968, but was loosely related to the numbers and proportions of black students. In particular, none of the districts with very large numbers of black students underwent extensive desegregation.

The percentage black among public school pupils increased in most of these districts. The measures of exposures of black pupils to white and of white pupils to black also increased. The changing racial composition of district enrolment typically did not vitiate the intended racial desegregation of the public schools.

## Choice and Constraint

The third section of this book presents a series of empirical studies which attempt to disentangle the spatial effects of the positive factors encouraging ethnic groups to maintain their clustering and the negative forces that prevent dispersal. This task is compounded by the host of economic and demographic factors which may underlie segregation, and also operate relatively independently of ethnicity. Thus if a group is more concentrated into the working class than is the rest of the population, its limited disposable income is likely to reduce the amount of housing choice. If ethnic groups are disproportionately working class, the housing available to them will be disproportionately restricted and some degree of segregation will be inevitable. Similarly, if the families of ethnic minorities tend to be larger than average, the distribution of housing adaptable to large families is likely to influence their spatial distribution. As dwellings which may be so adapted are not randomly distributed, this feature alone will restrict the extent of ethnic dispersal. Moreover, just as a low economic position may not be independent of host society attitudes, any apparently positive desires to maintain ethnic identity may not be independent of host society hostility. Thus while it is appropriate and helpful to separate the positive and negative aspects of segregation for analytical purposes, it is more conceptually satisfying to envisage a state of tension between the two, wherein ethnicity is more or less likely to be adopted as a principle of social

organisation and spatial behaviour, depending on the balance dictated
by a much wider range of variables. There are four essays in this
section which all bear on the problem of the relative contribution of
ethnic cohesion and host group rejection to patterns of segregation.


## American Experience

Peter Jackson develops a paradox first noted by Taeuber and Taeuber
(1964) and Kantrowitz (1969). Puerto Ricans arrived later than blacks
in US cities, they are also of lower economic status, have fewer
educational attainments and experience greater difficulties with the
English language, which is not their mother tongue. The discovery
that Puerto Ricans are less segregated than blacks raised the
suggestion that they must therefore be more racially acceptable to
whites. Jackson however shows that it is the higher-income and
better-educated Puerto Ricans who live in census tracts where they
are least concentrated as a group; and that of all tracts containing
Puerto Ricans, it is only in those with the highest mean incomes and
best education that they are residentially dispersed. Those Puerto
Ricans with most choice clearly choose to live in non-Puerto Rican
areas, but increasingly, the bulk of the population reside with American
blacks. It seems likely that Puerto Ricans are themselves being 'pulled
apart' along racial lines. Black Puerto Ricans are becoming more
concentrated into black areas while rich (presumably white) Puerto
Ricans are breaking away from them.

The dynamics of such processes, however, remain speculative.
While Gottmann (1961) found that 'The Puerto Ricans, white and
black together, gain access to housing in deteriorating tenements
that are still closed to American Negroes' (1961: 705), reflecting
Wakefield's (1959) assertion that Puerto Ricans broke the colour
barrier in housing and automatically enabled blacks to cross the line
afterwards, Rosenburg (1974) suggests the opposite, that
Puerto Ricans move into areas first opened up by blacks. It is
possible that the 'elite' of both groups reflect most accurately the
trade off between choice and constraint factors influencing
residential location. Puerto Ricans face less discrimination; American
blacks are better equipped to overcome economic constraints. The
latter group are the focus of the second paper in this section.

Harold Rose examines the housing preferences of part of the elite
black group in order to see whether their preference is for white,

black or mixed areas. Studies in this field have usually been carried out by census manipulation such as indirect standardisation. This attempt is by the more difficult but more direct use of a questionnaire, although its selective response means that findings are suggestive rather than conclusive.

Rose illuminates some facets of a black professional class. A pioneer group, willing to participate in non-white housing markets, they nevertheless prefer (or feel restricted to) mixed rather than dominantly white or black neighbourhoods. Their attitudes thus seem likely to discourage any attempts to pioneer 'all white' areas. The element of choice accorded to this relatively high-income group is apparently limited when dispersal beyond ethnically mixed areas is envisaged.

## British Experience

A more complex picture emerges from the British studies, where segregation within the Asian community along national, religious and linguistic lines highlights the importance of choice as a factor in ethnic clustering. Robinson demonstrates that although the Asians in his northern textiles town are highly segregated from the white British population, very high levels of intra-Asian segregation also exist. Gujerati speakers are separated from Punjabi speakers, Muslims from Hindus, East African Asians from those born on the subcontinent. This pattern was perpetuated even when council housing became widely available. In Blackburn, neither municipalis-ation nor suburbanisation was indicative of desegregation. Moreover, records of council house offers and preferred estates prove this to be a voluntary outcome, not a result of discriminatory allocation procedure. Municipalisation brought an extension of ethnic territory reflecting a positive desire to remain spatially encapsulated, and reasserting the strength and persistence of voluntary clustering.

Aldrich, Cater, Jones and McEvoy adopt a different approach to the economic encapsulation of Asians. They argue that restricted opportunities for economic advance led to the development of small-scale entrepreneurial activity in the form of shopkeeping. Such restrictions are seen as particularly significant given the possibility that business success may act as a catalyst for social advance. 'At one extreme, groups such as the Chinese and Jews are identified with commercial success and social mobility, while at the other pole, the under-development of black business is associated with continuing social and economic disadvantage' (Chapter 8). Paradoxically, the business 'success' of Asians in Britain now has to lie in shielding themselves from economic equality. An economically segregated commercial sector is able to serve a socially segregated population, but this precludes integration or desegregation in either sphere. Apparent choice is in fact a constraint dictated by economic and social marginality.

It is likely, however, that the role of the Asian shopkeeper varies among the different ethnic subgroups. There is, for example, a considerable difference between Punjabi Muslims from Pakistan and Gujerati Hindus from East Africa. The role adopted by Asian shopkeepers in Bradford may have more to do with the Punjabi peasant origin of the bulk of the Asian immigrant population there than with a universal Asian attempt to avoid catering for the native British population. East African Asians in other cities seem economically more integrated into the total market, rather than restricted to the small scale and to their own ethnic group. In fact, Ward and Sims (Chapter 10) go as far as to suggest that Asians have a 'Jewish' future in Britain while West Indians face an 'Irish' future.


**Social and Physical Distance**

The inspiration for the view that connects the social processes of interaction and assimilation to spatial patterns of ethnic distributions stems directly from the work of R.E. Park. Park, in the central paper which enunciates this relationship, saw sociology as having ultimately the structure of the classical physical sciences.

> Reduce all social relations to relations of space and it would be possible to apply to human relations the fundamental logic of the physical sciences. Social phenomena would be reduced to the elementary movement of individuals, just as physical phenomena, chemical action, and the qualities of matter, heat, sound and electricity are reduced to the elementary movements of molecules and atoms. (Park, 1926 (1975: 27) )

Retrospectively, it may seem that he overstated his case (Duncan and Duncan, 1955, say as much), and more recently, the contribution of his more subjective interactionist sociology to the humanistic side of geography has received elaboration (Entrikin, 1980; Jackson and Smith, 1981). Yet the central importance of his formalist view is seen in the fact that it continues to generate fruitful hypotheses for investigation half a century later.

Peach's essay extends the logic of Park's conception. If social inter-action is related to spatial intermixture, then it follows that little interaction between highly segregated groups is likely. From this theoretical starting-point, Peach re-examines the concept of the Triple Melting Pot which claimed, among other things, high inter-marriage rates between the 'Catholic' nationalities: Irish, Italians and Poles. Since the Irish, Italians and Poles were quite highly segregated from one another in most US cities, Peach re-examined the postulated intermarriage rates and found them to be spurious. He goes on to demonstrate the ultimate triumph of Park's view, proving that rates of segregation between ethnic groups *can* predict the degrees to which these groups intermarry.

With Park as touchstone, an explanation of the significance of ethnic residential segregation depends first on confirming that spatial pattern is significant in terms of social interaction; it depends secondly on distinguishing the ethnic component of segregation from other contributory factors. The two remaining papers address this question, drawing inspiration from Max Weber's sociology in an attempt to make explicit the role of social structure as it mediates between interaction and segregation.

A frequently recurring question in the segregation literature centres on the extent to which residential segregation can be explained by economic class rather than by race. The class component is commonly controlled for by using techniques of income standardis-ation (Taeuber and Taeuber, 1965; Taeuber, 1968; but see Kantrowitz, 1973). Weberian sociology, however, accords other factors equal weight with economic class as dimensions of social stratification. Their spatial expression is equally significant. Classes, status groups and parties comprise the main axes by which power is distributed and life chances dispensed.

Two papers illustrate the relevance of these major sources of stratification to the spatial pattern of ethnic residential segregation. First, Ward and Sims apply Weber's model of social stratification to the housing market and interpret segregation as a spatial by-product of social relationships amongst status groups and property (housing) classes. Secondly, Boal focuses on space as a resource, conserved as a group attribute in its own right. He employs Parkin's (1979) extension of Weber's social closure model, and as his work is set in Northern Ireland, it leads naturally on to a consideration of 'parties', a third structural consequence of the differential distribution of power. Together, therefore, these two papers evince that the spatial structure of social relationships is crucially mediated by a group's position with respect to class, status group and party.

Ward and Sims investigate the significance of class and status components of ethnic residential segregation. Using the case study of Birmingham they combine two theoretical models: a market model, which is applied to post-war changes in the housing market in so far as they affect access to different types and tenures of housing; and a status model, which is employed to explain white suburbanisation as a response to the deteriorating life-style and declining status associated with inner-city residence. However, they recognise that ethnicity does not slip easily into these class or status groupings. Weber himself saw ethnic groups as the most enigmatic source of social action, likening them to classes in that they lend a propensity for communal social action (a propensity which need not be realised), and to status groups in the sense that 'ethnic honour' is analogous to that social honour claimed generally by status groups seeking to maximise their symbolic rewards.

In an attempt to assess the extent to which patterns of ethnic segregation reflect the class and status positions of ethnic minorities rather than structures negotiated by ethnicity itself, Ward and Sims build a racial discrimination factor into the two models. Market discrimination affects locational options by forcing blacks to pay more than whites for equivalent housing. Status discrimination imposes similar restrictions when white 'gatekeepers' withhold property from blacks, even against their own economic interests.

Ward and Sims' conclusion, that ethnic segregation would occur even without discrimination, that it is contingent largely upon market processes and a quest for the status implied in suburban life-styles, is in effect an attempt to provide a theoretically more sophisticated explanation of the *constraints* on desegregation. Their chapter does not elucidate a corresponding element of *choice* exercised by the segregated minorities. But Boal's chapter confirms that this does exist. While powerful groups preserve their status by seeking success in suburban life-styles, the less powerful may also engage in a search for security which may prompt solidarity culminating in 'closure by usurpation'. Mounted in response to group experience of exclusion, usurpationary closure is the 'upwards' use of power in an attempt to eat into resources already claimed by more powerful strata (Parkin, 1979: 74—88).

Boal identifies space itself as one of these resources, providing a territorial base from which to claim political power. He explains this theoretically in terms of the two main forms of closure, exclusion and usurpation, which together provide the means by which communities of any standing can lay claim to, or defend, territory. The main requirement to effect such a strategy is the availability of an appropriate social or physical group attribute by which to define, and therefore include or exclude members. It is not surprising that race and ethnicity are common convenient devices for the monopolistic protection of interests through closure. Neither is it unexpected that Northern Ireland provides an appropriate context in which to demonstrate that segregation is not only underlain by claims to status and market position, but also by the claims on territory required to effect political action. 'Party', like status and class, is integral to the nature of ethnic residential segregation.

By focusing upon residentially mixed areas of Belfast, Boal is able to examine claims on territory effected both by exclusion and by usurpation. Changing residential patterns among Catholics and Protestants reveal the deliberate choice of closed rather than open relationships: groups perceive that their interests, in terms of security, psychological and material satisfaction, are better served by adopting monopolistic tactics than by openly negotiating rewards. In these transitional areas, where large Catholic or Protestant majorities are found, the dominant group appears able to exclude the minority. However, some areas have small and declining Protestant majorities, providing evidence of usurpation by Catholic groups extending their ethnic territory.

Interestingly, the mixed areas which are not transitional are mainly occupied by the middle classes. They are mixed partly because other means are available by which to effect social distance, and partly because resource scarcity among the working classes makes conflict between them more marked than among the more affluent middle classes. This requires some eplanation.

It would be expected when scarce resources are unequally distributed between different income groups, that conflict based on a lack of resources would occur between high- and lower-income groups; between middle and working classes rather than among the working class themselves. Explanations for the relative absence of this conflict have been both general, in terms of working-class parochialism and 'false consciousness', and specific to Northern Ireland, for instance, Boserup's suggestion that a period of transition between indigenous and external monopoly capitalism explains the disruption of a normal cleavage between bourgeoisie and proletariat (Boserup, 1972). Parkin, however, introduces the notion of dual closure to explain exploitation within as well as against the working class. It is based on the notion that exclusion within the working class is most often directed at socially visible targets.

> It probably always requires considerably less expenditure of political energy to effect exclusionary closure against a visible and vulnerable minority group than to mount collective usurpatory action against a powerful dominant class.
> (Parkin, 1979: 95)

At the local level, members of the different ethnic groups are easy to detect. At this level roles are easily defined and territorial claims unambiguously made by the excluding majorities or the usurping minorities. In Ireland, at a larger scale, roles become more ambiguous. Protestants, the majority in Northern Ireland, are the minority in the island as a whole. The territory over which struggles occur consequently varies perceptually between religious groups. Perhaps this ambiguity explains why neighbourhoods in Belfast portray such clear geographical examples of social closure as a response to spatial stress. Where social, economic and political positions nationally are unclear, groups can at least assert their ethnicity in the immediate environment.

In conclusion we would stress the stubborn persistence of ethnic residential segregation, despite the cycle of dispersal and assimilation traditionally expected by academics and policy-makers alike. The city continues as it was envisaged by the Chicago ecologists, a pattern of territoriality maintained by social interaction. Accommodation, not assimilation, is the process by which rewards and life chances are secured. But conflict is latent in accommodation. The 1960s race riots in the USA, recent disturbances in Brick Lane and Southall, London, unrest in St Paul's, Bristol, riots in Brixton and violence in Miami, Florida, illustrate some of the consequences of failed negotiations. Official recognition of the existence, persistence, legitimacy and quality of ethnic residential segregation is a first step towards accommodation based on equality. In this volume an international group of academics make their contribution to an understanding of the issues involved.

## Bibliography

Boserup, A. (1972) 'Contradictions and Struggles in Northern Ireland', *Socialist Register*, Merlin Press, London

Castells, M. (1977) *The Urban Question*, Edward Arnold, London

Cortese, C.F., Falk, R.F. and Cohen, J.K. (1976) 'Further Consideration on the Methodological Analysis of Segregation Indices', *American Sociological Review*, 41, 889–93

Duncan, O.D. and Duncan, B. (1955) 'A Methodological Analysis of Segregation Indexes', *American Sociological Review*, 20, 210–17

Entrikin, J.N. (1980) 'Robert Park's Human Ecology and Human Geography', *Annals, Association of American Geographers*, 66, 615–32

Gordon, M.M. (1964) *Assimilation in American Life*, Oxford University Press, New York

Gottmann, J. (1961) *Megalopolis: the Urbanized Northeastern Seaboard of the United States*, Twentieth Century Fund, New York

Harvey, D. (1973) *Social Justice and the City*, Edward Arnold, London

Jackson, P. and Smith, S.J. (eds.) (1981) *Social Interaction and Ethnic Segregation*, Academic Press, London

Kantrowitz, N. (1969) 'Ethnic and Racial Segregation in the New York Metropolis', *American Journal of Sociology*, 74, 685–95

Kantrowitz, N. (1973) *Ethnic Residential Segregation in the New York Metropolis: Residential Patterns Among White Ethnic Groups, Blacks and Puerto Ricans*, Praeger, New York

Park, R.E. (1926) 'The Urban Community as a Spatial Pattern and a Moral Order', in E.W. Burgess (ed.), *The Urban Community*, re-printed in Ceri Peach (ed.) (1975), *Urban Social Segregation*, Longman, London

Parkin, F. (1979) *Marxism and Class Theory: a Bourgeois Critique*, Tavistock, London

Rosenburg, T.J. (1974) *Residence, Employment and Mobility of Puerto Ricans in New York City*, Research Paper Number 151, Department of Geography, Chicago

Shah, S. (1979) 'Aspects of the Geographic Analysis of Asian Immigrants in London', Unpublished D.Phil. Thesis, Oxford University

Taeuber, K. (1968) 'The Effect of Income Distribution on Racial Residential Segregation', *Urban Affairs Quarterly*, 4, 5–14

Taeuber, K. and Taeuber, A. (1964) 'The Negro as an Immigrant Group', *American Journal of Sociology*, 69, 374–82

Taeuber, K. and Taeuber, A. (1965) *Negroes in Cities: Residential Segregation and Neighborhood Change*, Aldine, Chicago

Wakefield, D. (1959) *Island in the City: the World of Spanish Harlem*, Houghton-Mifflin, Boston, Massachusetts

# PART ONE:

# ATTACKS ON THE CONVENTIONAL WISDOM ON SEGREGATION

# 1 URBAN SEGREGATION AND INNER CITY POLICY IN GREAT BRITAIN

John Rex

It is very widely believed, and it is an underlying assumption of much
government policy in Britain, that many of the problems of ethnic
minorities arise from the fact that they live in the inner city and that
they share these problems with all of the inner-city poor. Consequently
it is argued that the solution of many of the problems of the ethnic
minorities lies in an assault on the inner-city problem as such, and that
this relatively popular political policy will enable government to deal
with ethnic problems in a low profile way. This paper argues the
opposite view. The problems of ethnic minorities do not arise solely
from their location in the inner city. They arise partly from the
simple fact that the minorities are relatively new immigrants and
much more from racial discrimination. The consequence of these
processes affecting the minorities is that they are located in the inner
city. In coming to be located there, they find their own problems
exacerbated, while at the same time contributing a new ethnic
dimension to the inner-city problem. This paper also argues, however,
that it is no answer to the segregation which has occurred merely to
'thin out' the immigrant minorities under a slogan or policy of
'getting a better racial mix'. Indeed the danger is that policies of
desegregation and dispersal might well be the principal threat to
immigrant minority communities today.

## Immigration, Lodging-houses and the Twilight Zone

Racial discrimination against immigrant minorities meant, in the
fifties and early sixties, that they were denied access to the main
forms of housing available to the native-born middle and working
classes, i.e. to mortgages, which would make them owner-occupiers,
and to council tenancies. Although in the immediate post-war period
local councils made special provision for the housing of key workers
needed by local industry, it was thought normal to deny immigrants
access to the list for periods of five years or more when a large part
of those immigrants were more clearly visible because of their skin

25

colour. This bar against immigrants involved *de facto* or indirect discrimination and forced them into the private housing market. Entry into this market, however, was controlled by the building societies and prior to the 1968 Act there was nothing to stop building societies discriminating in overt as well as covert ways against coloured peoples. They were the gatekeepers to legitimate private housing and they effectively closed the gates.

It must quickly be added that the operation of this system of largely indirect, though systematic, discrimination in the public sector, and direct discrimination in the private sector, was not something which was proven through direct challenges to its operation, nor that *all* coloured immigrants were housed as they were, not out of choice, but because of discrimination. In the first place, once a discriminatory system operates, many potential applicants will take it for granted that it is not worth applying. Secondly, once discrimination produces residential concentrations of minorities, other members of those minorities will actually prefer to live in the concentrated areas. Thirdly, as Dahya (1973) has pointed out, there will be some who, for ethnic reasons, or because of their own migration strategy, actually prefer not to seek housing through the two main legitimate channels. None of these considerations should lead one to conclude, however, that discrimination does not play an important part in ethnic concentration.

Some of the problems of ethnic minorities do not, of course, arise either from discrimination or from ethnic choice, but from the special needs of immigrants. A council house or a privately-owned semi are obviously not useful forms of housing for male working-class immigrants establishing a base before they bring in their families. But once the immigrant phase is past — and it is now past for most West Indian and Asian immigrants in Britain — these special immigrant conditions will not be the prime source of their problems. The problem for them will be that 'immigrant' becomes a permanent label and status which assigns them primarily to inferior housing conditions.

In my study with Robert Moore (Rex and Moore, 1967) of Sparkbrook, Birmingham, in the period from 1963 to 1965, I laid special emphasis upon one particular type of inferior housing, namely the multi-occupied lodging-house. It seemed to me then that what was happening in the larger cities was that, since the criteria of selection for council tenancies and mortgages were severely restrictive, there was bound to be a secondary illegitimate housing system if many thousands of people were not to be made homeless. In fact, in so far as the problem of homelessness affected working-class families with children, something was provided by the authorities, viz. hostels, halfway houses and accommodation in council-owned slums awaiting demolition. Such provision, however, was itself selective, and it was left to private enterprise to provide for the remainder of the population.

This private enterprise was not the respectable and legitimate private enterprise which worked within a framework set by public health law and more generally by *petit bourgeois* standards of respectability. It was the private enterprise of men who were often poor themselves and who had very special housing needs. I suggested that Birmingham relied for this ultimate safety net on the enterprise of immigrant men who needed large houses to house themselves and such of their kin as arrived from time to time, and that, in order to pay off their bank loans, they let off surplus rooms to those other people who had nowhere else to turn. The lodging-houses therefore fulfilled a very necessary social function, but they concentrated so many problems and problem people in particular places that those places became known as 'twilight zones', a term which came to refer not merely to the age of buildings, but to areas of 'violence and shame and despair'. While the city relied on such a system, it could not admit to doing so, and it set about vigorously punishing the landlords who set it up.

Moore and I were criticised for making so much of the lodging-house. Many immigrants, we were told, were in owner-occupied houses and were much better off than we had suggested. There is some basis for such criticism. The multi-occupied lodging-house was particularly important in 1963—5 because there were so many single men flooding in to the country to get in before the gates were closed by immigration control. Our more fundamental point, however, was not to point to the lodging-house as such, but to suggest an approach to a sociological theory of urban dynamics which we somewhat grandiosely referred to as the theory of housing classes (Rex and Moore, 1967; Rex, 1973; Rex and Tomlinson, 1979).

What this 'theory' suggests is the following:

1. In any city housing of different kinds will be regarded as having differing degrees of desirability in the main value system, although, of course, minorities will profess deviant values.
2. Access to desirable housing depends either upon market positions

or positions in relation to a politically governed bureaucratic system of allocation.
3. Max Weber's equation, class-situation = market situation (Weber, 1968: 926) has some application here, and an individual's position in the market or in relation to the allocative system might be thought of as placing him in a particular housing class.
4. 'Classes-in-themselves' become 'classes for themselves' in the sphere of housing as elsewhere. Privileged groups particularly organise and unite to exert a monopolistic closure over the kinds of access which they command (Parkin, 1979). There is therefore a tendency for urban politics to be based upon housing parties with different interests in the housing allocation system.

If we take as a starting point something like the oversimplified Sparkbrook model of 1965, it will be noted that there we have referred to four basic housing-class situations; those of:

1. the owner-occupier of a single-family-occupied mortgaged house;
2. the council tenant of a purpose-built council house;
3. the potentially homeless, placed in hostels or patched housing awaiting demolition;
4. the owners of multi-occupied lodging-houses and their tenants.

**Intermediate Solutions; Housing Action Areas, General Improvement Areas and Council Mortgages**

With this system operating in the mid-sixties, city councils faced a dilemma. On the one hand they could not relieve the condition of the lodging-house population by giving them council tenancies. On the other hand, they could not allow the continuation of the obviously scandalous conditions in the twilight zones. Intermediate solutions had thus to be invented and these intermediate solutions brought into being new types of housing and new housing classes.

The new types of housing which became important were not, of course, newly-built houses. What happened after 1967 was that government policies towards certain kinds of housing changed. Fitted into the housing system now was a new category of house, which could neither be allowed to stand as it was nor be scheduled for demolition. Regardless of ownership the government and local authorities set out to persuade, cajole and compel people to improve their houses up to a certain standard. Large parts of the city became, first, General Improvement Areas, and then Housing Action Areas.

The decision not to carry out a second wave of slum-clearance in the late sixties was epoch-making from a purely housing point of view (HMSO, 1966; 1968). Up till that time, government and local authorities alike had faced the legacy of nineteenth-century building and had looked forward to a continuous programme or urban renewal. Now the intention was to try to patch and improve rather than to destroy and replace. It quickly became apparent, however, that the General Improvement Areas and Housing Action Areas were to include houses so poor and squalid that, however strong the intention to improve them, they would still be the most squalid in the city.

The decision not to demolish these houses was not, however, taken on grounds of housing alone. It was obvious to government and local authorities alike that, if the occupants of this type of housing, which had been left out of the slum-clearance programme, were to be rehoused, there would be an enormous influx of, amongst others, 'coloured' immigrants on to council estates. Something else had to be done. Improvement was the second-best answer.

Housing Action Areas were a refinement of the improvement system (HMSO, 1973). They enabled the local authorities to keep their options open, to discriminate between one house and another *within* the areas of improvement, offering to demolish some and rehouse their tenants, while suggesting only improvement for others. *Prime facie* this could have been a system which enabled the councils to offer rehousing to those it favoured (especially the native British) and to refuse it to others. We do not know to what extent this was true because there has been little monitoring of the Housing Action Programme. It was less true than it might have been, however, because many of the native white owners and tenants of these areas resisted rehousing even though they disliked living with immigrant neighbours.

The General Improvement Areas and Housing Action Areas were not, however, merely areas which had a higher proportion of immigrant residents than did the slums at the outset. New policies were pursued which *directed* immigrant families into them. The most important of these were council mortgage schemes and conversion by housing associations.

The building societies had realised early on that there would be risks in lending on property in the inner areas. The local authorities on the other hand had a problem in the existence of large numbers of potential applicants for rehousing whose demand could not be met. The solution therefore lay in the councils lending on mortgages of property in the improvement areas and allowing immigrants more chance of getting these mortgages than they would a council tenancy. Banks too would make short-term loans on property and to people who would be excluded from building society lending.

Not all those excluded from the council lists could, however, afford council mortgages. These others would, in the early sixties, have obtained rooms in privately-owned lodging-houses. What happened now, however, was that, as the old lodging-houses were squeezed by the public health departments, so housing associations bought up and converted properties. They now became not inconsiderable landlords of rented property and landlords with different criteria for obtaining tenancies than those operated by the city councils. The housing associations operated particularly in the improvement and Housing Action Areas and were quite amenable to housing immigrants.

## An Emergent Housing Class

If one looks at the housing conditions of West Indian and Asian descended minorities in Britain today, it is striking that a higher proportion of them than of the population at large are owner-occupiers. This does not mean that they are privileged. As David Smith (1977a; 1977b) and Valerie Karn (1977) have pointed out, they are owners, but owners of the worst housing in the city. If, moreover, one looks at sources of housing finance, one finds that bank loans and private borrowing amongst Asians and council mortgages amongst West Indians are as important as building society loans. Amongst West Indians there is also a significant proportion who are housing association tenants.

A new type of housing and a new housing class have thus emerged, namely the housing of the improvement areas and its occupants. One might perhaps differentiate here between owner-occupiers and tenants, but, since the owners are dependent upon public mortgages and subject to considerable interference by the authorities, and the tenants are relatively protected by the conditions under which housing associations operate, the difference may not be great.

The West Indian or Asian descended occupant of a house in the improvement areas is trapped there. Once he gets a house of his own or a housing association tenancy, he comes off the council's list. Moreover it may not be easy for him to sell his property. Immigration control has meant that the improvement areas (often perceived as the immigrant areas) are actually areas of low inward immigration. Together with white flight this means that the sole possible buyers of houses will be newly-formed immigrant households. There seems to be a recipe for ghetto-formation here.

For the moment, however, this process is not complete. We know that whites will not buy into these areas, and that young white couples are leaving them. But the old residents stay on, stubbornly refusing all other options and suggesting that, rather than rehousing them, the council should consider moving out the blacks. There is some chance, as we shall see, that they may not be wholly unsuccessful.

If one looks at a typical group of inner-city wards such as those which we studied in Handsworth (Rex and Tomlinson, 1979), one finds the following elements in its population. First, there is a white population in which the majority of adults are over sixty and who have the natural desire for peace and quiet of a population of that kind. Secondly, there are the West Indians who are much younger, and whose children, and particularly the young males, are evident through their ebullient presence on the streets. Thirdly, there are the relatively withdrawn Asians, not so obvious through their street life, but noted for their frugal living and for their distinctive and alien shops. The difference in the age structure between the first of these groups and the other two is such that population ratios of 51 per cent, 22 per cent and 27 per cent respectively in one ward in 1971 ensures that today the schools, especially at primary level, are over 90 per cent immigrant.

The term used to describe the old lodging-house areas like Sparkbrook was 'twilight zone' and it referred to a kind of moral twilight. The term used to describe the improvement areas and their problems is 'inner city'. This term is ambiguous in its reference. Of course it refers to a particular physical fact (not actually, it should be noted, the literal inner city, but rather the secondary ring containing the worst housing, after the slum-clearance programme was complete) but it also refers to a *social* fact of the coexistence of white and black and of two quite disparate immigrant communities, the Asian and the West Indian.

As will be shown later, the term inner city has other meanings in discussions of social policy, but it also has a very specific, highly-charged emotional meaning which connects it with the sorts of areas that have been discussed. This highly charged meaning raises the expectation amongst whites, not merely that the physical fabric will be improved, but that the racial tensions arising from the co-existence of incompatible populations should somehow or other be made to disappear.

## The Inner City Ideology and Policy

Unfortunately this relatively simple set of inner-city problems, defined as the problems of the improvement areas and their populations, is now swallowed up in an inner-city ideology which has its roots in America but which has also become the focus of larger political anxieties in this country.

### British Perspectives on the US Situation

Middle-aged academics who read social science literature about the United States cannot but be struck by the change of emphasis in writing about cities between 1950 and 1970. New York in 1950 still appears as an exciting cosmopolitan metropolis, a centre of capitalism, but also a centre of high culture and vigorous urban social life. Chicago, it is true, is famous for its gangsters, but it too is an exciting place, where Park and Burgess's zone of transition is still thought of with sentimental affection. By the early sixties, however, the image has changed. There has been a flight from the central city by the respectable white middle classes, that central city is blighted and, as the black ghetto decays further, its young unemployed population expand into the city and terrorise it. Poverty programmes, civil rights programmes and inner-city programmes thus become the staple stuff of urban politics.

It is not surprising that, as British cities continued to decay, as their respectable middle classes fled the city, and as race became a main political theme, these ideas should have been taken over in Britain. Quite commonly it was suggested that American experience provided Britons with a warning and that policies should be developed here which would arrest the drift towards urban deterioration and racial conflict more effectively than had been done in America.

## British Policy Perception

These perceptions affected the thinking of many different government departments which addressed themselves to the problems of the disadvantaged poor. The Plowden Report on the worst of the schools (HMSO, 1967) led to the setting up of 'Educational Priority Areas'; the Ministry of Housing set up General Improvement Areas; the Urban Programme offered special government aid to areas with high indices of pathology; Community Development Programmes were set up to assess the needs of inner-city populations not yet provided for; and, in the Ministry of Health and Social Security, the Minister, inspired by Moynihan in the United States, called for an investigation into the possibility of a cumulative cycle of pathology in families.

Probably none of these moves in social policy, however, were as determined and influential as the set of studies initiated by Peter Walker as Secretary for the Environment leading to the White Paper *Policy for the Inner Cities* (HMSO, 1977a), eventually introduced by his successor, Peter Shore. It was very widely thought that the policies announced in the White Paper would deal not merely with problems of the environment, but with all the problems which were part and parcel of an increasing urban despair, including the problem of racial conflict.

## British Policy Reality

If one looks at the White Paper, however, one finds something rather different and more specific. The diagnosis is that there is an environmental problem and a problem of unemployment and poverty. The cure is to be found in united action in partnership by central government and local authorities to provide resources and a will to action, which will bring both prosperity and environmental improvement to the inner city. What is envisaged is the transfer of the kinds of resources which produced the New Towns to the inner city, the creation of more modern jobs and offices there in place of derelict industrial sites, and the improvement or replacement of the existing housing stock so that those who work in the new industries will have a worthy community life. Along with the formal mechanisms for achieving these goals, the Inner City Partnerships are also to be empowered to help voluntary organisations which are responding to the needs of the population in continuation of the work of the Urban Programme.

What will be the effects of this policy in general and what specific effects will it have upon either segregation or the severity of racial conflict? It is widely believed that the policy is about the problems of and the problems presented by West Indian and Asian immigrants and their children and the Minister, Peter Shore, reinforced this impression in the presentation of his White Paper. If one looks at the content, however, one gets a very different impression.

There are only two implicit references to the condition of the immigrant population in the White Paper. The first is almost wholly negative, pointing out that the White Paper deals with the problems of the disadvantaged inner-city poor and that while the policy proposed might incidentally help black people, the problem of racial discrimination is a matter for the Commission for Racial Equality (HMSO, 1977a, para. 19). The second refers to the unskilled, semi-skilled and retired who at present live in the inner city and of them it suggests that they would do better to move to the periphery (HMSO, 1977a, paras. 66—9).

By way of comment on these points, it should be noted that, so long as there is racial discrimination, those members of the disadvantaged inner-city poor who are also black might well ask whether it is certain that aid designed, say, to help the housing of the inner-city poor as such, will really come their way. The second point made in the set of paragraphs about population movements prompts the question of whether it is not actually the intention of the White Paper that black people, many of whom are at present underemployed in unskilled and semi-skilled jobs, should be excluded from any benefits arising from industrial and environmental employment. Against this, the charitable activities of the Partnerships through their Urban Programmes can do very little to alter the position of the minorities.

## Workplace and Residence

One point which the White Paper does emphasise is the close relationship between environmental deterioration and social problems on the one hand, and employment on the other. This has led many social scientists and politicians of left-wing persuasion to welcome it. What is not often recognised, however, is that one can hold that the best way to deal with poverty and social problems is to provide full employment in a prosperous economy, without holding that that employment should be provided on the worker's domestic doorstep. Moreover, so far as the ethnic minorities are concerned, their problems do not necessarily arise primarily from employment and, in so far as they do so, very largely arise from discrimination in employment, which this White Paper says is not its concern.

There is, in my view, very little relationship between the availability of employment in the immediate vicinity and poverty, either for the population at large or for the ethnic minorities in particular. Most workers from the ethnic minorities live where they do because of discrimination in the allocation of houses, and willingly face a slightly longer journey to work at those places which do not discriminate against them. What the location of new factories in the inner city will do is to improve the physical appearance of some industrial waste land and enable the planners to attract industry to locate in formerly residential areas, which they have allocated to industrial use. Such industries are likely to be manned by commuting workers and managers and may actually damage both the physical and the social environment of those who live close to them. Far more beneficial to the inner city would be the development of efficient transport which would take its workers to their jobs, coupled with the re-zoning of former industrial land to residential use in the inner city itself. Segregation of industry and residential community is, in fact, a very valuable principle in town planning. It is taken for granted in the suburbs and commuter towns. One is bound to ask why opposite principles should apply in the inner city. Is it not perhaps assumed that it is inevitable that the poor and the disadvantaged and the unemployed will live as they always have, tucked in amongst the factories?

The sections on population movement do, of course, suggest both that the residential environment will be improved sufficiently to attract back suburban families and that the present population may be encouraged to move away from the factories altogether. What is lacking is any consideration of whether there are, in the existing inner-city population, skills which could be used in new industry wherever it is located. The notion that the present inner-city population is entirely lacking in skill is belied by the evidence. Immigrant workers are usually underemployed in relation to their education (Rex and Tomlinson, 1979: 190–1) and it is also clear that their children will aspire to and be capable of better jobs than their parents. Even if one were to accept the racist assumption that all West Indian children do badly at school, it is clear that Asian children of unskilled foundry workers are doing as well as or better than their English peers.

*Residence and Environment*

The second aspect of the Inner City White Paper is that which refers
to environmental as distinct from industrial improvement. In order
to assess its efficacy therefore we have to understand what the
environmental problem is. In my view, the elements of this problem
are hardly understood by the planners: the most they are ever likely
to achieve by present methods is the piecemeal improvement of
streets of houses.

The first thing to notice about most so-called inner-city areas is
the grandeur of their pasts. Mostly these were classy middle-class
suburbs or at least suburbs where the respectable working class
came to live. The central features therefore tend to be the
splendidly conceived park, complete with lake and bandstand and,
overlooking it, the villas of the higher-class residents and the shopping
parade. Around this core there were terraces of houses of varying
sizes, including quite large houses once occupied by white-collar and
skilled workers, and orderly redbrick terraces with their pubs, chapels
and corner stores and, usually, a football ground, built for the working
classes.

That is the inner-city suburb of the past. What is it like today?
Take for instance Small Heath in Birmingham which was the subject
of one of the inner-city studies (HMSO, 1977b).

The park is largely deserted. Its boating lake is unstaffed and unused.
The bandstand rots away and attaches to itself newspapers blowing in
the wind. For whatever reason the park is humanly deserted and, the
more deserted it becomes, the more it becomes a suitable place for
muggings and murders. Most of the large villas have gone over to
multi-occupation. Other terraces are in improvement or Housing
Action Areas.

What strikes one most about the area, however, is the number of
deserted sites. These sites are either scheduled for housing development, but remaining deserted for long periods because of the
slowness of the council's building programme, or scheduled for
industry but unable to attract firms to locate there. In general the
area is living through a long transition. In the long run it may be
beautiful and prosperous, but in the long run the present inhabitants
will all be dead, so that their reality is the pock-marked present.

The football ground is a permanent environmental problem. It
stands amid a sea of rubble and ash, the houses which used to
surround it having long ago been knocked down. Very few of the
present supporters live in the neighbourhood, and those who come

in from outside find it a suitable terrain for their tribal wars and wars against the police. No one knows what to do about this problem. It simply adds to the human undesirability of living in the vicinity and ensures that those who cannot get housing elsewhere, particularly immigrants, will come here to live.

There is no longer much sign of the commerce which once flourished in the Parade along the side of the park, but, as the Small Heath study noted, one form of commerce does remain. Very few shops, whether in the main road or in the backstreets, remain un-occupied. There are literally hundreds of new shops and businesses and, one supposes, such commerce must induce a demand for whole-saling and manufacture. Very little is said in the recommendations of the report about this commerce, however. It remains a part of a different world from the industry which the Partnerships will be offering inducements to locate here. In all likelihood many of the present shops will be bulldozed away to clear sites for factories.

The proposals of the Inner City Policy for dealing with the environment involve essentially more of what has gone before. In so far as resources are available some of the deserted sites will have houses built on them. On others new factories will appear. In the improvement areas, houses will be improved and sometimes walls will be built around them and trees planted. Improvement will be especially concentrated on those streets where remaining white working-class families live, because the criteria as to what properties and people should benefit will be devised by politicians for the benefit of their constituents. Inevitably the immigrant community, in this case Pakistanis, will be driven to live in the interstices of the plan. The environment will not be developed for their benefit or with sensitivity to their culture and purposes and, though their tight-knit community thrives, they will seem a nuisance, only under-mining what the council regards as public health standards.

The one occasion in recent years when Small Health Park served a function was when hundreds of young Pakistani workers held a prayer meeting there on the occasion of the execution of the former Pakistani premier, Mr Bhutto. For once the community, or a good part of it, came together and used the social facilities available to them. But this is not the sort of activity that the planners take into account. Neighbouring Sparkbrook has a block of houses around its park where 90 per cent of the inhabitants are Pakistanis from Campbellpur and it is a natural focus for many Asian activities. Yet, when Samuel Lloyd's old mansion in the park became available for

use, the planners' most inspired idea was that it should be used to
locate a branch library. No one for a moment asked whether it might
not be used as an Asian studies centre.

What I am suggesting is that planning should be addressed to
providing for the needs of minority communities which exist rather
than simply regarding them as a public nuisance to be abolished. This
does not mean, however, that there will be no place for white people
to continue to live in Small Heath nor that all Pakistanis will be
trapped in such areas for all time.


### Accepting Ethnic Segregation in Planning?

First, I would like to emphasise that we should plan with and for the
Pakistani (or other immigrant) community in the inner city. At the
moment planning takes no notice of their needs and their community
life, even though they eventually become the majority. What one
sees therefore is a society and a culture surviving from its own internal
strengths and against the odds posed by the environment. Of course
this is to some extent accepted by the immigrants because the waste-
land of Small Heath is quite acceptable after the poverty of Mirpur.
But surely we do not have to assume that this culture implies the
drab environment that it inhabits. The richly coloured silks worn by
the women and children belie that. Surely then it should be possible
to consult with community leaders and with the population at large
on what sort of environment they want to see and provide that at the
highest possible level which the community can support.

So far as the remaining whites are concerned, it must be made clear
to them that the disappearance of their ethnic neighbours is a utopian
fantasy which can no longer be realised. They should have the option,
if they so wish, of being rehoused elsewhere, but, if they choose to
stay, they should first be reassured by the fruits of planning in the
ethnic areas that the existence of ethnic neighbourhoods need not
imply filth and squalor, and then work out their ways of maintaining
an effective English life with the most effective buildings and social
institutions possible within a multi-racial area. Creating and planning
such an area is a considerable challenge to planners, but one they
have hardly begun to consider.

The acceptance of partial segregation and of multi-cultural, multi-
ethnic areas by planners need not, of course, imply that all ethnics
will always remain ethnics, or be condemned to live forever in the

ghetto. Two other possibilities will open for the younger generation. Some will choose to change their allegiance, become culturally English, and disappear into suburbia. Others will migrate from the ghetto, produce a more liberal, flexible and open version of the culture else-where and keep in touch by transport and telephone with the riches of their grandparents' world (a process which some liberal American Jews call 'being a Jew by telephone').

Of course it may be asked whether, since the long-term process of assimilation is inevitable, the commitment of planning resources in the inner city on an ethnic basis is not ill-considered. On this two things may be said. One is that the sort of community we are discussing is likely to take root in the area for a period of fifty years or so. The other is that, even when an urban area is not purpose-built and planned, it will acquire an ethnic character and one ethnic group will gradually be displaced by another, as is the case for example with the succession of the Jews of Chapeltown, Leeds, first by the Poles and then by West Indians.

It might seem strange and offensive to liberal opinion to advocate policies appearing to imply planned segregation in British cities. But this is by no means because the city is based upon a concept of equal rights and planning for assimilation. The fact of the matter is that neither at a political level nor at the local government level is there any clear policy towards immigrant minorities. At best the policies which have been evolved have been piecemeal compromises to deal with contingencies as they arise. But even this pragmatic policy will be informed by other purposes, namely those of urban reform in the interests of the native working class. Such a policy inevitably sees immigrants as a nuisance and a threat. The first reaction was to keep them off the suburban estates. But when this produced the 'twilight zone' or the 'inner city' perceived as a social problem, the reform envisaged was one which would involve bringing the inner city up to standard, by eliminating *precisely those conditions which made it possible for immigrant minorities to live there*, e.g. by substituting single-family-occupied rented housing for the lodging-houses and for terrace houses in improvement areas.

## Summary

In short, far from the immigrant minorities having problems because they live in the inner city, it is because they have the basic problem of

being denied access to normal housing that they are in the inner city.
As a result, some, though not all, so-called inner-city areas (which
are actually the next worst areas of housing left after slum clearance
is complete) have become increasingly immigrant areas, and it is
precisely those areas where there *is* a high proportion of immigrants
which are thought of as problematic. (The area of east
Sparkbrook, which in 1964 had a population which was only some
25 per cent Pakistani, now has a population which is 70 per cent
Pakistani. In the four wards commonly designated Handsworth, the
percentage of those born in the New Commonwealth went up from
about 11 per cent in 1961 to 27 per cent in 1971; by 1977 62 per cent
of the population were of Asian or West Indian origin, and by 1979
several of the secondary schools were more than 90 per cent 'black'.)
Studies of house purchase by our Unit colleagues show that the white
working class have now ceased to buy the sort of terraced property
that exists in the improvement areas. In these areas inner-city improvement is often guided by the notion of getting rid of the kinds of
housing in which immigrants have lived and it is thought to be an
achievement to 'get a better racial mix'. Such aims do not in any way
help to solve the problems of immigrant minorities. If the planners
achieve their goals, the 'immigrant' will constitute a smaller proportion of the population than before and no one will know where the
lost remainder have disappeared to.

Meanwhile, even though the inner-city policy is intended to
improve the inner city, many of those concerned with improving the
situation of ethnic minorities argue that they should be helped to
leave it. Thus, for example, the Social Research Association has
supported the idea of an ethnic question in the census to ascertain
*inter alia* 'whether members of racial minorities are managing to
escape from inner city areas of job loss and environmental decline'.
Which policy, one may ask, is operating? Where are the resources to
go? Where should people go if they are to share in allocated resources?

In my view, the policy is one of saving the 'inner-city' areas mainly
be developing them along lines which were previously worked out in
areas like the North-east. There will be advance factories, and housing
will be replaced and improved as far as possible up to post-war
standards in the area. Because this will not happen very rapidly, given
the meagre resources available to the Partnerships, there will remain
patches and pockets within which the minority communities will
survive.

I do expect, however, that the intense segregation in some areas which we have seen will decline, partly because some minority members become sufficiently affluent to buy their way into the suburbs and partly because of the salvage operation carried out by the planners. If this happens, where will the minority communities go? That is the next chapter in the story of urban ethnic segregation. I do not expect, however, that this process will be planned, and such ethnic colonies as do develop will do so not because of the planners but despite them.

In suggesting that this is the scenario of inner-city planning, it is *not* suggested that our urban planners are racialist. What is suggested is that the concepts which govern their thinking derive from the reforming ideals of the native working class. If and in so far as members of the minorities develop a life-style like working-class Englishmen they will find that they fit into and are provided for in the new order. In so far as they do not, they will move on to form colonies wherever there are gaps in the urban system into which they can fit.

I have sometimes been called a moral nihilist because in writing on matters such as these I do not appear to be giving advice on what should be done. Let me, therefore, stress that I think that ethnic minority communities, having emerged as a means of surviving both the trials and tribulations of migration and the injustice of discrimination, should now be assisted and be given the physical means to exist. However, I do not think that this will happen. The idea of a multi-ethnic, multi-cultural society is not a very important element either in our political ideologies or in the professional ethos of planners. If it does play a part in their thinking it is far more likely to do so as a rationalisation of discrimination.

We should, of course, recognise that the White Paper on Inner City Policy does not *support* discrimination. It only says that discrimination is not its responsibility. Whether the Commission for Racial Equality, whose responsibility it is, will be able to make a difference to the planning process is a matter yet to be decided. My own assessment of its capacities, based upon three years' experience of the operation of the new Act, is that it is unlikely to do so, and that it is the confused environmentalist ideology of the inner city planners which will set the framework within which ethnic minorities have to work out their community life.

Finally, it may be asked what relevance this review of housing and planning has to the general theory of urban segregation. It is, simply, that the policy of desegregation alone will not necessarily reduce racial injustice. What is eminently desirable is that all ethnic groups should have choice. Instead of this, majority backed housing and planning policies have created a situation in which, first assimilation, and then segregation are denied as possibilities. The result is to leave the minorities in limbo, without choice and without adequate facilities for a reasonable social life.

## Bibliography

Dahya, B. (1973) 'Pakistanis in Britain – Transients or Settlers', *Race*, 14, 246–66

HMSO. (1966) *Our Older Homes*, London

HMSO. (1967) *Children in their Primary Schools* (The Plowden Report), London

HMSO. (1968) (Cmnd. 3602) *Old Houses into New Homes*, London

HMSO. (1973) (Cmnd. 5339) *Better Homes – The Next Priorities*, London

HMSO. (1977a) (Cmnd. 6845) *Policy for the Inner Cities*, London

HMSO. (1977b) *Unequal City – Final Report of the Birmingham Inner Area Study*, London

Karn, V. (1977) 'The Financing of Owner Occupation and its Impact on Ethnic Minorities', *New Community*, 6, 49–65

Parkin, F. (1979) *Marxism and Class Theory*, Tavistock, London

Rex, J. (1973) *Race, Colonialism and the City*, Routledge and Kegan Paul, London

Rex, J. and Moore, R. (1967) *Race, Community and Conflict*, Oxford University Press, London

Rex, J. and Tomlinson, S. (1979) *Colonial Immigrants in a British City*, Routledge and Kegan Paul, London

Smith, D. (1977a) *Racial Disadvantage in Britain*, Penguin, Harmondsworth

Smith, D. (1977b) 'The Housing of Racial Minorities – Its Unusual Nature', *New Community*, 6, 18–27

Weber, Max (1968) *Economy and Society*, Bedminster Press, New York

# 2 ETHNIC SEGREGATION: SOCIAL REALITY AND ACADEMIC MYTH

Nathan Kantrowitz

## American Ethnics and American Sociology

In recent years, ethnicity has become a popular idea in America as
identifiable groups asserted their own version of the American
experience. However, this assertion has come into political collision
with the black civil rights movement which has been firmly entrenched
as a liberal cause in the American intellectual establishment. The
stereotype of European ethnicity is usually expressed as the 'hard
hat' element or the working-class descendants of European immigrants
from Eastern Europe, the Mediterranean and Roman Catholic Ireland.[1]
In this political controversy between ethnics and blacks, the social
science 'establishment' has played a baleful role which reflects the
conflicts and provides the ideological theory.

To demonstrate this, this paper examines a recent and authoritative
sociological statement on ethnic segregation in America. It demonstrates
that the above conclusion rests upon unexamined cultural attitudes
which informed the original approach of American sociology,
exemplified in the work of Robert Park published in 1914. After that
first analysis, the paper discusses some of the unfortunate consequences
for public policy, and concludes with some observations for the future.

## The Received Wisdom

In general, establishment sociologists believe that ethnic segregation
is non-existent or vestigial. One form of this opinion appears in a
deposition submitted to the Supreme Court of the United States
over a recent trial concerning school desegregation (Billingsley *et al.*,
1979: 70). It was signed by 39 scholars whose personal and
institutional affiliations range considerably in status. However, they
include three past presidents of the American Sociological Association
and perhaps two dozen others of equivalent status in social science
disciplines, professors at the more prestigious universities, and
principals in the expenditure of millions of dollars in research

funds over the past decade. (This is an adequate definition of an academic establishment, I believe.) The group opinion was also published; it appears to be carefully objective:

> This statement emphasizes findings on which there is broad scholarly agreement, and avoids issues about which the evidence to date does not permit reasonably clear conclusions to be drawn.
>
> Although ethnic enclaves are a long-established feature of urban residential and commercial organization, the recent experience of blacks and Hispanic minorities in American cities has been far different than the historical experiences of persons of European descent. Some first and second generation European immigrants were discriminated against and were subject to restrictions on the housing they could obtain. Nevertheless, their degree of residential segregation declined rapidly from the peak levels attained during periods of rapid immigration, and those peak levels were never as high as the levels typical for blacks and Hispanic minorities today. The ethnic enclave for whites was temporary and, to a large extent, optional . . .

The establishment conclusion is clear: 'The ethnic enclave for whites was temporary' is a simple declarative sentence in the past tense. Moreover, there is consensus among scholars, at least among the 39 signatories; as we shall see, however, it flies in the face of the evidence. The relationship of ethnic to racial segregation is outside our main concern, but its political implications are important to an understanding of academic views. It is no accident that our quotation links denial of the existence of ethnic segregation with denial of the similarity between ethnic and racial segregation, for it is important to the lawyers' argument. The rejection of any racial and ethnic parallel is an important strategy against any opposition claim that blacks will automatically progress as the European ethnics have progressed in American society. The importance of this strategy can be attested to from personal experience. I have consulted with many lawyers for local school boards, and have been asked 'Isn't the black experience "just like" that of the European ethnic?' When I answered that the black experience was *not* 'just like' the ethnic — there were some similarities, some differences — I knew by the mental thud which followed that I had just told another lawyer what he did not want to hear. The political linkage between race and ethnicity is the

driving passion which has converted the outworn ideas of Robert Park
on ethnic assimilation into the *idée fixe* of the federal courtroom. The
position of my school board lawyers is clearly an ideological pose to
win in the courtroom; it must be realised that of the academic
establishment is exactly the same, although opposite.

The burden of my argument is that the cast of mind freighted with
Park's intellectual baggage has influenced our interpretation of the
empirical statistics. Since it is impossible to present definitive evidence
of why anyone chose a particular mode of interpretation, it is best I
begin with one I know best, myself. When I questioned the received
wisdom that ethnic segregation had precipitously declined (1969), I
did not do so out of any flash of inspiration. Rather it was the result
of painful rethinking. The segregation indices I had calculated for the
1960 New York metropolis startled me, and I could make no sense
of them, for they contradicted my expectation that they should be
very low. It was only after puzzling over them that it dawned on me
that perhaps my assumptions were wrong, something which led
me to re-read the scholarly literature in a different light.

Invisibly, we are prisoners of language and thought. Some social
linguists seem to suggest that certain combinations of language
cause the mind to stop, because we have attained an 'explanation'.
For example, when I re-read Lieberson (1963), I realised that nowhere
did he state that European ethnics had disappeared or were about to
disappear, yet he is a standard authority for precipitous decline. All
that really exists, however, is an academic prose, so suffused with
'assimilation' and conjugations of 'decline', 'lowering' and such,
combined with a model which implied the passage of time, the
passing of generations, movement outward from the city centre,
and the group-think descended from Robert Park, that it is no
wonder readers thought the end was near. The analytic terms suggest
as much.

A small content analysis of my work shows my own change of mind.
In 1969, I find seven statements of my agreement that ethnic
segregation had declined; in the revised (1973) version, there were
only four. Moreover, the semantics had changed from a willing agreement with decline in 1969 to a grudging concession of a moot point
in 1973. But what really gives the game away was my (1973) prediction that the 1960–70 New York ethnic segregation would remain
stable, with but a slight decline. My tacit assumption was the existence
of decline in the past, however small, followed by a decline in the
future, however small. Unfortunately for me as prophet, Peter Jackson

(1981) found that New York's inter-ethnic segregation actually registered a slight increase from 1960 to 1970. There is nothing in my text to indicate I dreamed it would increase; my only contribution was to say the decrease would be trivial. The fact that I erred in *direction* indicates a mind-set that did not comprehend increase. In my dénouement as seer, I can claim penance for pointing out in 1969 that ethnic segregation did indeed exist. Since then, there has been a mass of scholarship confirming my observation, which makes the continued denial of the establishment embarrassing; there is no longer the slightest question that ethnic segregation exists, only disagreements as to its causes.

I suspect New York's 1960–70 increase is not unique, for Uyeki (1976) and Guest and Weed (1976) concluded that Cleveland experienced a decline in ethnic segregation until 1960, after which it stabilised or increased slightly during 1960–70. Beyond this, ethnic persistence has been documented almost to the point of boredom, as for example in Bleda's (1975) comparative studies of nearly all metropolitan areas; Darroch and Marston's (1971) study of Toronto, Canada; Hershberg *et al.*'s (1979) study of Philadelphia; Kantrowitz's (1979) study of Boston, or Klaff's (1979) of Wilmington. Yet the establishment persists, even to Hawley's (1981: 94) latest conclusions. How did we get into such a predicament, and worse, what have been the consequences?

## Cultural Attitudes and Intellectual Interpretation

The idea of ethnic decline appears to originate with Robert Park, one of the most creative thinkers of twentieth-century sociology. The earliest example of his ideas on ethnicity were included in an essay he wrote just before the First World War, in which he portrayed a belief in rapid assimilation of the European immigrant (1914: 607):

> The growth of modern states exhibits the progressive merging of smaller, mutually exclusive, into larger and more inclusive social groups. This result has been achieved in various ways, but it has usually been followed, or accompanied, by a more or less complete adoption, by the members of the smaller groups, of the language, technique, and mores of the larger and more inclusive ones. The immigrant readily takes over the language, manners, and social ritual, and outward forms of his adopted country. In America it

has become proverbial that a Pole, Lithuanian, or Norwegian cannot be distinguished, in the second generation, from an American born of native parents.

Not only was Park sensible for his time, but it was a liberating contrast to the common intellectual dislike of the Catholic and Jewish poor, as expressed for example in Henry Adams's *Education*, or in Madison Grant's *The Passing of the Great Race*.

During the ensuing decade, Park's thought developed, and in 1926 he linked his ideas of assimilation, social organisation and the meaning of physical space (reprinted in Peach, 1975: 25):

Such segregations of populations as these take place, first, upon the basis of language and of culture, and second, upon the basis of race. Within these immigrant colonies and racial ghettoes, however, other processes of selection inevitably take place which bring about segregation based upon vocational interests, upon intelligence, and personal ambition. The result is that the keener, the more energetic, and the more ambitious very soon emerge from their ghettos and immigrant colonies and move into an area of second immigrant settlement, or perhaps into a cosmopolitan area in which the members of several immigrant and racial groups meet and live side by side. More and more, as the ties of race, of language, and of culture are weakened, successful individuals move out and eventually find their places in business and in the professions, among the older population group which has ceased to be identified with any language or racial group. The point is that change of occupation, personal success or failure – changes of economic and social status, in short – tend to be registered in changes in location.

Here Park posits that assimilation proceeds rapidly, and that it requires residential desegregation. He also introduces the idea that segregation is 'bad', within a Social Darwinist mode of thought. This is based upon the then common idea of a higher *kultur* in the wider society to which the best of any people aspired. Although this probably had its biases in a glorification of the upper classes and of White-Anglo-Saxon-Protestant (or WASP) culture, it was also part of the nineteenth-century belief in 'Progress'.

This view persisted among sociologists. For example, Louis Wirth did not specifically deal with ethnics or their segregation in his famous essay 'Urbanism as a Way of Life' (1938), a tribute perhaps to their presumed unimportance. But his general orientation within Park's view is made clear on pp. 20–1, and even more specifically on p. 23:

> In view of the ineffectiveness of actual kinship ties we create fictional kinship groups. In the face of the disappearance of the territorial unit as the basis of social solidarity we create interest units. Meanwhile the city as a community resolves itself into a series of tenuous segmental relationships superimposed upon a territorial base with a definite center but without a definite periphery and upon a division of labor which far transcends the immediate locality and is world-wide in scope.

This view continued as a reasonable one, considering the empirical knowledge of the time. In an influential statement made 35 years ago, but still cited today, Hawley (1944: 37) wrote:

> The histories of various European nationality groups settling in the United States are illustrative. So long as they remained compact units they kept their national traits and group structures. Under such circumstances they were also subject to attacks and subordination by the native population. On various occasions the Irish, Greeks, Italians, Poles and many others have known the meaning of minority status. The progeny of immigrants, however, drift away from the foreign settlement and merge with the general population. Eventually the group itself disappears unless it is replenished by fresh immigration.

Hawley's 1944 statement is a masterful interpretation of the theories and research then extant – primarily work done in the 1920s and 1930s by sociologists at the University of Chicago. Moreover, Hawley reaffirmed Park's earlier view that segregation was 'bad', when he wrote (1944: 674):

> Redistribution of a minority group in the same territorial pattern as that of the majority group results in a dissipation of subordinate status and an assimilation of the subjugated group into the social structure.

However, Hawley rejects Social Darwinism in favour of environmentalism (1944: 672):

Segregation, whether voluntary or involuntary, is a restriction of opportunity; it hampers the flow of knowledge and experience and, thus, impedes diversification of interests and occupations. Migrants settling in a new and strange community are for the most part fitted for only the least specialized functions. And to the extent that they establish a segregated existence in the new community the alien individuals tend to retain their uniformity.

Moreover, for Hawley, the end of segregation means the end of social existence (1944: 672–3). He asserts that:

. . . a group whose members become widely distributed sooner or later loses its ability to act in concert and hence its identity as a group. It may possibly be reconstructed as a statistical class, but it cannot be regarded as a group in the sociological sense.

Thus, by the Second World War, we have the Wisdom of the Elders: ethnic segregation is 'bad' whether for Social Darwinist or environmental reasons; but we should not fear, for ethnic groups and their segregation are rapidly disappearing.

## Consequences for Social Policy

More recently, social conflict over race has shaped concern with ethnicity. After the Second World War, a large part of the social agenda of the United States became the quest for social justice for the black population. An important part of this centres on residential segregation, with race tied to black inner-city slums and white middle-class suburbs, and the denial of opportunity of decent schools or good jobs to blacks. With the barriers coming down at last, supporters of the black civil rights movement bitterly resented any group who created another hurdle.

European ethnics became part of the issue because opponents of programmes for the amelioration of the conditions of black Americans sometimes claimed such programmes were unnecessary. They pointed to the purported social progress of European ethnics as examples of what could be attained by blacks. This position did nothing to endear the ethnics to supporters of the black civil rights movement. Not everyone who pointed out ethnic progress was trying to stop that of the blacks, but they were suspect. Real conflicts developed when blacks moved into areas where ethnics already lived. Not everyone who pointed out ethnics living in spatial community was trying to prevent blacks from having decent housing, but they were suspect. And, of course, as the school desegregation issue moved into northern cities, residential segregation became enmeshed further in another conflict, the organisation of school districts. Not everyone who defended neighbourhood schools wished to keep blacks from decent education, but they were suspect.

But these were objective conflicts. Intensifying them was an intellectual cast, created by the academic establishment and growing out of the perspective we have just discussed: since European ethnics were rapidly desegregating, those who still lived in spatial and social community were atavistic. Moreover, since segregation was 'bad', *per* Park's Social Darwinism or Hawley's environmentalism, the identifiable ethnics were seen as unworthy. In such a situation we may expect the worse and we have it. Situations where blacks and ethnics had discrete areas of conflict have been converted to total conflict. The pragmatic genius of American local politics for counting votes and buying compromise no matter what the dispute, was converted into a manichean holy war. So, for instance, competition for inner-city housing became not a question of how somehow to coexist, but rather whose community would be destroyed. As one consequence, there have been no ethnic-black coalitions of note in American cities. Academic denigration of the ethnics was not the sole cause, but the intellectual ideological imprimatur was important.

Throughout, the academic establishment has ignored suggestions that ethnics maintained spatial cohesion. The first, minor suggestion of ethnic continued self-segregation was submerged in Wallace's (1953) dissertation; my own doubts were originally voiced in 1967 and published in 1969. Of course there is contrary evidence, notably the Taeubers's (1964) study of Chicago. But the establishment sees only one side. A remarkable example of this is found in Hawley and Rock (1973: 8):

> Historically, ethnicity and race have also played a role in shaping the pattern of residential distribution of the population. In varying degree, immigrant groups retained a sense of communal solidarity derived from a common language and culture. These groups tended to cluster together until their members were ready to disperse amid the larger society.
>
> Historical analogies between the Blacks in America and those

ethnic groups are inappropriate in several respects.

The assertion is unequivocal, the source is impeccable, for the senior author is the Dean of American Social Ecologists. Moreover, the authors speak *ex cathedra*. The United States Department of Housing and Urban Development asked the National Academy of Sciences to address the basic question (Hawley and Rock, 1973: 2), 'What is known about the feasibility and desirability of "social mixing" in residential areas?' This basic question was carefully examined by: a Social Science Panel of the National Academy of Sciences; the Division of Behavioral Sciences of the National Reasearch Council; the National Academy of Engineering's Advisory Committee of the US Department of Housing and Urban Development; and finally, 'key officials' of the US Department of Housing and Urban Development. One could hardly ask for a greater concentration of weighty minds in high places, or for a better operational definition of an establishment. In the end, this labour brought forth the conclusion that the major factors were race and social class, and as in our quotation above, excluded other factors, including ethnic segregation. Such a conclusion is congruent with the National Academy in general, for its retiring president in his last report bemoaned the recent glorification of ethnicity (Reinhold, 1980).

An example of how this mind-set affects intellectual understanding can be seen in the interpretations of the racial conflict which has pervaded Boston in the wake of its school desegregation controversy. For example, Professor Robin Williams (1976: 17—18) who recognised the ethnic component interpreted it as follows:

In South Boston, Massachusetts court-ordered desegregation plan in 1974 was met by mass turbulence and violence (formerly attributed stereotypically to the 'Little Rock' syndrome of the Deep South) among Irish Catholic Whites. The area, containing 38,000 people, is a geographically and socially separate section of Boston, inhabited largely by working-class people and characterized by cultural homogeneity, low social mobility, strong particularistic and ascribed social ties, considerable interpersonal violence, social authoritarianism, and aversive attitudes toward 'outsiders.' In short, it exhibits *the characteristics that cultural isolation and social segregation typically produce, including rigid ingroup-outgroup distinctions, closed social horizons, extreme exclusiveness, and hostility toward social change and extralocal groups.* (Note: italics in original.)

It is evident that Professor Williams dislikes the Boston Irish. Perhaps with his own demographic authority, for (1972: 6), Professor Karl Taeuber speaking of the Boston Italians told the US Court in Boston of 'the third, fourth and fifth generation Italians who have scattered about the city (and may not even know their own ancestry)'. If the establishment believes that by the third generation ethnics have scattered and do not even know their own grandparents' origins, obviously those who do and who remain in enclaves must be the dregs. This is 1914 Robert Park, pure and simple.

The issues have hardly been only intellectual. Husock (1979) depicts Boston as a city consumed by racial hate, particularly by its ethnic population's reaction to school desegregation.

However, the real intensity of dislike comes not from formal academic prose, but rather from such marketplaces of ideas as the Editorial Section of the *New York Times*. Although this journalism reaches beyond residential segregation into ethnicity in general, the spatial component is crucial. For example, in 1976 when President Ford and candidate Carter were courting the ethnic vote, Professor Richard Sennett of New York University wrote (1976) on the 'Op-Ed' page (part of the Editorial Section where non-staff members contribute essays selected by the editor):

> Given the actual facts of ethnic community life in America, there is something obscene about politicians like Gerald Ford or Jimmy Carter celebrating 'our precious ethnic heritage.' The history of most ethnic groups in America, white as well as black, is appalling . . .
>
> Celebrating ethnicity *per se* means celebrating the badges of cultural inferiority American society forced the agrarian immigrants to wear . . .
>
> Finally, the issue of ethnic identity is a painful one between the generations in many ethnic families. People who have grown up in ethnic communities have often felt suffocated by them; when they leave, the old feel the ethnic culture is being abandoned . . .

More recently, in another essay on the same page, Professor Orlando Patterson of Harvard University began (1978):

> The ethnic revival sweeping the United States is another example of this nation's retreat from its constitutional committment to the ideal of equality.
>
> The fact that the movement has the strong support of many

so-called liberals and minority activists makes it all the more in-
sidious and disturbing. The harmless, if vain, search for ancestral
roots and communal solidarity is the tip of an ideology that is both
reactionary and socially explosive.

Finally, Professor Patterson ends his essay:

> The fact that the ethnic revival is largely ideological should not
> lead us to underestimate it. We know from the history of ethnic
> movements that ideology, under the right circumstances, can trans-
> form reality. European fascism was first and foremost an
> ideological movement, and, in a disturbing parallel with modern
> America, fascist ideology had its roots in the romantic revolt
> against the enlightenment — a revolt that, in its early phases, was
> generally liberal, very concerned with the social and human cost
> of 'progress,' and espoused the principal of ethnic pluralism.
>   The time has come when all genuine humanists who cherish the
> great ideal of the Constitution — that all human beings are created
> equal — must awake from their slumber and meet head on the
> challenge of the chauvinists.

In between opening with ethnicity as the apology for reaction, and
ending with it as the leading edge of fascism, Professor Patterson
makes other points, a few of which are that: real ethnicity was but
temporary protection and assimilation has eliminated it; ethnicity is a
mask for racism; ethnic pluralism is an ideology antithetical to the
Judeo-Christian ethic. A few weeks later, on 14 March 1978, the
*New York Times* printed a letter from Professor Marvin Harris,
of Columbia University, extolling Professor Patterson for attacking
the ethnic 'mania'. The *Times* did not print any letters from academics
in disagreement. One can always find attacks on many kinds of groups
such as Jews, Catholics or blacks. But these are rarely acerbic essays
by academic 'insiders' published in the editorial section of an
'establishment' outlet such as the *New York Times*.

These are the real issues, those of social justice and self-interest, of
the politics of race. Not all academics share the virulence of Professors
Harris, Patterson and Sennett, but I think it fair to say the predominant reaction of the academic establishment is negative.
Stretching back from Professors Harris, Patterson and Sennett is the
same sentiment in Professor Williams's academic prose. And rising
above these professions of dislike is a mind-set of disbelief in ethnic

existence, in Hawley and Rock and in the authoritative document submitted by the academic establishment to the United States Courts. And all this comes naturally with intellectual assumptions which stretch back to the insights of Robert Park.

## Conclusion

By any reading, the overwhelming weight of evidence is that European ethnic segregation has not disappeared. But the academic establishment still marches to Robert Park's drumbeat of 1914. Also, there is a long tradition going back to Park's Social Darwinism or Hawley's environmentalism that segregation is 'bad'. These have contributed to the negative view of ethnic segregation, and I suspect, a negative view of ethnics' role in the quest for social justice for black Americans.

Segregation simply is. Many universities boast of self-segregation of their faculty: liberal groups such as Quakers or suburban Jews are not randomly scattered throughout the metropolis. There is no reason to expect desegregation of Italians or Irish, so long as these ethnics constitute some sort of viable social group. Although segregation is wrong where it is caused by discrimination against black Americans, this is no reason to derogate the European ethnics.

Some ethnics may be racist, but I think of them as a people who are not immune from protecting their self-interest. Some blacks may be racist, but I think of them as a people who want their piece of America which has for too long been unjustly denied them. There are inevitably conflicts which will arise between these groups over neighbourhoods in cities. What is surprising is that so far the conflict has been of confrontation, with no sign of politicians building bridges between groups. I think it has been a strategic mistake that black politicians have not seen that ethnic segregation has an existence and legitimacy, or that ethnic politicians have not seen that black claims to some part of what ethnics value has its own legitimacy.

Nor do I see much constructive contribution by the academic establishment. If research has any role to play, it is to assess empirically the reality and mythology of ethnic life, particularly segregation at *all* class levels, generations and into suburbia. The image of the lower class which hangs about the idea of ethnicity may be unwarranted. I suspect the corporate board room is just as ethnic and just as 'culturally isolated' as Boston's South End, and their major difference is money, which, as Nancy Mitford wrote, is 'such a comfort'. My guess is that upper-class suburbia, more spatially diffused by acreage and automobiles, may be just as much, say, Scottish or Swedish (or specific types of combination of WASPs) as inner Boston is Irish or Italian. No more relationship to contemporary Scandinavia or Scotland than contemporary Ireland or Italy, but shaped by origins and experience. Or there may be webs linking exurbia Irish to city Irish. If so, the defended neighbourhood of the inner city and the exclusionary zoning laws of exurbia may not be separate phenomena. There is no end to the speculation in which we may engage. Perhaps my guesses are wrong, and in the end ethnicity may be only a passing lower-class phenomenon. But I think some research would be worthwhile, for if ethnicity is as pervasive as I suspect, our present society may have to change considerably to see blacks, Roman Catholic ethnics, and others become dominant in the WASP corporate world — the interlocking of the board room, the locker room, and the marriage bed may be too invisibly resilient to change.

## Note

1. Ethnicity has a bewildering variety of definitions and often refers to blacks, Hispanics, American Indians and others who have suffered discrimination. For this essay, I mean only European ethnics, the immigrants and their descendants of the primarily Roman Catholic poor who reached the United States around the turn of the century. The Irish among them began migrating a half-century earlier during their famines. The impoverished Central European Jews who shared this turn-of-the-century migration with the Roman Catholics play an anomolous role, being on one hand another ethnicity, and on the other, *nouveau arrivées* in some of the social science establishments dominated by White Anglo-Saxon Protestants (or WASPs). Imprecise as it is, I generally omit the Jews from the paper.

## Bibliography

Billingsley, A. *et al*. (39 signatories) (1979) 'School Desegregation and Residential Segregation', *Society*, July/August, 70–6

Bleda, S.E. (1975) 'Socioeconomic, Demographic, and Cultural Bases of Ethnic Residential Location in Selected Metropolitan Areas of the United States', unpublished PhD thesis, Ohio State University

Darroch, A.G. and Marston, W.G. (1971) 'The Social Class Basis of Ethnic Residential Segregation: The Canadian Case', *American Journal of Sociology*, 77, 491–510

Guest, A.M. and Weed, J.A. (1976) 'Ethnic Residential Segregation: Patterns of Change', *American Journal of Sociology*, 81, 1088–111

Hawley, A.H. (1944) 'Dispersion versus Segregation', *Papers of the Michigan Academy of Science, Arts, and Letters*, 30, 667–74

Hawley, A.H. (1981) *Urban Society*, John Wiley, New York

Hawley, A.H. and Rock, V.P. (eds.) (1973) *Segregation in Residential Areas: Papers on Racial and Socio Economic Factors in Choice of Housing*, National Academy of Sciences, Washington, DC

Hershberg, T., Burstein, A., Ericksen, E., Greenberg, S. and Yancey, W. (1979) 'A Tale of Three Cities: Blacks and Immigrants in Philadelphia, 1850–1880, and 1970', *Annals of the American Academy of Political and Social Science*, 441, 55–81

Husock, H. (1979) 'Boston: The Problem That Won't Go Away', *New York Times Magazine*, 25 November, Section 6

Jackson, P. (1981) 'A Social Geography of Puerto Ricans in New York', unpublished D.Phil. thesis, Oxford University

Kantrowitz, N. (1969) 'Ethnic and Racial Segregation in The New York Metropolis, 1960', *American Journal of Sociology*, 74, 685–95

Kantrowitz, N. (1973) *Ethnic and Racial Segregation in the New York Metropolis: Residential Patterns Among White Ethnic Groups, Blacks, and Puerto Ricans*, Praeger, New York

Kantrowitz, N. (1979) 'Racial and Ethnic Residential Segregation in Boston, 1830–1970', *Annals of the American Academy of Political and Social Science*, 44, 41–54

Klaff, V.S. (1979) 'The Structure of Racial and Ethnic Segregation Patterns in Metropolitan Areas', unpublished manuscript

Lieberson, S. (1963) *Ethnic Patterns in American Cities*, Free Press, New York

Park, R.E. (1914) 'Racial Assimilation in Secondary Groups With Particular Reference to the Negro', *American Journal of Sociology*, 19, 606–23

Park, R.E. (1926) 'The Urban Community as a Spatial Pattern and Moral Order', reprinted in Peach (1975)

Patterson, O. (1978) 'Hidden Dangers in the Ethnic Revival', *New York Times*, 20 February, Op-Ed page

Peach, Ceri (ed.) (1975) *Urban Social Segregation*, Longman, London

Reinhold, R. (1980) 'Academy Reports Spark Debate Over its Objectivity', *New York Times*, 10 June, p. C1

Sennett, R. (1976) 'Pure as the Driven Slush', *New York Times*, 10 May, Op-Ed page

Taeuber, K.E. (1972) 'Report to the Court', United States District Court for the District of Massachusetts, Civil Action 72-911-G, 4 December

Taeuber, K.E. and Taeuber, A.F. (1964) 'The Negro as an Immigrant Group: Recent Trends in Racial and Ethnic Segregation in Chicago', *American Journal of Sociology*, 69, 374–82

Uyeki, E.S. (1976) 'Ethnic and Race Segregation, Cleveland 1910–1970', paper presented at the Annual Meeting, Population Association of America, Montreal. *Ethnicity* (forthcoming)

Wallace, D. (1953) 'Residential Concentration of Negroes in Chicago', unpublished PhD thesis, Harvard University

Williams, R.M. Jr. (1976) 'Conflict Resolution and Mutual Accommodation: The Case of the Schools', paper prepared for the Annual Meeting, American Sociological Association, New York

Wirth, L. (1938) 'Urbanism as a Way of Life', *American Journal of Sociology*, 44, 1–24

## Acknowledgement

I would like to express my appreciation for the assistance of Dr Joanne Spencer Kantrowitz.

# PART TWO:

# METHODS AND APPLICATIONS

# 3 AN ASYMMETRICAL APPROACH TO SEGREGATION

Stanley Lieberson

## Conventional Approaches

The index of dissimilarity (ID) has been the most widely used measure of residential segregation in sociology for nearly 25 years. Even now its main challenge is only in terms of statistical significance and biases introduced by differences in composition (witness, for example, Cortese, Falk and Cohen, 1976; 1978). There is much to be said for this index: it is easy to compute; has a simple and clear operational meaning; ranges from zero to 100; and avoids the influence of population composition since it is confined purely to describing differences between groups in their proportional distributions among specified subareas of a city or metropolitan area. The author has employed the measure extensively in studying residential segregation of racial and ethnic groups, language groups and differences in other spatially-based phenomena such as banking activites. To be sure, the ID has been used in situations where it is inappropriate, such as in settings where the data have some rank ordering to them and where it is unwise to ignore that ordering. Examples are using the ID to summarise differences between two groups with respect to their educational distributions, occupational distributions or income distributions. All of these being instances where the index fails to distinguish differences between adjacent categories from differences between distant categories (see Johnson, 1973; Lieberson, 1975).

The computation and interpretation of the ID is well known, having been described in many sources (for example, Duncan and Duncan, 1955a; Lieberson, 1963; Taeuber and Taeuber, 1965; Peach, 1975). Consider columns 1 and 2 of Table 3.1, which provide hypothetical population distributions of blacks and whites in the subareas of a city in which there are no other groups. The numbers in each column are converted to percentage distributions (see columns 4 and 5). Of the 200 blacks living in the city, 60 reside in subarea A. Hence 60/200 = 0.30, or 30 per cent. Likewise, 20/200 of blacks are found in subarea B; hence 10 per cent of the black population are located therein, etc. In similar fashion, the percentage

**Table 3.1: Computation of the ID and P\* Index**

| Subareas | Blacks | Number Whites | Total | Per cent Black | White | Black proportion of subarea total |
|---|---|---|---|---|---|---|
| A | 60 | 370 | 430 | 30 | 37 | 0.140 |
| B | 20 | 290 | 310 | 10 | 29 | 0.065 |
| C | 0 | 300 | 300 | 0 | 30 | 0 |
| D | 120 | 40 | 160 | 60 | 4 | 0.750 |
| Sum | 200 | 1,000 | 1,200 | 100 | 100 | |

distribution for the 1,000 whites living in the city may be calculated (shown in column 5, based on numbers in column 2). By converting to percentage distributions, the ID intentionally ignores the absolute numbers involved in each group, but simply compares the two percentage distributions to determine how similar they are to each other. This is done by summing differences between the black and white percentages in each subarea (ignoring signs). The ID is one-half the sum of these differences (or alternately and ignoring rounding errors, the sum of the positive differences, or the sum of the negative differences). In the example at hand the index is ( $|30 - 37|$ + $|10 - 29|$ + $|0 - 30|$ + $|60 - 4|$ ) $/2 = 56$ on a scale of 0 to 100. The ID ranges from zero (in which case there is no segregation because the percentage distribution is identical for each group) to 100 (which would occur in the maximum case of segregation such that blacks would be found only in subareas where whites were absent and vice versa).

The index is not only easily computed, but has the added attraction of being readily interpreted. It describes the percentage of one group or the other which would have to move if there was to be no segregation between the groups. A symmetrical variant of this, which takes composition into account in order to determine the minimum percentage of the population that would have to move, is the replacement index (Walker, Stinchcombe and McDill, 1967). The ID can also be used in multiple group situations, for example, to determine the segregation between pairs of occupational or ethnic groups or between a given group and the total population (even when the total consists of many different groups). A procedure also exists for avoiding the part-whole problem that occurs if group X is compared with the spatial distribution figures for the total population (a set of figures which also includes group X).[1]

The dominance of the ID is due to a justifiably influential paper by the Duncans (1955b) which, along with their empirical study of occupational segregation published in the same year (1955a), and later work, played a key role in settling what Peach (1975: 3) has labelled as the 'index war' between 1947 and 1955. A wide variety of measures had been proposed and evaluated during that period (see the literature reviewed in Duncan and Duncan, 1955b, and Taeuber and Taeuber, 1965, Appendix A), but the Duncan and Duncan study (1955b) raised a number of serious objections about many of them. Of particular importance for the issue at hand is their consideration of several indices which were affected by population composition. Turning back to Table 3.1 again, it can be readily shown that if there were only 100 whites in the city instead of 1,000, but if they still had the same percentage distribution among the subareas (in other words, if the number of whites in each subarea was divided by ten), then the index of dissimilarity would remain unchanged. By contrast, there were a number of indices that would be affected by such changes in population composition since the groups' relative numbers affected the index value.

Duncan and Duncan showed that the correlations reported by Jahn, Schmid and Schrag (1947) between intercity differences in black-white segregation measured by Gh, an index affected by composition, and three dependent variables were grossly misleading. The correlations originally found between intercity differences in Gh and variation in the tuberculosis death rates, degree of overcrowded housing and Thorndike's 'G' measure all declined sharply when composition was directly taken into account (1955b: 215). For example, the correlation between Gh and the percentage of overcrowded housing in a city went from 0.40 to 0.02 after partialling for composition.

Following up on the Duncans' lead, Taeuber and Taeuber (1965: 218) correlated various measures of segregation obtained for 188 cities in 1950 with percent black. For the three segregation indices that use composition in their formulas, Taeuber and Taeuber found 'moderately high' correlations between the indices and composition, ranging from 0.69 to 0.79. By contrast, there was no association between composition and either the ID or the closely related Gini index. None of this was likely to encourage further use of indices which take composition into account. After distinguishing between those affected and not affected by composition, the Duncans had been cautious about which was a more desirable property for an index (1955b: 216–17). Indeed, they then went on to suggest that no single index would be sufficient for all purposes. To my knowledge, however, they did not use composition-based measures of segregation in their work. The Taeubers reached a stronger conclusion in favour of a symmetric approach towards the degree of unevenness of two groups' spatial distributions and in opposition to measures which create 'distortions' due to composition (1965: 214). Indeed, they go on to argue against any asymmetrical approach, 'The basic notion of unevenness is symmetrical: if Negroes are segregated from whites, whites are equally segregated from Negroes' (p. 243).

A modification by Bell (1954) in the index of isolation proposed by Shevky and Williams in their social area analyses (1949) is relevant both to developments later in this paper and to the Duncans' findings with respect to Gh. On the one hand, Bell's measure was found by Duncan and Duncan to be identical with the square of a standard statistic, *eta* (1955b: 213). In turn, *eta* was found to have a close linkage to the non-white ghetto index, Gh. On the other hand, one component of the Bell formula is the basis for the asymmetrical measures described below.

## An Asymmetrical Approach

Despite all of these objections, this paper reconsiders and elaborates on one component of a composition-linked segregation measure, namely what can be called the P*-type indices. The resurrection under consideration here is not entirely due to chance, but rather reflects some concerns raised when using the index of dissimilarity. The apparent immunity of the ID from compositional influences is not always a desirable feature because the effect of a given ID on other social phenomena will be influenced by the relative numbers of the groups involved. The implications of the same index value will depend on the percentage of the population in each group. In a city with relatively few blacks, for example, the probability of black interaction with whites will be much greater than in another city with a bigger black component were the ID to be identical in the two cities (Lieberson, 1969: 859). If one is examining segregation in order to consider its impact on group patterns, then the ID by itself does not tell enough. Observe that for other purposes, the ID could be ideal, but not in this case. In dealing with language behaviour, for example, suppose one wishes to determine the influence of segregation on the propensity of immigrant groups to learn the host society's language. If group X has a higher ID than group Y, say 80 and 40 respectively, but the latter is 14 per cent of the population whereas X is 3 per cent, how do we combine the two factors influencing language behaviour? If there are enough groups, then perhaps a multiple regression might be possible, although it is not necessarily entirely clean. If there are two groups then such steps are not possible even though we still want to know about the relative isolation of groups X and Y. Moreover, multiple regressions — even when appropriate — do not come up with a parameter which combines the two factors in an operational manner such as is possible with asymmetrical measures.

Also, there are times when one would want to take into account the asymmetric quality of group interaction. Namely, the probability of a given member of group X interacting with a member of Y is not the same as the probability of a given member of group Y interacting with an X in the usual situation where the size of the two groups are different. (This difference in probabilities is similar to that developed theoretically by Blau, 1977.) For example, if 100 out of 1,000 married Protestants have Catholic mates and 100 out of 400 Catholics are married to Protestants, then 10 per cent of Protestants are intermarried whereas 25 per cent of Catholics are married across religious lines. The meaning and consequences for the two groups are different. If one recognises that there is not one best measure for all possible circumstances, then clearly the ID is at a relative disadvantage when compared with composition-based measures for some problems.

In a recently completed monograph on blacks and South-Central-Eastern Europeans in the United States, the author found it fruitful to use measures of segregation that simultaneously take into account differences in group size as well as spatial patterns (Lieberson, 1980, Chapter 9). By not assuming symmetry in the segregation between two groups, such as is the case with the ID, but by viewing X's isolation from Y as not necessarily the same as Y's isolation from X, a somewhat different perspective was gained on the patterns of segregation. As will be shown below, the average black's isolation from whites was found to increase during a period when the average white's isolation from blacks decreased. Such a conclusion is perfectly possible with an asymmetrical approach but is not likely to be reached under the bilateral assumptions inherent in the ID.

The aforementioned monograph was primarily concerned with the substantive results obtained with these asymmetrical indices rather than with the methodological issues pertaining to the measurement of segregation. However, if these asymmetrical measures do provide a way of thinking about residential segregation and measuring it that could alter existing conclusions regarding the actual direction and magnitude of residential segregation in cities and its causal linkages with other social phenomena, then a direct comparison is in order. Because the index of dissimilarity has been used so widely and for such a long time, receptivity to a different measure should be minimal, if only because there are so many cities and periods for which segregation has been measured through the ID. Indeed, unless there are significant and very clear advantages to using an alternative, the arguments for simplicity, comparability and standardisation of measurement would all weigh strongly for continuation of the ID. There are three goals to this paper: an exposition of the asymmetrical measures of segregation; a comparison between the proposed measures and the ID based on the inferences obtained with actual data; and a formal mathematical comparison between the ID and the asymmetrical measures.

## P* Indices

The index of isolation (II) proposed by Shevky and Williams (1949) and later modified by Bell (1954) can be viewed as the quotient of two measures. 'The numerator is an approximation to the probability P that the next person a random individual from group 1 will meet is also from group 1. The denominator is an approximation to the hypothetical probability $P_h$ that the next person a random individual from group 1 will meet is also from group 1 assuming group 1 is homogeneously mixed in all the census tracts of the city' (Bell, 1954: 357–8). The numerator of this ratio, what Bell then calls P*, is of special interest here since it can provide a direct and simple way of describing the combined effects of composition and non-random residential patterns on the isolation of ethnic or racial groups from either the remainder of the population or specific subgroups. It is, of course, false to assume that interaction within subareas is a random event. First, the groups are not likely to be randomly distributed within the area. Beyond this, it is unlikely that actual contacts between people within the areas will ignore the origins of the persons involved. Nevertheless, if these facts are kept in mind, then the operational quality of the P* measure is appealing, to wit, describing for a specified group in the city the average probability of interacting with some specified population based on the distribution of persons by subareas and the assumption that interaction is with someone in the same subarea. The measures described below are essentially an elaboration and extension of the initial P*-type index.[2]

Let the subscripts preceding and following P* indicate, respectively, the group from whom and to whom interaction is directed. Thus, for a randomly selected member of group X in a city, the probability that someone else selected from the same residential subarea will be a member of group Y is denoted by $_xP_y^*$. Only in the exceptional case, where the number of X and Y in the city is identical will $_xP_y^* = {_y}P_x^*$; normally the isolation of the average X from Y will not be of the same magnitude as the isolation of the average Y from X. This is due, of course, to the fact that the numbers of Xs and Ys in the city are taken into account along with the dissimilarity of their spatial distributions. $_xP_x^*$ refers to the isolation experienced by members of group X in the city, that is, for a member of group X randomly selected in the city, $_xP_x^*$ gives the probability that someone else chosen from the same residential area will also be a member of group X. In other words, it gives the average proportion X is of the population in each subarea weighted by the number of Xs residing in each of these subareas (Farley and Taeuber, 1968: 956). Likewise, $_yP_y^*$ refers to the average isolation experienced by members of group Y in the city. One cannot only measure the isolation of a given group, say X, from other specific groups such as Y and Z, but also its total isolation from all others.

In its most general form, the equation for the index is:

$$_xP_y^* = \sum_{i=1}^{n} \left(\frac{x_i}{X}\right)\left(\frac{y_i}{t_i}\right),$$

where X is the total number of members of group X in the city, $x_i$ is the number of group X in a given subarea, $y_i$ is the number of group Y in the subarea, and $t_i$ is the total population of the subarea. (It is possible for $y_i$ to refer to group X when the simple isolation of the group is being measured.)[3]

The computation of P* is quite simple and an illustration will help the reader gain a conceptual understanding as well. Suppose one wishes to know about the probability of blacks interacting with blacks. One determines the total population in each subarea, $t_i$ (Table 3.1, column 3), and then divides the number of blacks in each subarea, $b_i$, by this total. The resulting black proportions in each subarea (column 6) are then weighted by the proportion of all blacks in the city who live in each subarea, $b_i/B$. Thus using the data in Table 3.1, the P* index for blacks interacting with fellow blacks is:

$$_bP_b^* = \sum_{i=1}^{n} \left(\frac{b_i}{B}\right)\left(\frac{b_i}{t_i}\right) = \left(\frac{60}{200}\right)\left(\frac{60}{430}\right) + \left(\frac{20}{200}\right)\left(\frac{20}{310}\right)$$

$$+ \left(\frac{0}{200}\right)\left(\frac{0}{300}\right) + \left(\frac{120}{200}\right)\left(\frac{120}{160}\right) = 0.4983$$

This means that the average black in the city lives in an area where 0.4983 of the residents are black. This figure can be readily compared with the value that would occur if there was no segregation in the city and if there were no random fluctuations from area to area. This is simply the proportion blacks are of the total city population; in this case B/T = 200/1,200 = 0.1667. The difference, 0.4983 − 0.1667 = 0.3316, is the excess proportion encountered by the average black compared to the value expected if the black component in each subarea was the same as the black proportion of the entire city population. (Of course, it is unlikely that the distributions would be exactly identical even if race was irrelevant: see Cortese, Falk and Cohen, 1978.)

Assuming there are only two groups in the city, whites and blacks, the average proportion of whites (w) encountered by blacks in their residential areas is simply 1 minus the proportion of blacks encountered by blacks. Thus $_bP_w^* = 1 - {_bP_b^*} = 1 - 0.4983 = 0.5017$. Since whites comprise 0.8333 of the city population (1,000/1,200), the difference between $_bP_w^*$ and the proportion that would occur in the absence of segregation is 0.5017 − 0.8333 = −0.3316, the same value as obtained above except in the opposite direction. This figure gives the decrease in contact with whites for blacks compared to what would occur in the absence of any segregation.

An important quality of P* is that the results are asymmetrical for the groups, that is, $_bP_w^* \neq {_wP_b^*}$, $_bP_b^* \neq {_wP_w^*}$. Hence, if we saw above that the average black in the city lives in a residential area where 0.5017 of the residents are white, this does not mean the probability for a randomly selected white having contact with blacks is also 0.5017. In point of fact, except for the rare case when the two groups have exactly the same number of residents in the city, it is certain that the other index will be different. In the present case, one would weight the black proportion in each subarea population (Table 3.1, column 6) by the number of whites (column 2) rather than the number of blacks (column 1), if the goal is the proportion of blacks living in the average white's subarea ( $_wP_b^* = 0.1.003$). (For those oriented to demographic standardisation methods, these differences are analogous to the effect of using different population weights for a given set of rates.) We shall make good use of this difference in probabilities.

In the course of this generalisation of P*, an exact equation was developed for determining $_wP_b^*$ if $_bP_w^*$ is known. This is:

$$_wP_b^* = (_bP_w^*) \ (B/W).$$

From this equation, which can be used to derive either index from the other as long as the relative size of B and W are known for the city, it follows that a change in one P* of a given magnitude has a different effect on the other index, the difference being a function of the ratio between W and B. Thus, if $_w\Delta_b$ represents a change in $_wP_b^*$, it follows that the change in the $_bP_w^*$ index, $_b\Delta_w$ , will be function of B/W as such:

$$_b\Delta_w = \frac{_w\Delta_b}{B/W}$$

This is extremely important because it means that the greater the difference between two groups in their total numbers in the city, the greater will be the differential consequence of a change in segregation. This property has important substantive implications.

Finally, given a group's isolation index, a conversion exists for determining the other group's isolation in the simple case where only two groups are present.

$$_bP_b^* = 1 - [ \ (\frac{W}{B})(1 - _wP_w^*) \ ] \ .$$

There are, of course, a number of other technical issues in the computation of segregation indices, for example, the spatial grid used, the number of spatial units, and the like, but these have been carefully considered elsewhere and there is no point rehashing the discussion at this point (see Taeuber and Taeuber, 1965; Lieberson, 1963). The key issue is determining whether these P* indices have a significant function in research on segregation that cannot be met adequately with the ID.

## Empirical Applications

Rather than speculate on these matters, both the ID and the $_iP_i^*$ measures are applied to some actual data sets. The first of these sets are data initially reported in my monograph (Lieberson, 1980) that had previously been analysed exclusively with P* indices. In this case, the results are first examined in terms of the index of dissimilarity to see what the inferences would normally be and then considered in terms of the P* values obtained earlier.[4]

Indices of dissimilarity were computed between blacks and whites for 17 large non-Southern cities in the United States in each decade between 1890 and 1930.[5] The results, summarised in Table 3.2, indicate that the average level of segregation at first increased only slightly and then more rapidly during the period at hand. Between 1890 and 1900, the average increased just under 2 points from 44.06 to 45.96. Indeed, there were eight cities experiencing declines compared with nine increases (the average increase for the latter outweighed the average decline for the former to generate this change). In each succeeding decade, an increasing number of the 17 cities experienced gains in segregation, with the average increment going up. It seems reasonable to conclude that residential segregation between blacks and whites increased during the span, possibly reflecting the growing numbers of new blacks migrating to these Northern cities. But, whatever the reason, certainly one would conclude that a jump in the average index of residential segregation from 44 to 62, a change of about 40 per cent, represents increased residential segregation between the two groups.

By contrast, what do the P*-type measures tell us about the same period? The mean value of $_bP_b^*$ increased during this period from about 0.07 to 0.30. In 1890, the average black in these cities lived in a ward where 7 per cent of the residents were black; in 1930, the average black resided in a ward in which 30 per cent were black. The much more rapid increase reflects the fact that two forces were working

**Table 3.2: Black-White Segregation, 17 Leading Northern United States Cities, Wards, 1890–1930**

| Year | Index of dissimilarity | | $_bP_b$ | | $_wP^*_w$ | |
| | Mean | Number of cities increasing over preceding year | Mean | Number of cities increasing over preceding year | Mean | Number of cities increasing over preceding year |
| --- | --- | --- | --- | --- | --- | --- |
| 1890 | 44.06 | | 0.0666 | | 0.9720 | |
| 1900 | 45.96 | 9 | 0.0760 | 12 | 0.9686 | 4 |
| 1910 | 49.72 | 11 | 0.0972 | 13 | 0.9698 | 10 |
| 1920 | 54.37 | 12 | 0.1677 | 17 | 0.9614 | 1 |
| 1930 | 62.14 | 16 | 0.2992 | 16 | 0.9540 | 5 |

Note: For list of cities, see Table 3.4.

in the same direction. Namely, the spatial dissimilarity between blacks and whites increased, as indicated by the ID, *and* the average percent blacks also increased. The results are a four-fold increase in black isolation. The change for whites is quite different however. Although the ID went up, white isolation declined slightly during the same period from 0.9720 to 0.9540. The reason is simple enough; the isolation of whites declined because the increases in spatial dissimilarity were not of a magnitude sufficient to compensate for the increase in the black proportion of the cities' populations. Hence the isolation trends (to wit, the combined product of spatial dissimilarity and population composition) are different for whites and blacks in the North in the early decades of this century. Blacks were becoming more isolated, but whites were becoming slightly less isolated even though the differences in spatial distribution were increasing.

There is no immediate way such a distinctive interpretation could occur if we knew changes in population composition and added those to patterns of change in the ID. The black average proportion in these 17 cities increased from 0.0295 (1890) to 0.0331 (1900) to 0.0333 (1910) to 0.0458 (1920) to 0.0648 (1930). Would that be enough to decrease the average isolation of whites in these cities even though the ID increased? It is hard to answer by just combining the ID values with the compositional information. To be sure, one could correlate composition with the ID, either in static fashion or in terms of changes over time. But if one wishes to draw some inferences about the levels of isolation and/or changes in these levels over time, the P*-type provide a distinctive perspective.

Consider some actual cases. The index of dissimilarity between blacks and whites in Philadelphia increased from 47.11 to 51.03 between 1920 and 1930. During the same period the black proportion of the population also went up, from 0.0736 to 0.1126. In terms of the actual isolation of blacks, we know that the changes are in the same direction, that is, there is both greater dissimilarity in spatial distribution *and* a larger black proportion of the population. But what is the combined effect? On the other hand, from the white perspective, the increase in the black-white ID measure will be counterbalanced to some unknown degree by the decrease in the white proportion of the population. Again, it is rather hard to put these facts together except through the use of P* measures. In this case, $_bP_b^*$ increased from 0.2078 to 0.2727 during the decade; $_wP_w^*$ dropped from 0.9371 to 0.9078, even though the ID increased.

Use of P* indices suggests a rather different interpretation of the events transpiring during the early part of the twentieth century in the urban North. With the movement of blacks to the urban North, the upward shifts in the ID are not necessarily a function of a change in white attitudes towards blacks, but rather the increases in the ID represent nothing more than an effort to maintain the same level of white isolation from blacks at a time when the compositional shifts are working in the opposite direction. The level of black contact with whites, $_bP_w^*$ (which in the two-group case is nothing more than $1 - {_bP_b^*}$ ), declines at the same time as an increase in the average white's contact with blacks (Lieberson, 1980, Chapter 9). Hence, not only does the P* approach permit combining the net consequences of both population composition and dissimilarities in spatial distribution into one indicator with a clear operational meaning, but the asymmetrical approach gives new substantive understanding to the spatial patterns observed in a city.

To be sure, it is possible for one to misanalyse P* indices by forgetting that they are partially reflecting limits set by the group's proportion in the city. The minimum $_iP_i^*$ is always equal to the group's proportion of the total population. Thus if one visualises a graph displaying $_iP_i^*$ on I/T, the range of possible values will occur only in the part of the graph above a line set by $_iP_i^* = I/T$. Still there is more going on than changes in percent black to explain the events between 1890 and 1930. The indices of black isolation increase progressively in each decade from 1900 through 1930 even when regressed on the black percentage in each city (and restricting the analyses to comparable ranges of I/T values). Hence there is genuine change possible in levels of isolation between groups that are not merely a function of changes in population composition (Table 3.3).

**Table 3.3: Comparisons Between Adjacent Decades in the Regression of $_bP^*_b$ on the Black Proportion of the Population, 17 Leading Non-southern Cities**

| Year | r | b | a |
|------|------|--------|--------|
| 1900 | 0.81 | 1.2621 | 0.0365 |
| 1910 | 0.87 | 1.8393 | 0.0373 |
| 1910 | 0.88 | 1.8887 | 0.0343 |
| 1920 | 0.69 | 2.4384 | 0.0618 |
| 1920 | 0.67 | 2.0846 | 0.0722 |
| 1930 | 0.63 | 3.3280 | 0.1127 |

Note: First year shown in a pair includes all 17 cities; second row is for those cities 10 years later with a black proportion of the population falling within the range existing in the first decade of the pair.

The asymmetrical possibilities of analysis presented by P* are extremely valuable for some problems, not the least of which is understanding the actual consequences for each group. After all, it is easier to assume that people are responding to the relative numbers of blacks and whites in their home turf rather than to the inequality of the spatial distributions between the groups. Massive differences between cities in their IDs during this period are far more comprehensible when the degree of white isolation is considered (to wit, jointly taking into account composition and differences in spatial distributions). Table 3.4 gives information for the 17 specific Northern cities in both 1930 and 1890. In both cases, observe the substantial intercity variation in the ID obtained between blacks and whites. In 1890 the index ranges from 17.64 and 21.44 for Kansas City and Los Angeles, respectively, to the mid-60s for Chicago and Milwaukee. Likewise, there is a wide range in the ID for 1930, ranging from 33.64 in Minneapolis and 40 in Indianapolis to the mid-80s for Chicago and Milwaukee again. The average ID between blacks and whites has gone up considerably during this

**Table 3.4: Black-White Segregation in 17 Specific Cities, by Wards, 1890 and 1930**

| City | ID 1890 | ID 1930 | $_bP_b^*$ 1890 | $_bP_b^*$ 1930 | $_wP_w^*$ 1890 | $_wP_w^*$ 1930 |
|------|------|------|------|------|------|------|
| Boston | 56.50 | 67.76 | 0.0849 | 0.1923 | 0.9831 | 0.9782 |
| Buffalo | 38.10 | 79.91 | 0.0107 | 0.2420 | 0.9957 | 0.9816 |
| Chicago | 63.65 | 84.90 | 0.0811 | 0.7041 | 0.9879 | 0.9780 |
| Cincinnati | 45.06 | 65.78 | 0.0943 | 0.4449 | 0.9630 | 0.9342 |
| Cleveland | 60.70 | 80.16 | 0.0467 | 0.5094 | 0.9890 | 0.9574 |
| Detroit | 57.02 | 59.52 | 0.0553 | 0.3115 | 0.9840 | 0.9429 |
| Indianapolis | 41.95 | 40.07 | 0.1727 | 0.2601 | 0.9215 | 0.8984 |
| Kansas City | 17.64 | 59.83 | 0.1262 | 0.3159 | 0.8994 | 0.9269 |
| Los Angeles | 21.44 | 68.20 | 0.0329 | 0.2562 | 0.9752 | 0.9759 |
| Milwaukee | 66.99 | 83.71 | 0.0143 | 0.1636 | 0.9978 | 0.9890 |
| Minneapolis | 40.02 | 33.64 | 0.0163 | 0.0165 | 0.9921 | 0.9911 |
| Newark | 34.59 | 46.55 | 0.0404 | 0.2282 | 0.9776 | 0.9256 |
| New York City | 42.35 | 64.08 | 0.0349 | 0.4177 | 0.9851 | 0.9711 |
| Philadelphia | 42.74 | 51.03 | 0.1170 | 0.2727 | 0.9655 | 0.9078 |
| Pittsburgh | 45.22 | 51.51 | 0.0814 | 0.2681 | 0.9688 | 0.9346 |
| St Louis | 33.50 | 75.55 | 0.1089 | 0.4655 | 0.9437 | 0.9313 |
| San Francisco | 41.58 | 44.14 | 0.0134 | 0.0179 | 0.9939 | 0.9941 |

period, from 44 to 62.

Consider, however, the conclusions generated by a separate analysis of black and white P* indices. As is the case for the ID, there is considerable variation between cities in the isolation of blacks. In 1930, $_bP_b^*$ ranges from less than 0.02 for Minneapolis and San Francisco to 0.51 for Cleveland and 0.70 for Chicago. Observe by contrast the steady nature of white isolation, both with respect to changes between 1890 and 1930 (a decline in the mean $_wP_w^*$ from 0.97 to 0.95) and in terms of the rather small variation between cities in each period. In 1890, the indices were rather uniformly high, ranging from lows of 0.8994 and 0.92 in Kansas City and Indianapolis to highs in excess of 0.99 in four cities. In 1930, the lows again were about 0.90 (for Indianapolis and Philadelphia), with $_wP_w^*$ exceeding 0.99 in two cities (Minneapolis and San Francisco). The enormous stability in the magnitude of white isolation, in the face of increases in the ID, black isolation and the black proportion of the population, is certainly consistent with the hypothesis that at least part of the fluctuations in segregation are nothing more than the dominant white population attempting to maintain the same high level of isolation from blacks as before. The point of all this is to illustrate the kinds of problems that are attractive to study through an asymmetrical approach to segregation.

However, one might object to the above example on the grounds that the analysis was necessarily confined to rather large spatial units, wards. It may be that the increases over time in both the ID and black isolation simply reflected the filling in of the ward units over time. If a group's total population in the city is smaller than the population of most of the spatial units used in the analysis, it is difficult adequately to measure segregation. Even if all members of the group are in one spatial unit, the ID will necessarily be less than 100 (see Lieberson, 1963: 36–7). Although these spatial units affect both the P* and dissimilarity indices, a certain reservation is healthy. Particularly when the period from 1890 to 1930 may have covered some important shifts in urban spatial structure due to changes in transportation. Another data set is available which allows one to overrule such issues. Based on data for 13 cities experiencing special censuses in the 1960s, Farley and Taeuber (1968) compared the segregation between blacks and whites in 1960 with the data for later in the decade. Of particular value for the purposes at hand, they present both the ID and what they call the 'Homogeneity index', the latter being a P* index computed separately for both blacks and whites, $_bP_b^*$ and $_wP_w^*$ respectively.

Table 3.5 indicates the ID between blacks and whites, the P* indices for each group, and the proportion of the population black. Since computations were based on the census tract distributions of the groups, the ward objection is eliminated. Here too we see the ID goes up in all but two of the cities in the 1960s. Again, the patterns are quite different for the specific racial groups. Although black isolation increases in all cities, a very mixed pattern exists for whites: increases in four cities, declines in three, and no change in six. The pattern is very much in keeping with the notion that whites are simply trying to maintain a certain constant high level of isolation from blacks. White isolation varies only narrowly in both periods, ranging from 0.88 to 0.97 in 1960 and from 0.89 to 0.97 later in the decade. By contrast, there is much greater variation between cities in the ID (or in $_bP_b^*$ for that matter). In both periods Sacramento has the lowest ID, in the high 50s; Cleveland has the highest ID in the first period and second highest later in the decade, 85 and 87 respectively. Does it make sense trying to understand massive differences between such cities in their indices of dissimilarity when the levels of white isolation are actually so similar? Indeed,

**Table 3.5: Black-White Segregation in 13 Cities, by Tracts, 1960 and Later**

| City | ID 1960 | ID later | $_bP^*_b$ 1960 | $_bP^*_b$ later | $_wP^*_w$ 1960 | $_wP^*_w$ later | Percent black 1960 | Percent black later |
|------|------|------|------|------|------|------|------|------|
| Buffalo | 84.5 | 85.1 | 0.65 | 0.74 | 0.95 | 0.95 | 13.2 | 17.0 |
| Providence | 64.2 | 70.3 | 0.23 | 0.30 | 0.96 | 0.94 | 5.4 | 7.4 |
| Rochester | 76.7 | 79.3 | 0.44 | 0.53 | 0.96 | 0.95 | 7.4 | 10.4 |
| Cleveland | 85.2 | 87.2 | 0.81 | 0.86 | 0.92 | 0.92 | 28.6 | 34.1 |
| Des Moines | 76.7 | 77.3 | 0.35 | 0.40 | 0.97 | 0.97 | 4.9 | 5.3 |
| Evansville | 76.9 | 80.5 | 0.54 | 0.61 | 0.97 | 0.97 | 6.6 | 6.9 |
| Fort Wayne | 79.8 | 79.2 | 0.38 | 0.52 | 0.95 | 0.95 | 7.5 | 10.2 |
| Greensboro | 83.8 | 89.1 | 0.83 | 0.88 | 0.94 | 0.96 | 25.8 | 26.7 |
| Louisville | 78.6 | 81.2 | 0.68 | 0.73 | 0.93 | 0.93 | 17.9 | 20.2 |
| Memphis | 79.3 | 83.7 | 0.79 | 0.86 | 0.88 | 0.89 | 37.6 | 42.6 |
| Raleigh | 75.0 | 78.0 | 0.72 | 0.74 | 0.92 | 0.93 | 23.4 | 23.4 |
| Shreveport | 82.5 | 85.1 | 0.81 | 0.85 | 0.90 | 0.92 | 33.1 | 34.7 |
| Sacramento | 58.2 | 57.2 | 0.24 | 0.29 | 0.95 | 0.94 | 6.5 | 8.3 |

Source: Farley and Taeuber, 1968, Tables 1 and 3.

whites are slightly more isolated in Sacramento than in Cleveland.

To be sure, there are cases where the levels of isolation may indeed be truly different. An analysis of Southern cities, for example, indicates sharply lower white isolation than in the North throughout the 1890–1930 period. It is not so crucial, for the purposes at hand, to draw any definite conclusions about attempts by the dominant white population to maintain their distance from blacks in the face of the latter's increasing proportions. Of concern here is that these indices provide a distinctive approach to segregation — one that cannot be matched adequately by dealing with spatial dissimilarity and population composition as two separate variables.

## Linkages between the ID and P*

It is therefore very important to consider closely the linkage between P*-type indices and the combined effect of the ID and population composition. If knowledge of the ID and population composition would allow the investigator to determine the value of P* or even closely to estimate its value, then the P* measures could be generated with existing data on the ID and population composition.

At the extreme values of the ID such an exact linkage exists with P*. When the ID between groups I and J is 100, then $_iP_i^* = 1.0$ and $_jP_j^* = 1.0$. When $D_{ij} = 0$, then $_iP_i^* = I/T$ and $_jP_j^* = J/T$. However, the measures are not so closely linked in the situations commonly encountered when segregation is neither absent nor total. Through trial and error processes the following bounds are inferred for a given index of dissimilarity, $ID_{ij}$:

$$\text{Maximum } _iP_i^* = I/T + [\,(ID_{ij}/100)\,(1 - I/T)\,]$$

$$\text{Maximum } _jP_j^* = J/T + [\,(ID_{ij}/100)\,(1 - J/T)\,]$$

The minimum P* for a given ID, is somewhat more complicated.

$$\text{Minimum } _iP_i^* = \frac{(0.50 + ID_{ij}/200)^2\,(I)}{[\,(0.50 + ID_{ij}/200)\,(I)\,] + [\,(0.50 - ID_{ij}/200)\,(T - I)\,]}$$
$$+ \frac{(0.50 - ID_{ij}/200)^2\,(I)}{[\,(0.50 - ID_{ij}/200)\,(I)\,] + [\,(0.50 + ID_{ij}/200)\,(T - I)\,]}$$

Two important conclusions follow from these equations. Holding $ID_{ij}$ constant, the range of possible values for $_iP_i^*$ increases as I/T gets smaller. If I/T is very large, then the range of possible values for $_iP_i^*$ is relatively small. Second, the range of $_iP_i^*$ is affected by the level of $ID_{ij}$, holding I/T constant, but in a more complicated manner. If I/T = 0.5, then the range of $_iP_i^*$ is greatest when the ID is 50, becoming progressively smaller as the ID approaches either extreme of 100 or 0. As I/T moves towards either a smaller or larger proportion, the peak range for $_iP_i^*$ occurs at increasingly large values of $ID_{ij}$. This is relatively insignificant as I/T approaches 1.0 because, as pointed out above, the range is so constrained anyway.

Table 3.6 converts these formulae into actual values, giving the reader some understanding of the $_iP_i^*$ range that can be encountered with a given index of dissimilarity and when group I is some specific proportion of the population. The range of $_iP_i^*$ is narrow, in both an absolute and relative sense, when I/T is large (especially when the ID is relatively small). Hence, when I/T is 0.9 and the ID is 10, $_iP_i^*$ ranges from 0.90 to 0.91. But the range is considerably wider in a two-group situation where the other group, J, is one-tenth. With an ID of 10 $_jP_j^*$ ranges from 0.10 to 0.19 (nearly double the bottom limit). A quick

**Table 3.6: Limits in P\* Indices, given ID and Population Composition**

| I/T | Δ = 10 | | | Δ = 30 | | | Δ = 50 | | | Δ = 70 | | | Δ = 90 | | |
|---|---|---|---|---|---|---|---|---|---|---|---|---|---|---|---|
| | Max. | Min. | Range | Max. | Min. | Range | Max. | Min. | Range | Max. | Min. | Range | Max. | Min. | Range |
| 0.05 | 0.14 | 0.05 | 0.09 | 0.34 | 0.07 | 0.27 | 0.52 | 0.11 | 0.41 | 0.72 | 0.20 | 0.52 | 0.91 | 0.48 | 0.43 |
| 0.10 | 0.19 | 0.10 | 0.09 | 0.37 | 0.13 | 0.24 | 0.55 | 0.20 | 0.35 | 0.73 | 0.33 | 0.40 | 0.91 | 0.64 | 0.27 |
| 0.30 | 0.37 | 0.31 | 0.06 | 0.51 | 0.35 | 0.16 | 0.65 | 0.45 | 0.20 | 0.79 | 0.61 | 0.18 | 0.93 | 0.85 | 0.08 |
| 0.50 | 0.55 | 0.50 | 0.05 | 0.65 | 0.54 | 0.11 | 0.75 | 0.62 | 0.13 | 0.85 | 0.74 | 0.11 | 0.95 | 0.91 | 0.04 |
| 0.70 | 0.73 | 0.70 | 0.03 | 0.79 | 0.72 | 0.07 | 0.85 | 0.77 | 0.08 | 0.91 | 0.83 | 0.08 | 0.97 | 0.93 | 0.04 |
| 0.90 | 0.91 | 0.90 | 0.01 | 0.93 | 0.90 | 0.03 | 0.95 | 0.91 | 0.04 | 0.97 | 0.93 | 0.04 | 0.99 | 0.96 | 0.03 |
| 0.95 | 0.96 | 0.95 | 0.01 | 0.97 | 0.95 | 0.02 | 0.98 | 0.95 | 0.03 | 0.99 | 0.96 | 0.03 | 0.995 | 0.95 | 0.045 |

survey of Table 3.6 shows many instances with much wider ranges in situations that could easily be encountered in occupational, educational or racial and ethnic situations in a variety of settings. A group that is 30 per cent of the population and has an ID of 70 could range from an average level of isolation of 0.61 to 0.79; a similar index for a group amounting to 10 per cent of the population could mean a $_iP_i^*$ anywhere from 0.33 to 0.73.

In short, there are certain extreme cases when the P* index of isolation will have a very narrow possible range, regardless of the level of the ID. But under those very conditions, there will have to be one or more other groups in the community whose members make up a small proportion of the population and hence for whom a wide range of possible P* values will exist. It is therefore almost certain that in any segregation study, IDs, coupled with information on composition, will not permit a sufficiently exact determination of the P* indices without a direct computation.

The range is quite substantial, given the composition and indices of dissimilarity encountered with actual data. In the late 1960s data set for 13 cities reported in Table 3.5, the range in $_bP_b^*$ for the average city was 0.27, hardly a trivial matter. Since the black proportions of the population were even smaller in the 1930 data set reported in Table 3.4, the range of possible black isolation indices was even greater, running from 0.29 and 0.33 in Indianapolis and Minneapolis respectively to 0.64 in Buffalo and 0.72 in Milwaukee. Hence, at the moment, the information obtained through a compositional variable and the ID cannot provide a substitute for measurement of the P* index (except where the formulae provided above indicate that the possible range of P* is acceptably narrow). To be sure, more needs to be done with this issue since there is no knowledge about the distributions actually occurring across the possible range of values.


## Conclusion

What are the arguments for and against the P*-type index? The existence of a large body of existing data with ID values is not a trivial matter, if only because standard data are not that common in the social sciences and there is enough difficulty comparing segregation between places and across periods as it is, without complicating the matter by introducing a different segregation measure. The second objection stems from the fact that the measure is correlated with population composition. All things being the same, differences between cities in P* indices will be correlated with differences in population composition. Hence the investigator is apt to run into serious and sticky problems when correlating P*-type measures with composition. (Even here, it is possible to analyse the linkage with composition in different periods and places by considering the regression of P*-type indices on composition, such as was described earlier in this paper and reported in Table 3.3.)

On the other hand, a P* index describes the actual isolation of a group either from all others or from a specific group in a manner which takes into account the joint influence of population composition and spatial distribution. The operational definitions possible with these measures are appealing and readily understood. Hence, by taking composition into account, it is possible with one number to pull together the two forces most likely to mean isolation; namely, differences in spatial distribution and relative numbers. In so far as the investigator wishes to know this, we have seen that combining the index of dissimilarity with a separate measure of composition is an inadequate substitute in many cases. Considering only indices of dissimilarity can easily be misleading since it is all too easy to assume that this measure of spatial differences in distribution is describing the actual spatial isolation of the groups. I believe, also, that the asymmetrical approach is full of interesting research and substantive possibilities. Even in some of the studies where these measures have been used, the investigators have not taken full advantage of the implications of looking at the event from the perspective of each of the two groups (even more perspectives are possible when segregation is analysed in a multi-group setting). At the very least, it seems reasonable in many research projects to expect researchers to compute both the index of dissimilarity and P*-type measures — particularly since the same data inputs are necessary. As one moves away from describing dissimilarity in spatial patterns and gets into the question of the actual isolation of the groups, it is likely that P* will prove to be a more complete and adequate measure.

## Notes

1. If X/T is the proportion X is of the total population, then the index of dissimilarity between X and the total population (thus including X) is divided

by $1 - (X/T)$ to obtain the ID that would occur between X and non-X.

2.  See also Erbe (1975) who developed her analysis of socio-economic race segregation on the basis of Bell's work. Apparently unaware of the residential segregation literature, Coleman, Kelly and Moore (1975, pp. 7–9) independently rediscovered both the revised II index and P* some 20 years later, calling them $r_{ij}$ and $s_{ij}$ respectively. In the same way that II was found inadequately to take composition into account, one could make the same conclusion with respect to $r_{ij}$ in the controversial study of school desegregation. Also apparently unaware of Bell, Schnare (1977) has likewise independently developed the measure.

3.  In the case where one computes a group's probability of interacting with fellow members of the same group, that is, where the subscripts before and after P* are identical, it is convenient to alter the true probability by in effect assuming sampling with replacement (Bell, 1954: 358).

4.  The figures for P* in some cases differ slightly from those reported in Chapter 9 of Lieberson, 1980. With one small exception, this reflects rounding.

5.  Non-whites other than blacks are included with whites. This is of no consequence in nearly all of the cities, but facilitates the analysis and illustrations by avoiding a multiple group situation.

# Bibliography

Bell, W. (1954) 'A Probability Model for the Measurement of Ecological Segregation', *Social Forces*, 32, 357–64

Blau, P.M. (1977) *Inequality and Heterogeneity*, Free Press, New York

Coleman, J.S., Kelly, S.D. and Moore, J.A. (1975) *Trends in School Segregation, 1968–73*, The Urban Institute, Washington, DC

Cortese, C.F., Falk, R.F. and Cohen, J. (1976) 'Further Considerations on the Methodological Analysis of Segregation Indices', *American Sociological Review*, 41, 630–7

Cortese, C.F., Falk, R.F. and Cohen, J. (1978) 'Understanding the Standardized Index of Dissimilarity: Reply to Massey', *American Sociological Review*, 43, 590–2

Duncan, O.D. and Duncan, B. (1955a) 'Residential Distribution and Occupational Stratification', *American Journal of Sociology*, 60, 493–503

Duncan, O.D. and Duncan, B. (1955b) 'A Methodological Analysis of Segregation Indexes', *American Sociological Review*, 20, 210–17

Erbe, B. Mach (1975) 'Race and Socioeconomic Segregation', *American Sociological Review*, 40, 801–12

Farley, R. and Taeuber, K.E. (1968) 'Population Trends and Residential Segregation since 1960', *Science*, 159, 953–6

Jahn, J., Schmid, C.F. and Schrag, C. (1947) 'The Measurement of Ecological Segregation', *American Sociological Review*, 12, 293–303

Johnson, M. (1973) 'A Comment on Palmore and Whittington's Index of Similarity', *Social Forces*, 51, 490–2

Lieberson, S. (1963) *Ethnic Patterns in American Cities*, The Free Press, New York

Lieberson, S. (1969) 'Measuring Population Diversity', *American Sociological Review*, 34, 850–62

Lieberson, S. (1975) 'Rank-sum Comparisons between Groups', in David Heise (ed.), *Sociological Methodology 1976*, Jossey-Bass, San Francisco

Lieberson, S. (1980) *A Piece of the Pie: Blacks and White Immigrants Since*

*1880*, University of California Press, Berkeley

Peach, Ceri (ed.) (1975) *Urban Social Segregation*, Longman, London

Schnare, A.B. (1977) *Residential Segregation by Race in U.S. Metropolitan Areas: An Analysis Across Cities and Over Time*, The Urban Institute, Washington DC

Shevky, E. and Williams, M. (1949) *The Social Areas of Los Angeles, Analysis and Typology*, University of California Press, Berkeley

Taeuber, K.E. and Taeuber, A.F. (1965) *Negroes in Cities*, Aldine, Chicago

Walker, D., Stinchcombe, A.L. and McDill, M.J. (1967) *School Desegregation in Baltimore*, Johns Hopkins Center for the Study of Social Organization of Schools, Baltimore

## Acknowledgement

The assistance of Donna K. Carter is gratefully acknowledged. This study is part of a project on asymmetrical segregation supported by the National Science Foundation (grant SOC — 7915358).

# 4 A DEMOGRAPHIC PERSPECTIVE ON SCHOOL DESEGREGATION IN THE USA

Karl E. Taeuber, Franklin D. Wilson, David R. James
and Alma F. Taeuber

Public education in the United States is organised spatially and
racially. During the last three decades the federal government, seeking
to reduce racial segregation in the public (state) schools, has intervened in the organisation of education. In hundreds of school districts,
the racial assignment of pupils to schools has been changed. Linkages
among race, residence and schooling have been altered, often massively.
Other consequences for race and place may follow, putatively white
flight and conceivably other types of residential change. Because
the timing and magnitude of school racial reassignments have varied
greatly from one school district to another, the school desegregation
process may be viewed as a national experiment to make over certain
features of ethnic ecology. This report presents a demographic
description of the direct changes in pupil distribution. Although the
empirical materials do not extend to any new analysis of white flight,
they do provide a basis for reconsideration of some of the scholarly
and polemic literature on the demographic consequences of school
desegregation.

To explain what is meant by a 'national experiment in ethnic
ecology', let us begin with the general observation that human
activities are spatially organised. In contemporary industrial nations,
the settlement pattern is elaborately differentiated. Much of the
population lives in densely settled urban or metropolitan regions.
Within these regions, activities vary in patterns of spatial concentration. Manufacturing and other major employment centres, wholesale trade, certain kinds of retail trade, some governmental facilities
and other specialised businesses and services tend to be highly concentrated. Convenience goods and services, including residential
facilities, tend to be more widely and evenly distributed.

The utilisation of residential space is organised along various
social and economic axes. Among these is ethnicity. The highly
structured and persistent racial residential segregation of US
cities is particularly pertinent for this analysis. There is also a
racial patterning of convenience goods and services. For most of

these establishments, the clientele are mainly of one race. Often there is racial patterning of personnel offering the services. There may also be racially patterned areal differences in the quantity or quality of services (including governmental services).

## School Desegregation in the United States: a Brief History

In the United States, the territorial structure of formal governmental administration is a complex overlay on the urban region. Educational services are typically administered by school districts that have varying degrees of geographic and political overlap with other administrative systems, particularly counties and municipalities. In many southern states, school districts tend to be county-wide. In northern states, each large municipality tends to be served by a school district with similar boundaries, although inclusion of additional territory and exclusion of some municipal area is common.

Elementary schools tend to be scattered through residential territory in the manner of a convenience service. Secondary schools serve a larger population base, but are also geographically dispersed. Prior to desegregation activities, most large school districts used residential location as a principal determinant of the school a child was entitled to attend. Geographic determination, however, was often quite incomplete. Overlapping zones, transfer provisions, enrolment provisions for schools offering special services, and other attendance rules complicated the system.

Among the attendance rules in the South was compulsory racial separation. A formally designated dual system persisted intact until 1954 and changed little for some years thereafter. Northern districts with large numbers of black pupils used attendance rules, personnel policies and other administrative strategies to operate substantially dual systems.

Although litigation against school segregation was only one tactic in a broad panorama of social actions and social movements affecting what Myrdal (1944; see also Kluger, 1976) called 'the web of discrimination', the 1954 *Brown* decision of the US Supreme Court, which declared school segregation unconstitutional, became the herald of the 'civil rights movement' and the 'civil rights era'. For some years, this symbolic effect of *Brown* was its chief effect. Not until 1955 did the Supreme Court issue an implementation decree for *Brown*, and then the task of devising appropriate remedies was placed under the jurisdiction of local federal judges, who could take into account the specific circumstances of each school district. Among these circumstances were strong political opposition to desegregation and the peculiar US balance between federal and state powers. The Supreme Court shied away from full clarification and implementation of its mandate, and the federal and state governments generally shied away from their enforcement responsibilities. In 1956 President Eisenhower sent federal troops to Little Rock, Arkansas, to enable seven black pupils to attend a 'white school', and for another decade most school desegregation was of a similar token sort.

In the mid-1960s the civil rights movement had become politically important, and there was a renewed flurry of judicial, legislative and administrative actions to foster school desegregation (Orfield, 1969). The Supreme Court issued a series of decisions tightening up the remedy requirements, Congress passed a major civil rights act, and both the Department of Justice and the Department of Health, Education and Welfare began actively instigating and watchdogging desegregation.

In 1973, in *Keyes*, the Supreme Court gave clear sanction to imposition of desegregation remedies on Northern districts. Two years before, in *Swann*, the Court had specified that those remedies could include bussing if transportation to schools geographically remote from residences was necessary to disestablish the dual system 'root and branch' and to create a system 'without black schools or white schools but just schools'. The *Swann* decision also authorised the use of racial balance — each school having the district-wide racial percentage — as a starting-point for the evaluation of the effectiveness of a remedy.

This brief history is incomplete, but it suffices to emphasise the ecologically significant features of the process. School desegregation activities during the last dozen years have been very much focused on the racial composition of schools. Rules for allocating children to schools have been altered in order to eliminate racial identifiability of schools and reduce school-by-school variation in racial percentages. Desegregation activities have thereby transformed the linkages among race, residential location and school assignment. Enforcement by judicial and administrative agencies has proceeded on a case-by-case basis. Desegregation has typically been implemented one district at a time, with various starting dates, various modes and rates of re-allocation, various criteria for desegregation, and various degrees of success in reducing racial segregation in the schools. This 'experiment'

has created enormous variance among cities in the timing and
scope of transformation in school attendance patterns. Social scientists
thus have the opportunity to anticipate and to study the ripple effects
of these changes on other features of the racial locational process.

## Data and Methods of Analysis

More than 2,000 school districts in the United States serve significant
numbers and proportions of minority pupils. To permit a graphic
portrayal of the varieties of experience, we chose a set of large
districts with large numbers of black pupils. The minimum size
criterion was 10,000 black pupils enrolled in public (state) schools in
autumn 1968. The 87 school districts that exceed this limit contain
more than one-half of the nation's black state school pupils. These
districts account for much of the judicial and administrative
difficulty in devising, implementing and evaluating desegregation
plans; they are the locus of the greatest and most persistent political
controversy and turmoil.

This report is based on autumn enrolment data for black and white
pupils in public (state) elementary and secondary schools for the
school years 1968–9 to 1976–7; no data were collected on a nationwide basis for autumn 1975. We used specially edited tape files
prepared for this project from the data files of the US Office for
Civil Rights, Department of Health, Education and Welfare. (Data
for some of these years have been published, e.g. US Office for Civil
Rights, 1970.) In several of the 87 districts the multi-ethnic nature
of the student body has played a role in the structure of segregation,
and in a few the desegregation process has explicitly distinguished
one or more of the other groups separately identified in the files
(Hispanic, Asian or Native Americans). For simplicity of presentation
and interpretation, attention here is given only to the black and white
groups. ('White' is, more specifically, non-Hispanic white, or 'Anglo'.)

Three measures of school racial segregation are used. (Formal
definitions of indices are given in the Appendix.) Many desegregation
plans are designed with complete racial balance as the approximate
target, and with a specified permissible tolerance range for the
variation of each school's racial proportion from the district racial
proportion. The tolerance range is often plus or minus 10 per cent, or
15 per cent. The index of dissimilarity (ID) is an adjusted weighted
average of the deviations of school proportions black from the district

proportion black, and thus is conceptually the most appropriate index for measuring school desegregation. It is also the most commonly used index for measuring racial residential segregation and other types of areal social segregation.

In the graphs the ID is expressed in percentage form, with 100 representing complete segregation (every school uniracial) and zero representing complete desegregation (every school with the same percentage black). Obviously this is a strictly demographic assessment of pupil segregation and desegregation, and takes no account of educational processes, resources and other aspects that may be specified in a desegregation plan and that would have to be included in an assessment of the educational effects of desegregation.

Two other measures of the demographic character of school desegregation will be used. These exposure indices, sometimes called racial contact measures, are measures of the average racial composition in the schools attended by pupils of a given race. The index of exposure of blacks to whites is the average percent white in the schools of black pupils. The index of exposure of whites to blacks is the average percent black in the schools of white pupils.

The ID is essentially independent of a district's racial composition. The exposure indices are very much constrained by that composition. To the extent that parental responses to desegregation are shaped by accurate perceptions of changes in the racial composition of their children's schools, the exposure indices may be more closely related to behavioural responses than are changes in dissimilarity. For this reason, and because exposure of each race to the other is one explicit goal of many proponents of desegregation, the exposure indices may usefully supplement the ID.

## Trends in Public (State) School Segregation

### Spatial Dissimilarity

Our empirical description of trends in public school segregation in the 87 districts from 1968 to 1976 is presented in nine figures. Each figure is a scatterplot; an asterisk locates each district at the point representing its value on the measures specified by the horizontal and vertical scales. In these computer-generated plots, if more than one district occupies approximately the same position on the scatterplot, the number of such districts is printed.

The general trend in degree of school segregation is portrayed in Figures 4.1 and 4.2, using the ID. The year-by-year dispersion of scores is plotted in Figure 4.1. If data were available for autumn 1953, before the Supreme Court ruled against racial segregation, all of the Southern districts would have been plotted at 100. During the 1950s and 1960s all of these districts took some actions to move away from complete racial segregation, but by the autumn of 1968, none of the districts (Southern or Northern) had undergone a desegregation programme comprehensive enough to bring the dissimilarity index below 50. Eight years later, 37 districts had scores below 50.

The strongest visual feature of Figure 4.1, the spreading down toward the bottom of the chart in 1971, reflects the implementation of many substantial desegregation efforts in that year. Less obvious in this plot is the steady downward movement of the average ID; the median dropped from 82 to 56 in eight years. To call attention to this trend, the location of the median district for each year is underlined.

To portray changes in school segregation for individual districts (Figure 4.2), dissimilarity indices for 1976 are plotted on the vertical

**Figure 4.1: Distribution of Dissimilarity Scores in Each Year, 1968 to 1976**

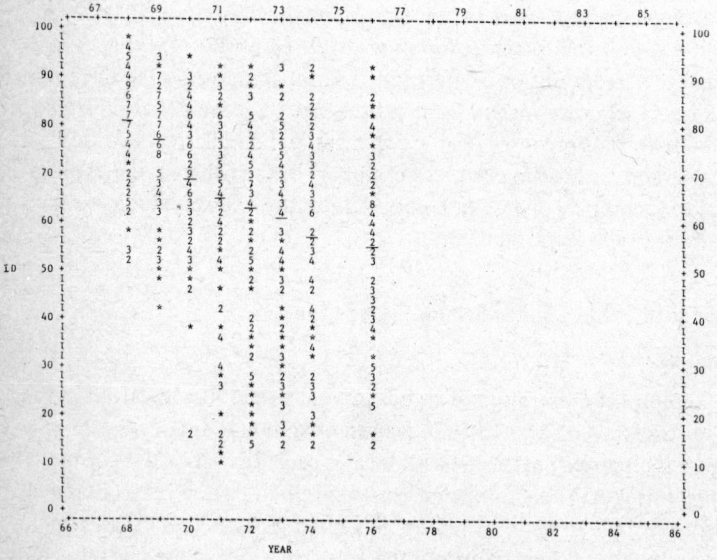

scale and indices for 1968 are on the horizontal scale. The compression of 1968 scores into the range from 50 to 100 and the dispersion of 1976 scores through nearly the full range is again evident. What this figure adds to the preceding one is an indication of no connection between initial (1968) and terminal (1976) scores. Either of two patterns might have been considered more likely than this lack of pattern. If private litigants and government agencies had directed their attacks on segregation largely towards the most segregated districts, Figure 4.2 might have been nearly empty in the upper right corner and much denser in the lower right, with a distinct negative correlation between 1968 and 1976 scores. Alternatively, those districts in which 1968 scores were below the median might have been those most receptive to past desegregation activities and most likely to engage in further desegregation, while those above the median might have been predicted, on the basis of having changed little from 1954 to 1968, to change little from 1968 to 1976. If this were the case, the points in Figure 4.2 would be clustered along

**Figure 4.2: Dissimilarity in 1976 (ID 76) v. Dissimilarity in 1968 (ID 68)**

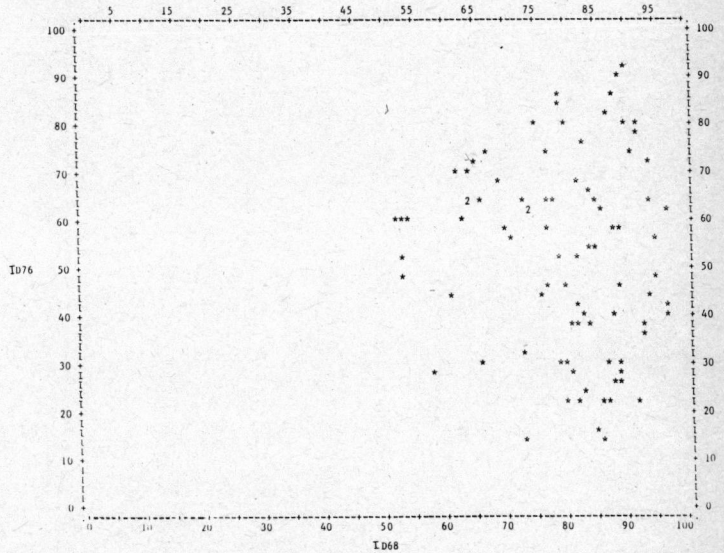

a line running from about 50 on the horizontal axis to the upper right corner. The correlation between 1968 and 1976 scores would have been distinctly positive. Neither of these patterns occurred, nor is the actual dispersed pattern a combination of the two. Whatever the selection process that resulted in some districts having sharply lower segregation in 1976 than in 1968, it did not select districts on the basis of their 1968 score.

The diagonal line that would be obtained by connecting the lower left and upper right corners in Figure 4.2 represents no change in segregation index. For twelve districts located above that line, the 1976 score was above the 1968 score, in each case by only a few percentage points. Nineteen districts, located in the lower right of the plot, experienced decreases of more than 50 percentage points during the 8-year interval.

From this examination of Figures 4.1 and 4.2, we conclude that there was a diversity of desegregation experiences among the 87 districts during this period. Viewing desegregation activities as an

## Figure 4.3: Dissimilarity in 1976 (ID 76) v. Number of Black Pupils in 1968 (B 68)

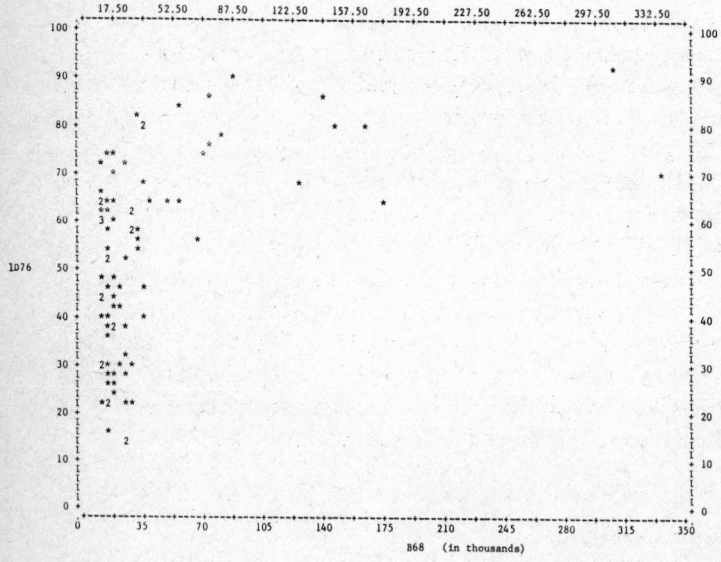

experiment, we see that these districts were exposed to a wide range of 'treatments'. The treatment was not correlated with the initial (1968) level of segregation. The next question we pose is whether the treatment is correlated with the percentage or the number of black pupils in the district.

The level of school segregation in 1968 was not related to the percentage black (among the total of black and white pupils in the district), but the segregation score eight years later was related to the initial percentage black. Districts in which the percentage black was below 50 in 1968 were more likely to have a large decline in segregation by 1976 than were those districts in which black pupils outnumbered white pupils. This pattern is clear, but imperfect; the correlation coefficient is 0.5. Districts at each level of percentage black display some diversity of desegregation experience.

Although the segregation score in 1968 was unrelated to number of black pupils, extensive desegregation during the next eight years did not take place in districts with very large numbers of black pupils (Figure 4.3). None of the 16 districts with an initial (1968) black pupil population greater than 40,000 had a segregation score below 50 in 1976. Of the seven districts with more than 100,000 black pupils (in order, from largest, New York, Chicago, Detroit, Philadelphia, Los Angeles, Washington and Baltimore), four experienced small increases in segregation and three experienced decreases of less than 15 points.

This general pattern is repeated in both North and South. Nine of the 16 districts with large black enrolments are in the South, seven in the North; none experienced desegregation substantial enough to result in a 1976 score below 50. In each region, many of the districts with smaller black enrolments experienced substantial desegregation, but there is a regional pattern. None of the smaller districts in the South had an increase in segregation score, 1968 to 1976, and 31 of 41 ended the period with scores below 50. Eight of 30 northern districts with smaller black enrolments had an increase in segregation, and only seven ended the period with scores below 50.

## Racial Exposure

The ID is a measure of dispersion of school racial percentages around the district average; what that average is and whether it changes during the course of desegregation are ignored. The exposure indices summarise the actual school racial compositions from the perspective of the typical black or white pupil. Effective implementation of a substantial desegregation programme simultaneously reduces the school-by-school variation in racial composition, increases the percentage white in the school of the typical black pupil, and increases the percentage black in the school of the typical white pupil. The magnitude of the changes in the three measures need not be identical. In the absence of a desegregation programme, or in response to a partial programme, the three indices may change in different directions, especially if the racial composition of the district is also changing. Some observers of desegregation in the United States suggest that because of the resistance of white parents to desegregation and the actions that those parents take to remove their children from racially mixed schools, the extensive activities designed to reduce dissimilarity in school racial percentages have not, in fact, resulted in much increased exposure of blacks to whites or whites to blacks. An empirical assessment of this aspect of the desegregation

**Figure 4.4: Exposure of Blacks to Whites in 1976 (EBW76) v. Exposure of Blacks to Whites in 1968 (EBW68)**

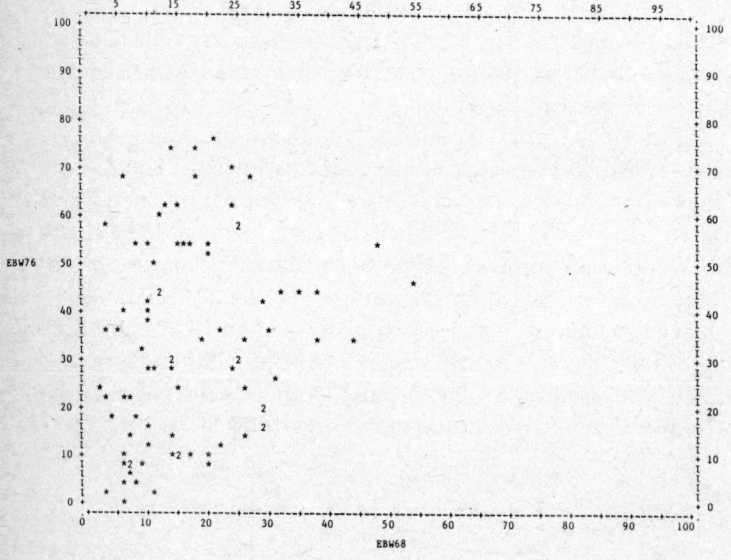

experience of our 87 districts during 1968 to 1976 may be made by examining changes in racial exposure indices.

The index of exposure of blacks to whites indicates the average percentage white encountered by black pupils in the schools they attend. Plotting the 1976 value for this index against the 1968 value (Figure 4.4) reveals a general pattern similar to that for the ID: a relatively constricted range in 1968 and a substantial dispersal in the direction of desegregation by 1976. In 1976, the median black-to-white exposure index was about 30 per cent, 22 districts were above 50, and 12 districts were below 10. Despite the general similarity in patterns of change, two differences between the trends for this exposure index and the trends in dissimilarity plotted in Figure 4.2 are apparent. First, the exposure index does not assume values near the extreme of the range; this is an artefact of the range not being 0 to 100, but 0 to the district percentage white. Second, about twice as many districts (25 v. 12) experienced decreases in black-to-white exposure as experienced increases in dissimilarity. Again this is partly

**Figure 4.5: Exposure of Whites to Blacks in 1976 (EWB76) v Exposure of Whites to Blacks in 1968 (EWB68)**

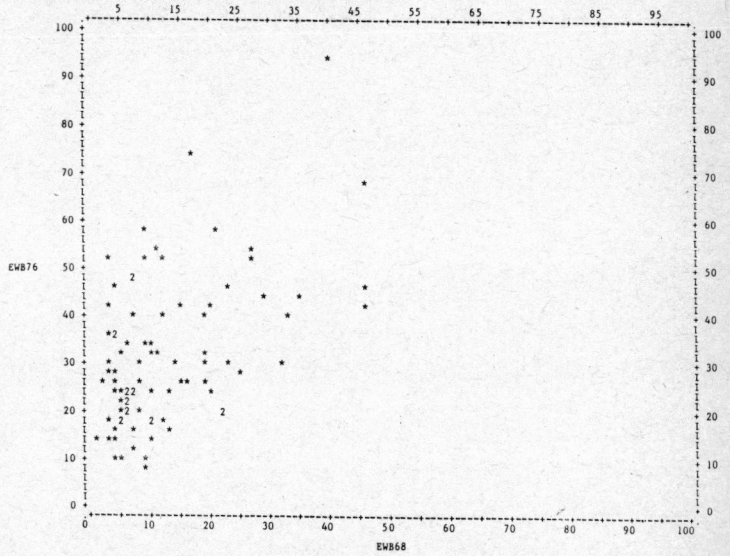

a reflection of the link between the exposure index and percentage white; with many districts having a decreasing percentage white there is a tendency for black-to-white exposure to drift downwards unless countered by desegregation activities.

The index of exposure of whites to blacks indicates the average percentage black encountered by white pupils in the schools they attend. Plotting the 1976 value for this index against the 1968 value (Figure 4.5) again produces a general pattern of a broader range and upward dispersal in 1976 as compared to 1968. In 1968, the median white-to-black exposure index was below 10; in 1976 it was about 28. In no district in 1968 was the average racial composition for white pupils a black majority; this was the case in 11 districts in 1976.

The specific value of an exposure index provides one perspective on the racial distribution in a district's schools. The value of an exposure index relative to the maximum value that it can take provides another perspective. The maximum value that an exposure

**Figure 4.6: Exposure of Blacks to Whites in 1976 (EBW76) v. Percentage Black in 1976 (P76)**

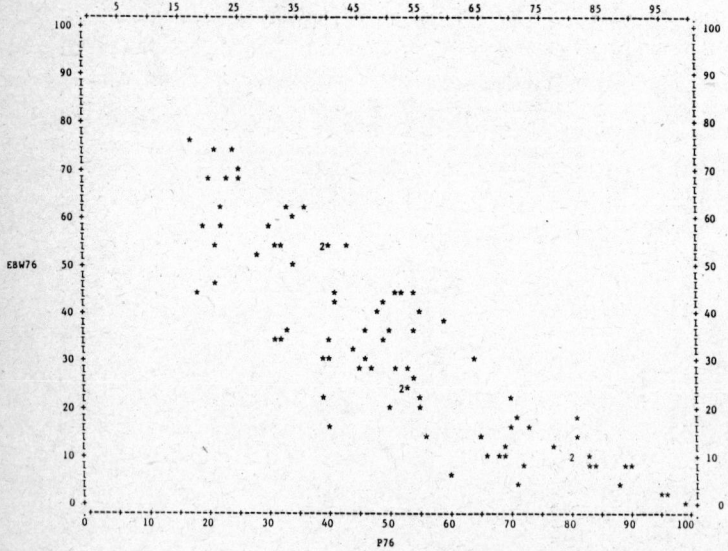

index can take is determined by the district racial composition. In Figures 4.6 and 4.7 the exposure indices for 1976 are plotted against the percentage black for that year.

For the black-to-white exposure index, the maximum value is 100 minus the percentage black. This maximum can be visualised as lying on the line running from the upper left to the lower right corners in Figure 4.6. In a similar plot for 1968 (not shown), black exposure to white pupils is well below the maximum. In 1976 (Figure 4.6), many districts lie close to the diagonal of maximum value. In 14 districts in 1976, the percentage black was above 75 and the exposure of blacks to whites was necessarily below 25 per cent. In the remaining 73 districts, the black exposure to whites was within 25 points of its maximum value in 69 districts. In 1968, only 12 of 84 districts were similarly within 25 points of the maximum black-to-white exposure.

The exposure of white pupils to black is plotted against percentage black in Figure 4.7. For this exposure index the maximum attainable value is simply the district percentage black. This maximum can be

**Figure 4.7: Exposure of Whites to Blacks in 1976 (EWB76) v. Percentage Black in 1976 (P76)**

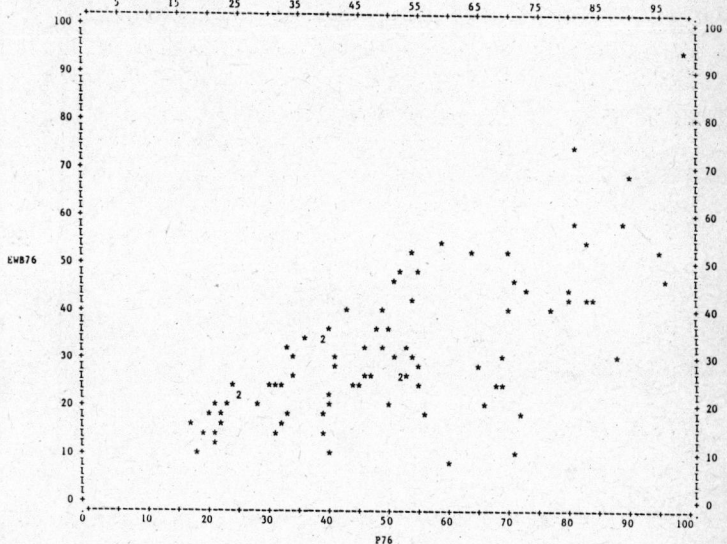

visualised as lying on a diagonal line running from the lower left to the upper right corner in the figure. The plot for 1976 as compared to that for 1968 (not shown) shows that many districts moved from near the bottom horizontal axis, representing little white-to-black exposure, to points closer to the diagonal. In 1976, 46 districts were within 25 points of the maximum, as compared to 28 districts in 1968. For white-to-black exposure, as for black-to-white exposure, comparisons of absolute scores and of scores relative to district racial composition reveal substantially increased exposure from 1968 to 1976.

In a segregated district, both exposure measures will be low; in a desegregated district, both will be high. How high depends on the racial composition of the district, and the two measures are asymmetrically affected. Under complete desegregation, when each exposure index is at its maximum, the two indices sum to 100. In Figures 4.8 and 4.9, the two exposure measures are plotted against each other, for 1968 and for 1976. A diagonal line running from the upper left to the lower right of each figure would represent the

**Figure 4.8: Exposure of Whites to Blacks in 1968 (EWB68) v. Exposure of Blacks to Whites in 1968 (EBW68)**

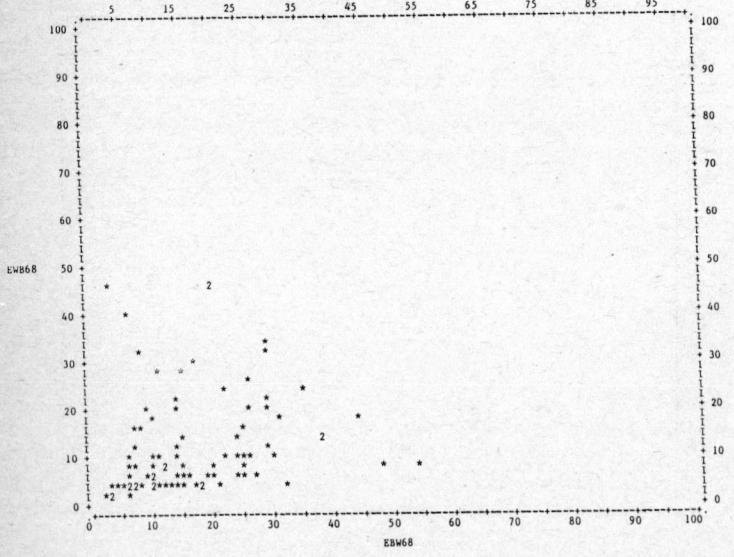

location of points that sum to 100. The nearer a point is to that line, the closer the exposure measures jointly are to their maximum values.

In 1968 (Figure 4.8), all 87 districts were segregated and none had high exposure of each race to the other. Only three districts were above 25 per cent on both exposure measures, eight more were above 25 per cent on white-to-black exposure only, and 19 were above 25 per cent only on black-to-white exposure. The remaining 57 districts were below 25 per cent on both measures. In 1976 (Figure 4.9), eleven districts were below 25 per cent on both exposure indices. Thirty-one districts in 1976 as compared to none in 1968 were within 25 points of their maximum sum.

## The Impact of School Desegregation

The restructuring of public education for the purpose of desegregation has been controversial in these 87 districts, and in hundreds of others,

**Figure 4.9: Exposure of Whites to Blacks in 1976 (EWB76) v. Exposure of Blacks to Whites in 1976 (EBW76)**

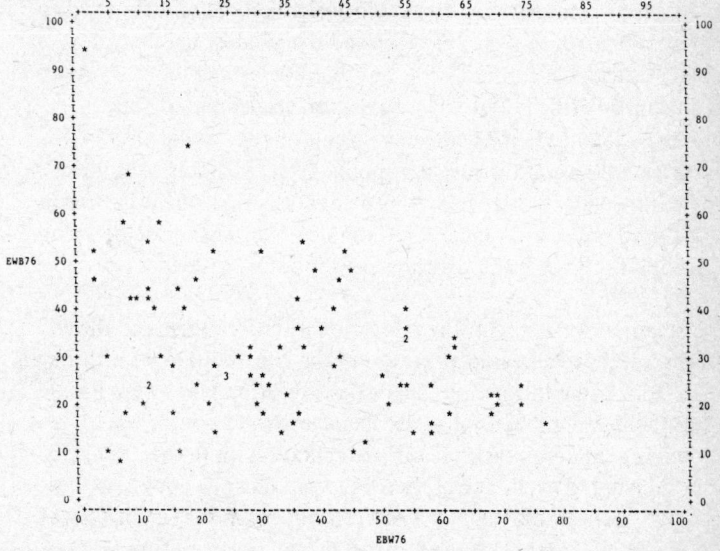

even in those that have as yet altered the school assignments of few
or no pupils. Opposition to proposed, newly implemented or
established desegregation programmes may take many forms. Political
controversy may be extraordinarily intense and sustained at fever
pitch for more than a decade, as in Boston, or it may be more subdued and shorter-lived as in most of the Florida county districts.
Study of the comparative dynamics of the political response to
desegregation has barely begun, yet must ultimately form a part of
any full interpretation of the demographic and ecological impact of
desegregation. The effects of school desegregation are not confined
to the actions of parents whose children's school assignments have
been altered. Great opposition to desegregation is also expressed by
adults without children in the state schools. Even in the short run, it
is not only the immediately affected parents who may respond to
desegregation with political protest or with a residential or educational
relocation. In the longer run, shifts in the resources devoted to —
and the perceived quality of — public and private education and
shifts in the patterns of residential demand will affect all the residents
of a metropolitan area, even if the immediate political issues are
resolved with relatively little disruption.

Among the demographic and ecological effects of school
desegregation, 'white flight' has received the greatest public and
scholarly attention. In the 1960s, Southern desegregation was often
accompanied by the growth of 'segregation academies', private
schooling alternatives for whites. Problems of cost and quality of
private schooling and the fact that public (state) schools continued
to offer free educational services made extensive use of the academies
a short-lived response in most Southern districts. They have persisted
on a limited scale in many districts and on a large scale in a few
(Orfield, 1978).

Residential white flight, the relocation of city residents to the
suburbs, received increased attention in the late 1960s and on through
the 1970s. During this period, major desegregation plans were implemented in a number of city districts, North and South, where
surrounding suburban districts offered schools with few or no black
pupils. Moving to avoid desegregation was an obvious option, and
the typical pattern of declining white enrolment in the public (state)
schools was apparent evidence that the option was being used. Some
commentators, including some judges ruling on remedies for past
segregation, thought that white flight made desegregation plans
ineffective, particularly those plans including compulsory reassignments

with bussing. It was claimed that the failure of white pupils to show up in their newly assigned schools meant the failure of such desegregation efforts. Others were concerned that the white flight further exacerbated prevailing urban problems connected with the loss of the middle classes to the suburbs. Scholarly studies documenting the existence and magnitude of white flight became weapons used by opponents of certain desegregation programmes and plans.

Proponents of desegregation began to use other studies as weapons in their political battles. Some of these studies emphasised the difficulty in distinguishing desegregation-induced white flight from the general white suburbanisation that has been a central feature of metropolitan America since the 1920s. Other studies called attention to examples of desegregation without white flight. Many such cases depend on the historic presence of blacks in the southern countryside and the prevailing county-wide organisation of school districts; in these circumstances residential white flight was not an option for escaping from desegregation.

Studies of white flight have thus become enmeshed in political and legal controversies. Most of the scholars have themselves become identified as partisans, and succeeding studies have often been designed as rebuttals to the other side or as documents for immediate courtroom use prior to publication for a professional audience. Most of these studies were facilitated by accumulation of the racial enrolment surveys conducted since 1967 by the government. These provide the basic data used in a series of studies that take 'change in white enrolment in the public schools' as the measure of white flight. Little effort has been given to a systematic chronicle of potential demographic effects of desegregation. Whites may shift their children to private schools, or relocate within a district to schools unaffected by the particular desegregation plan (because the schools are already racially mixed, or because the plan is not truly system-wide), or relocate to another district. Households which do not currently have children in the public (state) schools may also respond to desegregation, but their activities will not be captured by the usual school-enrolment data base.

Extensive use of the term 'white flight' has rather surprisingly not led to corresponding usage of the concept of 'black flight'. If assignment to non-local schools, or to inferior, overcrowded and unsafe schools, or to any school not chosen by the parents, is a source of such profound concern to white parents that they are willing to undergo the financial sacrifice of private school tuition or a disadvantageous home sale, might it not be supposed that some black parents have similar concerns and similar responses? If the concerns of black parents are similar but the responses differ, how much of the racial differential in flight behaviour should be attributed to the impact of the desegregation plan and how much to current or historical discrimination by private schools or the suburban housing market? Is there a trend towards black flight that, paired with white flight, augments the decline in city public school enrolments but avoids the 'resegregative' consequence of increasing the percentage black among the public school pupils? For black parents or white, how can studies based on enrolment data distinguish analytically between a response to desegregation, a response to the 'decline of the public schools', and a response inspired by the 'back to the basics' movement?

The white-flight literature is complex, polemic and becoming voluminous. A thorough review would be lengthy and, because of the shortcomings of data and method, inevitably inconclusive. For example, there was debate for some time over whether comparative multi-district studies produced acceptable evidence of any relation between indicators of desegregation and measures of white enrolment change. There then emerged a consensus that for large districts desegregating in the late 1960s or early 1970s, in the first year of desegregation the loss of white enrolment in the state schools was, on the average, greater than can be accounted for by any of the control variables. There is continued dissension over whether there are excess enrolment losses before year one (anticipatory effects), or after year one, and whether the excess year-one loss represents a permanent downward shift of the long-run white enrolment curve or only a temporary timing shift that is compensated in subsequent years by an upward shift of the curve (Coleman, Kelly and Moore, 1975; Farley, Richards and Wurdock, 1979; Rossell, 1979; Armor, 1980).

## Towards a Reformulation of Research and Policy Questions

Although the data that we have presented for 87 school districts with large black enrolments do not constitute a new study of white flight, we believe they can be helpful in reformulating the social science and policy questions to which empirical evidence may be directed. One policy conclusion nominally based on evidence is that desegregation is futile because (1) desegregation accelerates white flight, and (2) white flight proceeds inexorably to the point at which there are few whites remaining in a district's state schools. We believe there is ample reason to question the universality and inevitability of each of the two premises, but even granting them, the policy conclusion is not compelling. The data for 87 districts (Figures 4.4 and 4.5) show many large increases, 1968 to 1976, in within-school exposure of blacks to whites and whites to blacks. Although we have not used any direct measures of desegregation activities, it is obvious that in many districts desegregation has greatly increased interracial exposure in the schools. Perhaps all of these districts will have continually diminishing percentages of whites in the state schools, and the exposure indices will eventually begin a decline toward zero. Even were that inevitable, the policy conclusion that desegregation was futile would seem to be premature. Given the premises, the policy question that should be asked is whether the increased interracial exposure that desegregation brings about during an interim period should be sacrificed in order to slow by a few years the transition of a segregated school system to all black.

The study by Coleman, Kelly and Moore (1975) was influential in posing the terms of the policy debate about white flight and in suggesting the relevance of empirical analysis to that debate. We believe that they and many other commentators have given insufficient attention to two of their empirical conclusions. At the end of their white flight chapter they report nine conclusions, of which the final two are pertinent (Coleman, Kelly and Moore, 1975: 79):

8. The effect of desegregation on white loss has been widely different among different cities where desegregation has taken place.
9. Because, insofar as we can estimate, the loss of whites upon desegregation is a one-time loss, the long-term impact of desegregation is considerably less than that of other continuing factors. The continuing white losses produce an extensive erosion of the interracial contact that desegregation of city schools brings about.

With respect to conclusion 9, our empirical evidence seems to indicate that at any stage in a central district's presumed transition toward all-black public (state) school enrolment, there will be greater interracial exposure with desegregation than without. The presumption of a universal rapid transition toward an all-black enrolment may also be questioned. In Figure 4.7, consider the dispersal of points along the horizontal axis. Percentage black among the 87 districts is seen to be widely dispersed in 1976, with one of every six districts above 75 per cent black and one-half below 50 per cent. An upward shift in percentage black in these public school districts has been occurring but most districts are still enrolling substantial proportions of white pupils. Projection of a past trend into the future is one of the simplest forms of prediction, but the longer the future the less confident the prediction. Many scholars believe the era of increasing black concentration in the nation's largest central cities has ended. Within the last decade it became evident that: (1) the centuries-long era of metropolitan gain from net migration has come to an end; (2) regional migration patterns are changing for blacks and whites; (3) with few rural blacks remaining and with black fertility in both urban and rural areas down sharply, the pace of urban black population increase has also diminished sharply; (4) the pace of black suburbanisation has picked up sharply in many metropolitan areas; and (5) the fiscal and energy crises of the nation are altering the locational economics of housing choice. Simple projection of the trends of the 1950s and 1960s into the 1980s and 1990s may illuminate the consequences of an analytic model and its specific assumptions, but unwitting extrapolation is not a sound basis for evaluating the effects of past actions or forming policy about new actions.

Conclusion 8 of the Coleman study, quoted above, seems to us worthy of far greater attention than it has received. Even among scholars, interest in the empirical results has centred on the average effect. Yet the average effect is an average of 'widely different' effects among those cities where some amount of desegregation has taken place. Our empirical results, while not designed to evaluate the amount of white flight, show widely different amounts of desegregation and changes in interracial exposure. Indeed we chose to present the data in scatterplots because of the great degree of scatter in the experience of these 87 districts. The average value of any measure of desegregation-related experience should not be interpreted as representing the 'typical' or 'normal' experience. Each district has its own history, and only a very limited purpose can be served by efforts to describe or project that history on the basis of the average experience of the full set of 87 districts or the subset that has experienced some arbitrary amount of desegregation activity. If we regard desegregation as an experiment, we should describe the treatments being assigned to the subjects as being a diverse set of actions and inactions with respect to school desegregation, and the subjects themselves, the 87 districts, as heterogeneous in terms of their initial characteristics and their responses to treatment.

## Conclusion

To return to our introductory theme, we conclude that the rather dis-organised national desegregation experiment has indeed been altering the distribution of educational services as a convenience good. Flight to another school system, public or private, is not the only option for those upset with a new school assignment. Those of either race who object to the loss of convenient access to public schools may be able to restore that convenience by an appropriate within-district move. Most desegregation plans offer to many families the opportunity to send their children to geographically proximate public schools during some portion of the grade span. That portion is likely to be greater the more racially balanced is the local residential area. School desegregation plans may thus offer incentives for local moves that enhance residential integration. It would be entirely possible for school authorities or other public and private agencies to provide additional incentives for such residential behaviour, through information and referral services, assistance with residential finance, and other services (for an example, see Kentucky Commission on Human Rights, 1977). Although the US judiciary has repeatedly recognised the contributions of school authorities as well as many other public agencies to the creation and maintenance of residential segregation, it has shied away from incorporating explicit residential desegregation programmes into court-ordered school desegregation plans.

Among districts that have desegregated, several have boundaries that encompass all or much of a metropolitan area. In these districts, residential flight from desegregation is likely to be an unusually costly option, for no nearby white school districts are available. These districts provide a particularly clear opportunity to study what happens when one traditional determinant of residential choice is rendered inoperable. In these circumstances, as time passes, will the residential location process give compensatory weight to other segregative determinants, or, as has occurred with respect to religious residential segregation in Belfast during periods of diminished violence (Boal, Chapter 11), will there be some corresponding residential desegregation? An examination of data for Louisville, Kentucky, has suggested that the Belfast pattern is occurring (Kentucky Commission on Human Rights, 1977).

We conclude that analysis of school desegregation in the United States may be of broader than expected interest to students of ethnic segregation and the urban scene. The topic has interest beyond its applicability in the politics of school desegregation research. When national policies change a critical variable, the change often takes effect simultaneously nationwide, and it is hard for the social analyst to distinguish its effects from those of other temporal trends. By spreading out the timing and magnitude of desegregation activities, the US experiment with desegregation offers a rich lode for scholarly analysis, albeit studded with the false gold of political payoffs and technically difficult to mine.

## Appendix: Measures of School Segregation

The measures calculated are based on numbers of 'black' and 'white' pupils (ignoring pupils identified as 'Hispanic', 'Asian' or 'native American') enrolled in state elementary and secondary schools. Data refer to enrolment in autumn of the year specified.

In the formulas, total pupil enrolment in the $i$th school is $T_i$, the sum of $B_i$ black pupils and $W_i$ white pupils. $P_i = B_i/T_i$. The corresponding symbols without subscripts are district totals. Summations are taken over all schools.

Index of Dissimilarity, ID
  see Lieberson (Chapter 3).

Exposure of Black Pupils to White Pupils, EBW

$$EBW = \frac{\sum B_i (1 - P_i)}{B}$$

Exposure of White Pupils to Black Pupils, EWB

$$EWB = \frac{\sum W_i P_i}{W}$$

## Bibliography

Armor, D. (1980) 'White Flight and the Future of School Desegregation', in Walter G. Stephan and Joe R. Feagin (eds.), *School Desegregation*, Plenum Press, New York

Coleman, J.S., Kelly, S.D. and Moore, J.A. (1975) *Trends in School Segregation, 1968–73*, The Urban Institute, Washington, DC

Farley, R., Richards, T. and Wurdock, C. (1979) *School Desegregation and White*

*Flight: A Resolution of Conflicting Results*, Population Studies Center, University of Michigan, Ann Arbor

Kentucky Commission on Human Rights (1977) *Housing Desegregation Increases as Schools Desegregate in Jefferson County*, The Commission, Louisville

Kluger, R. (1976) *Simple Justice*, Knopf, New York

Myrdal, G. (1944) *An American Dilemma*, Harper, New York

Orfield, G. (1969) *The Reconstruction of Southern Education*, Wiley, New York

Orfield, G. (1978) *Must We Bus?*, The Brookings Institute, Washington, DC

Rossell, C.H. (1979) 'School Desegregation and White Flight, Postscript: 1978', in Nicolaus Mills (ed.), *Busing U.S.A.*, Teachers College Press, New York

US Office for Civil Rights, Department of Health, Education and Welfare (1970) *Directory of Public Elementary and Secondary Schools in Selected Districts: Enrollment and Staff by Racial/Ethnic Group, Fall 1968*, US Government Printing Office, Washington, DC

## Acknowledgement

This report is one in a series, 'Studies in Racial Segregation', supported by funds granted to the Institute for Research on Poverty at the University of Wisconsin by the Department of Health, Education and Welfare pursuant to the provisions of the Economic Opportunity Act of 1964, by Contract No. HEW-100-0196 from the Assistant Secretary for Planning and Evaluation, DHEW, and by Grant No. 5 RO1 MH 27880-02 from the Center for Studies of Metropolitan Problems, National Institute of Mental Health. Data acquisition and processing were supported in part by Population Research Grant No. 5 PO1-HD-0-5876 awarded to the Center for Demography and Ecology of the University of Wisconsin by the Center for Population Research of the National Institute of Child Health and Human Development. Conclusions and interpretations are the sole responsibility of the authors.

Note: Additional figures and a table showing the values of each measure for each of the 87 school districts for 1968 and 1976 may be obtained by requesting Discussion Paper 617–80 from the Institute for Research on Poverty, University of Wisconsin, Madison, WI 53706.

PART THREE:

CHOICE AND CONSTRAINT

# 5 PARADOXES OF PUERTO RICAN SEGREGATION IN NEW YORK

Peter Jackson

## Models of Ethnic 'Assimilation'

Contrary to conventional models of ethnic 'assimilation', which predict a consistent decline in residential segregation as an ethnic group improves its socio-economic position with the progress of time, ethnic segregation tended to increase slightly overall in the 1960s in New York. This trend was anticipated, to some extent, by Kantrowitz (1969a; 1973), who regarded the reported demise of ethnic segregation as exaggerated, and by Guest and Weed (1976), who concluded that patterns of segregation remained remarkably constant from 1960 to 1970 in their analysis of Cleveland, Boston and Seattle. Van Valey et al.'s (1977) analysis of a sample of 137 metropolitan areas at the census tract level similarly concluded ambiguously on the trend of black-white segregation during the 1960s, with over half of the sampled metropolitan areas experiencing net increases in segregation index scores.

A refined version of the 'assimilationist' model was Lieberson's (1961) demonstration of a persistent and consistent association through time for various ethnic groups between decreasing residential segregation and increasing similarity to native whites. Taeuber and Taeuber (1965) queried the applicability of the model to patterns of black segregation in a study of over 200 American cities, using the now familiar index of dissimilarity (ID).[1] Black residential patterns could not be explained on the model of previous ethnic groups: colour prejudice and racial discrimination perpetuated high rates of segregation despite socio-economic progress into the second generation and beyond for whom 'Negro' ethnicity remained just as 'visible' (Taeuber and Taeuber, 1964). Black segregation was high even in comparison with Puerto Ricans and Mexicans, who ranked lower than blacks in socio-economic terms, contrary to Duncan and Lieberson's (1959) thesis that an ethnic group's level of segregation was inversely related to appropriate measures of its socio-economic status.

Kantrowitz (1969a; 1973) epitomised the sceptical literature which followed, challenging the bland assurance that residential

segregation would decline simply with time. Even very similar intermarrying groups, such as Protestant Swedes and Norwegians, remained
fairly highly segregated into the second generation, suggesting that a
strong voluntary element may underlie ethnic segregation and explain
its persistence.

The importance of the Puerto Ricans, already less segregated than
blacks despite more recent migration and lower socio-economic status,
was emphasised by Rosenberg and Lake (1976) who argued that
neither existing model of ethnic 'assimilation' — decreasing segregation
with increasing similarity to native whites, nor continuing residential
concentration combined with rapid turnover and succession for blacks
— applied to the Puerto Rican experience.

### Ethnic Segregation in New York, 1960–70

The main data source for the present study was the US Census of
Population and Housing for 1960 and 1970. This paper differs from
earlier versions in that the original 1960 data were used to compute
indices on exactly the same basis as for 1970 data, rather than relying
on Kantrowitz's (1969a; 1973) analysis of the 1960 data.[2] The
census employed a 25 per cent sample for ethnic group totals in 1960
and a 15 per cent sample in 1970.[3] The reliability of the data is
limited by a widely acknowledged undercount of minority groups
(see, for example, *New York Times*, 2 October 1972). 'Foreign
stock' populations were subject to considerable change between 1960
and 1970 (see Table 5.1) and can no longer be assumed to refer to
the immigrants of the earlier part of this century. Post-war immigration
has contributed greatly to certain groups and the populations under
analysis are certainly not just 'quaint immigrant fragments'
(cf. Kantrowitz, 1973: 20). Although the metropolitan area 'foreign
stock' population declined by 332,055 over the decade, they were
more than compensated by blacks and Puerto Ricans who together
increased by 874,023. The populations to which the indices refer
(excluding 'all other and not reported') represent about 56 per
cent of the total metropolitan area population in both 1960 and 1970.

The analysis employs indices of dissimilarity to measure inter-
ethnic segregation and indices of segregation to provide 'average'
measures for each group (see footnote 1). The segregation index is
similar to ID, but includes a weighting factor to allow for the contribution which the group makes to the total population with which

**Table 5.1: 'Foreign Stock', 'Negro' and 'Puerto Rican' Populations in the New York Standard Metropolitan Statistical Area (SMSA); 1960 and 1970**

|  | 1960 | 1970 |
|---|---|---|
| United Kingdom | 272,685 | 207,524 |
| Eire | 399,748 | 315,061 |
| Norway | 54,221 | * |
| Sweden | 46,238 | 30,737 |
| Germany | 466,280 | 344,752 |
| Poland | 476,557 | 385,631 |
| Czechoslovakia | 79,757 | 66,466 |
| Austria | 271,759 | 197,524 |
| Hungary | 120,336 | 96,680 |
| USSR | 672,334 | 512,773 |
| Italy | 1,126,843 | 1,004,771 |
| Canada | 107,194 | 92,473 |
| Mexico | 8,260 | 9,872 |
| Cuba | * | 95,240 |
| Other America | * | 402,056 |
| All other/not reported | 791,129 | 799,726 |
| *Total foreign stock* | 4,893,341 | 4,561,286 |
| Negro | 1,227,625 | 1,885,303 |
| Puerto Rican | 629,430 | 845,775 |
| *Total Population* | 10,694,633 | 11,571,819 |

* = not available
Sources: US Census of Population and Housing, 1960 (Final Report) and 1970 (4th Count).

it is being compared.

The main disadvantage of such indices — that they are dependent on the size of the areal unit chosen, smaller units yielding higher indices *ceteris paribus* — scarcely applies in the present study as a common areal base (census tracts) was used for both 1960 and 1970 data. Changes in tract boundaries were considered insignificant as subdivisions were roughly balanced by aggregations. The New York Standard Metropolitan Statistical Area (SMSA) has nearly 3,000 census tracts with an average population size of 4,000 — an ideally-sized mesh for this kind of analysis. One other possible limitation of this method applies when individual population groups are small in relation to the number of census tracts employed, where a high degree of dissimilarity might be expected to occur through chance alone. This limitation applies in the present analysis, if at all, only

**Table 5.2: Segregation Indices for Various 'Foreign Stock' Ethnic Groups, Negro and Puerto Rican, for the New York Standard Metropolitan Statistical Area (SMSA), New York City, and the 'Suburban Ring': 1960 and 1970**

|  | New York SMSA 1960 | New York SMSA 1970 | New York City 1960 | New York City 1970 | 'Suburban Ring' 1960 | 'Suburban Ring' 1970 |
|---|---|---|---|---|---|---|
| 1. United Kingdom | 29.6 | 31.8 | 34.8 | 38.0 | 15.5 | 17.7 |
| 2. Eire | 39.6 | 40.6 | 44.2 | 49.2 | 19.4 | 21.5 |
| 3. Norway | 62.4 | * | 73.3 | * | 31.1 | * |
| 4. Sweden | 48.3 | 49.1 | 56.9 | 57.2 | 25.9 | 34.4 |
| 5. Germany | 32.8 | 33.5 | 39.2 | 41.4 | 16.5 | 17.2 |
| 6. Poland | 40.3 | 41.6 | 42.0 | 44.7 | 27.2 | 29.6 |
| 7. Czechoslovakia | 45.8 | 45.6 | 49.6 | 50.5 | 32.2 | 35.0 |
| 8. Austria | 38.6 | 39.8 | 39.5 | 42.7 | 26.4 | 29.8 |
| 9. Hungary | 43.8 | 43.6 | 45.8 | 47.7 | 25.9 | 29.5 |
| 10. USSR | 48.0 | 48.3 | 48.3 | 50.2 | 36.6 | 39.0 |
| 11. Italy | 44.3 | 41.7 | 49.7 | 49.9 | 25.7 | 24.4 |
| 12. Canada | 41.9 | 37.1 | 50.1 | 43.3 | 19.8 | 24.3 |
| 13. Mexico | 81.4 | 71.2 | 83.1 | 68.9 | 68.2 | 76.9 |
| 14. Cuba | * | 57.7 | * | 53.9 | * | 61.1 |
| 15. Other America | * | 50.3 | * | 44.8 | * | 37.6 |
| 16. Negro | 74.7 | 74.1 | 75.6 | 71.1 | 65.6 | 75.1 |
| 17. Puerto Rican | 71.9 | 68.6 | 68.2 | 63.5 | 53.7 | 54.1 |

* = not available
'Suburban ring' = that part of the SMSA outside New York City.
Source: US Census of Population and Housing, 1960 and 1970.

to the Mexicans, Norwegians and Swedes.

Table 5.2 presents segregation indices for fifteen 'foreign stock' ethnic groups, and for blacks ('Negro') and Puerto Ricans in the metropolitan area (SMSA), in New York City, and in the 'suburban ring' (that part of the SMSA outside New York City) for 1960 and 1970. Overall, and excluding the Mexicans and Norwegians because of their small group size, the most highly segregated groups were the blacks and Puerto Ricans, with blacks being consistently the more highly segregated. In the SMSA, only small changes occurred over the decade and no overall trend is apparent: of the fourteen pairs where comparison is possible, half increased and half decreased. In New York City almost all the groups experienced an increase, with four exceptions including the blacks and Puerto Ricans whose indices both declined (by 4.5 and 4.7 respectively). In the 'suburban ring', there was only one exception (the Italians) to the general trend of increasing segregation as measured by this index. Segregation levels

Table 5.3: Indices of Dissimilarity for Various 'Foreign Stock' Ethnic Groups, Negro and Puerto Rican, for the New York Standard Metropolitan Statistical Area (SMSA): 1960 and 1970

New York SMSA: 1960 and 1970

| | 1. | 2. | 3. | 4. | 5. | 6. | 7. | 8. | 9. | 10. | 11. | 12. | 13. | 14. | 15. | 16. | 17. |
|---|---|---|---|---|---|---|---|---|---|---|---|---|---|---|---|---|---|
| 1. United Kingdom | — | 33.0 | * | 40.3 | 27.9 | 45.3 | 43.8 | 40.6 | 43.0 | 48.4 | 44.8 | 30.6 | 72.8 | 64.8 | 66.5 | 81.3 | 79.8 |
| 2. Eire | 31.6 | — | * | 47.9 | 36.6 | 53.0 | 49.7 | 48.3 | 49.8 | 57.6 | 46.1 | 42.5 | 75.3 | 64.4 | 68.0 | 82.8 | 79.3 |
| 3. Norway | 56.2 | 61.9 | — | * | 43.9 | 60.5 | 56.8 | 56.5 | 58.1 | 63.3 | 54.2 | 43.6 | 77.8 | 74.9 | 75.4 | 85.8 | 85.5 |
| 4. Sweden | 38.1 | 46.9 | 48.9 | — | 46.6 | 44.8 | 42.0 | 39.0 | 42.1 | 66.3 | 43.4 | 36.1 | 73.9 | 64.7 | 66.8 | 82.7 | 80.6 |
| 5. Germany | 26.9 | 35.5 | 61.3 | 44.6 | — | 44.8 | 42.0 | 39.0 | 42.1 | 49.3 | 43.4 | 36.1 | 73.9 | 64.7 | 66.8 | 82.7 | 80.6 |
| 6. Poland | 46.2 | 53.1 | 70.8 | 61.7 | 45.2 | — | 47.5 | 22.8 | 37.4 | 22.3 | 52.5 | 49.6 | 76.2 | 65.2 | 69.9 | 84.6 | 81.5 |
| 7. Czechoslovakia | 45.3 | 49.1 | 62.9 | 55.6 | 45.2 | 47.5 | — | 43.3 | 39.9 | 51.3 | 53.4 | 48.7 | 76.2 | 65.2 | 69.9 | 81.9 | 79.1 |
| 8. Austria | 42.0 | 48.6 | 66.4 | 55.6 | 41.7 | 22.8 | 43.3 | — | 30.8 | 21.3 | 52.3 | 46.1 | 74.2 | 64.5 | 66.5 | 81.9 | 79.1 |
| 9. Hungary | 46.6 | 50.1 | 68.9 | 58.4 | 44.4 | 37.4 | 39.9 | 30.8 | — | 37.9 | 55.1 | 46.7 | 75.4 | 65.4 | 68.1 | 83.6 | 79.7 |
| 10. USSR | 52.1 | 58.9 | 76.3 | 66.3 | 52.4 | 21.5 | 55.2 | 23.2 | 40.5 | — | 59.6 | 51.8 | 76.3 | 67.9 | 68.1 | 82.2 | 80.3 |
| 11. Italy | 47.0 | 49.7 | 64.0 | 57.1 | 46.8 | 53.4 | 56.0 | 54.4 | 58.4 | 60.6 | — | 47.9 | 78.2 | 70.3 | 70.7 | 83.1 | 79.4 |
| 12. Canada | 37.1 | 45.3 | 55.0 | 47.5 | 42.2 | 54.1 | 52.7 | 49.5 | 50.4 | 57.9 | 53.3 | — | 74.4 | 67.6 | 68.8 | 82.1 | 80.4 |
| 13. Mexico | 82.3 | 83.9 | 76.8 | 77.1 | 82.6 | 82.9 | 77.5 | 78.8 | 78.1 | 84.9 | 86.2 | 68.3 | — | 70.9 | 72.8 | 80.4 | 71.7 |
| 14. Cuba | * | * | * | * | * | * | * | * | * | * | * | * | * | — | 52.0 | 72.8 | 68.3 |
| 15. Other America | * | * | * | * | * | * | * | * | * | * | * | * | * | * | — | 42.1 | 56.4 |
| 16. Negro | 79.5 | 80.5 | 88.3 | 83.8 | 79.8 | 78.8 | 82.0 | 79.9 | 81.0 | 81.9 | 80.5 | 82.7 | 87.3 | * | * | — | 55.9 |
| 17. Puerto Rican | 80.3 | 77.1 | 89.3 | 85.7 | 80.0 | 75.9 | 80.7 | 77.5 | 78.7 | 78.3 | 77.9 | 82.7 | 86.9 | * | * | 64.1 | — |

* = not available

Above the diagonal 1970; below the diagonal 1960

Source: US Census of Population and Housing, 1960 and 1970.

were generally higher in the city than in the SMSA, except for the Puerto Ricans in both 1960 and 1970 and for four other groups (Mexicans, Cubans, Other Americans and blacks) in 1970. Significantly, these groups were the five groups with the lowest proportion of their total in the 'suburban ring', where segregation levels were generally well below either city or SMSA levels (except for blacks, Mexicans and Cubans in 1970).

Even at this level of analysis, then, there is evidence to contradict the orthodox notion that ethnic 'assimilation' is a unidirectional, irreversible process. A more refined analysis of inter-ethnic segregation patterns, using the index of dissimilarity, helps to clarify the general trends and to indicate the Puerto Ricans' paradoxical experience.

Table 5.3 provides a matrix of IDs, comparing the same population groups as above, in the SMSA for 1960 (below the diagonal) and for 1970 (above the diagonal). Of the 91 pairs where comparison is possible, 32 increased in 1970, including 18 cases which involved blacks or Puerto Ricans. Black versus Puerto Rican segregation, however, decreased by the largest amount (from 64.1 to 55.9) except for a number of Mexican comparisons.

Table 5.4 presents similar figures for New York City, where 35 of the 91 pairs registered an increase, including 18 involving either blacks or Puerto Ricans. Again, black versus Puerto Rican segregation decreased dramatically (from 62.6 to 52.8). Table 5.5 completes this part of the analysis, with reference to the 'suburban ring', where there was a widespread tendency towards increased segregation with only three exceptions to the general trend, all involving European groups (Italy versus Germany; Poland versus USSR; and Italy versus USSR).

## The Paradoxes of Puerto Rican Segregation

While the trend towards increased segregation in New York during the 1960s is by no means unequivocal, and while small changes in particular indices may be of disputable significance, conventional 'assimilation' theory is clearly inadequate to explain the complex changes which have been reported. The remainder of this paper focuses on the Puerto Rican experience and suggests that a better understanding of the paradox of their uneasy position as neither a European ethnic group nor a racially distinct minority may yield more insight into the nature of residential segregation than the simplistic assumptions of

**Table 5.4: Indices of Dissimilarity for Various 'Foreign Stock' Ethnic Groups, Negro and Puerto Rican, for New York City: 1960 and 1970**

New York City: 1960 and 1970

| | 1. | 2. | 3. | 4. | 5. | 6. | 7. | 8. | 9. | 10. | 11. | 12. | 13. | 14. | 15. | 16. | 17. |
|---|---|---|---|---|---|---|---|---|---|---|---|---|---|---|---|---|---|
| 1. United Kingdom | — | 35.0 | * | 46.0 | 32.7 | 46.8 | 46.2 | 39.4 | 43.5 | 47.1 | 52.6 | 34.8 | 70.6 | 59.2 | 63.6 | 81.5 | 77.6 |
| 2. Eire | 31.9 | — | * | 52.7 | 41.8 | 58.7 | 55.8 | 52.8 | 55.0 | 61.5 | 54.5 | 48.0 | 75.3 | 62.9 | 69.3 | 84.4 | 78.9 |
| 3. Norway | 65.5 | 68.8 | — | * | * | * | * | * | * | * | * | * | * | * | * | * | * |
| 4. Sweden | 44.8 | 51.5 | 54.0 | — | 52.2 | 64.5 | 60.9 | 58.8 | 61.0 | 65.2 | 61.9 | 50.0 | 76.6 | 72.0 | 74.2 | 87.1 | 84.1 |
| 5. Germany | 30.7 | 38.1 | 72.7 | 53.5 | — | 47.7 | 44.0 | 39.2 | 43.4 | 50.1 | 51.6 | 42.7 | 72.2 | 59.9 | 65.5 | 83.2 | 79.2 |
| 6. Poland | 48.1 | 57.9 | 77.5 | 66.9 | 49.6 | — | 46.5 | 24.1 | 39.1 | 21.1 | 57.3 | 51.0 | 75.4 | 66.6 | 68.0 | 82.0 | 77.7 |
| 7. Czechoslovakia | 48.2 | 53.4 | 68.5 | 59.2 | 48.0 | 49.9 | — | 45.0 | 40.6 | 51.8 | 59.6 | 52.3 | 74.6 | 63.4 | 67.4 | 85.6 | 81.0 |
| 8. Austria | 41.9 | 52.4 | 71.4 | 58.8 | 43.2 | 23.3 | 44.7 | — | 32.7 | 20.9 | 58.0 | 45.8 | 72.3 | 63.6 | 63.6 | 82.9 | 79.0 |
| 9. Hungary | 47.8 | 54.1 | 74.4 | 61.0 | 45.9 | 39.7 | 40.5 | 32.7 | — | 39.8 | 61.7 | 46.5 | 73.8 | 64.7 | 69.3 | 84.7 | 79.7 |
| 10. USSR | 52.1 | 62.4 | 81.5 | 69.8 | 54.0 | 20.2 | 56.5 | 20.9 | 39.8 | — | 63.8 | 51.1 | 74.9 | 67.2 | 69.2 | 82.5 | 80.2 |
| 11. Italy | 52.7 | 55.7 | 71.3 | 63.7 | 52.5 | 57.4 | 60.9 | 58.6 | 63.1 | 63.4 | — | 55.1 | 79.0 | 70.7 | 71.8 | 84.6 | 78.6 |
| 12. Canada | 45.3 | 50.4 | 62.1 | 56.0 | 50.1 | 57.9 | 56.9 | 52.1 | 52.4 | 60.5 | 59.6 | — | 72.0 | 63.4 | 66.4 | 81.8 | 78.1 |
| 13. Mexico | 82.6 | 85.4 | 74.2 | 76.8 | 83.4 | 84.0 | 76.6 | 79.1 | 78.3 | 86.1 | 87.3 | 63.1 | — | 68.4 | 71.3 | 79.1 | 69.2 |
| 14. Cuba | * | * | * | * | * | * | * | * | * | * | * | * | * | — | 50.7 | 72.5 | 67.3 |
| 15. Other America | * | * | * | * | * | * | * | * | * | * | * | * | * | * | — | 40.0 | 55.8 |
| 16. Negro | 81.2 | 83.1 | 90.9 | 86.4 | 81.6 | 80.6 | 83.8 | 81.5 | 82.8 | 83.1 | 83.0 | 84.9 | 87.6 | * | * | — | 52.8 |
| 17. Puerto Rican | 78.3 | 76.3 | 90.1 | 85.2 | 78.4 | 75.1 | 80.3 | 76.9 | 78.7 | 77.8 | 77.2 | 82.0 | 87.1 | * | * | 62.6 | — |

* = not available
Above the diagonal 1970; below the diagonal 1960.
Source: US Census of Population and Housing, 1960 and 1970.

**Table 5.5: Indices of Dissimilarity for Various 'Foreign Stock' Ethnic Groups, Negro and Puerto Rican, for the New York 'Suburban Ring' (that part of the SMSA outside New York City): 1960 and 1970**

New York 'Suburban Ring': 1960 and 1970

| | 1. | 2. | 3. | 4. | 5. | 6. | 7. | 8. | 9. | 10. | 11. | 12. | 13. | 14. | 15. | 16. | 17. |
|---|---|---|---|---|---|---|---|---|---|---|---|---|---|---|---|---|---|
| 1. United Kingdom | – | 22.6 | * | 33.7 | 21.1 | 33.9 | 36.1 | 34.2 | 33.2 | 41.6 | 29.4 | 25.3 | 76.2 | 61.5 | 42.8 | 73.6 | 58.6 |
| 2. Eire | 17.2 | – | * | 35.0 | 23.4 | 36.9 | 35.9 | 36.0 | 34.5 | 44.9 | 27.7 | 28.5 | 76.0 | 62.7 | 44.7 | 73.6 | 57.1 |
| 3. Norway | 31.1 | 36.4 | – | * | * | * | * | * | * | * | * | * | * | * | * | * | * |
| 4. Sweden | 24.0 | 27.2 | 33.1 | – | 32.6 | 46.0 | 46.3 | 45.9 | 44.9 | 52.7 | 39.7 | 36.3 | 77.8 | 68.2 | 52.1 | 77.0 | 65.6 |
| 5. Germany | 18.2 | 21.4 | 29.3 | 23.5 | – | 32.0 | 36.1 | 33.3 | 33.0 | 40.9 | 27.0 | 26.7 | 77.3 | 64.3 | 43.7 | 76.0 | 58.3 |
| 6. Poland | 30.6 | 32.9 | 42.8 | 39.2 | 31.4 | – | 39.9 | 23.6 | 29.7 | 26.3 | 37.8 | 38.7 | 79.7 | 65.4 | 46.9 | 75.5 | 63.3 |
| 7. Czechoslovakia | 33.9 | 33.0 | 43.4 | 40.7 | 34.0 | 35.8 | – | 38.1 | 38.9 | 47.0 | 40.0 | 38.8 | 80.9 | 67.1 | 52.0 | 77.6 | 63.2 |
| 8. Austria | 30.8 | 31.8 | 44.9 | 39.0 | 30.1 | 20.5 | 35.4 | – | 26.3 | 22.2 | 37.0 | 38.1 | 80.8 | 64.0 | 46.9 | 76.6 | 63.8 |
| 9. Hungary | 29.3 | 30.5 | 42.4 | 36.3 | 29.6 | 26.1 | 34.8 | 21.3 | – | 31.5 | 36.4 | 36.0 | 81.7 | 65.8 | 48.3 | 78.0 | 62.3 |
| 10. USSR | 39.2 | 41.6 | 51.0 | 45.9 | 39.0 | 27.1 | 46.9 | 20.0 | 28.6 | – | 45.7 | 43.5 | 81.8 | 68.2 | 51.0 | 80.1 | 69.3 |
| 11. Italy | 29.0 | 27.4 | 38.8 | 35.6 | 28.2 | 35.8 | 38.4 | 36.3 | 34.8 | 45.8 | – | 33.6 | 76.2 | 61.7 | 43.8 | 73.4 | 57.0 |
| 12. Canada | 19.0 | 24.1 | 33.9 | 26.6 | 22.5 | 35.7 | 36.7 | 34.2 | 32.7 | 41.4 | 33.2 | – | 77.4 | 65.3 | 45.0 | 75.5 | 61.6 |
| 13. Mexico | 68.9 | 69.7 | 68.7 | 68.9 | 68.3 | 70.9 | 71.0 | 69.6 | 69.8 | 71.1 | 69.2 | 68.4 | – | 81.9 | 79.2 | 87.4 | 82.7 |
| 14. Cuba | * | * | * | * | * | * | * | * | * | * | * | * | 68.4 | – | 62.3 | 75.6 | 71.2 |
| 15. Other America | * | * | * | * | * | * | * | * | * | * | * | * | * | * | – | 56.0 | 59.0 |
| 16. Negro | 67.7 | 65.1 | 73.4 | 69.8 | 68.3 | 66.7 | 70.7 | 69.5 | 67.9 | 73.3 | 64.9 | 67.9 | 84.5 | * | * | – | 73.8 |
| 17. Puerto Rican | 57.4 | 56.4 | 57.9 | 61.0 | 57.0 | 59.9 | 57.0 | 59.6 | 57.7 | 65.2 | 54.6 | 57.3 | 77.8 | * | * | 69.9 | – |

* = not available.

Above the diagonal 1970; below the diagonal 1960.

Source: US Census of Population and Housing, 1960 and 1970.

existing models.

The particular interest of the Puerto Ricans to theories of ethnic 'assimilation' is in their distinctive ethnicity and in their rapid rate of spatial 'assimilation' in comparison with blacks. The Puerto Ricans are native Spanish-speakers, Roman Catholics and racially mixed. Their large-scale migration to mainland America was made possible by American citizenship, received as early as 1917, but it was delayed until the advent of cheap mass air transportation after 1945.[4] Despite American citizenship, Puerto Ricans are jealous of their 'nationality' (*patria*) and the unique political status of the island as a Free Associated State with Commonwealth status is a temporary and ambiguous recognition of this fact. Puerto Ricans generally have little enthusiasm for the spirit of American competitive individualism and the Spanish language and cultural heritage are often fiercely adhered to. The migration has always been two-way, and since 1970 consistently favours return to the island. Return migrants are now known to be a heterogeneous population (Torruellas and Vázquez, 1976), contradicting Rosenberg and Lake's (1976) argument about the adverse effects of selective return migration by only the more successful migrants. A close attachment to the island, however, clearly affects their commitment to 'assimilation' on the model of earlier (European) immigrants.

## Blacks and Puerto Ricans

Blacks and Puerto Ricans are among the most highly segregated groups in New York, yet while they are becoming generally more segregated from other ethnic groups, they are becoming simultaneously less dissimilar from each other, outside the suburbs at least. Rosenberg (1974) has commented on how Puerto Ricans have tended to settle in mixed ethnic areas, often with blacks, and Kantrowitz (1969b) has shown the close geographical association between black and Puerto Rican settlement patterns in his cartographical analysis of New York. The relationship of Puerto Rican 'foothills to Negro mountains' which he suggested for 1960 data remains true for 1970 (see Figure 5.1).

The minority of black Puerto Ricans tended, in 1960, to act as a binding group between black and white residential areas, being concentrated in Manhattan, for example, along a band of census tracts following Fifth Avenue — the conventional divide between black Central Harlem and substantially white East ('Spanish') Harlem. There is less reason for optimism from an analysis of 1970 patterns (see Figure 5.2). The evidence here is that the Puerto Ricans are being

**Figure 5.1: Distribution of Black and Puerto Rican Populations in New York City, 1970**

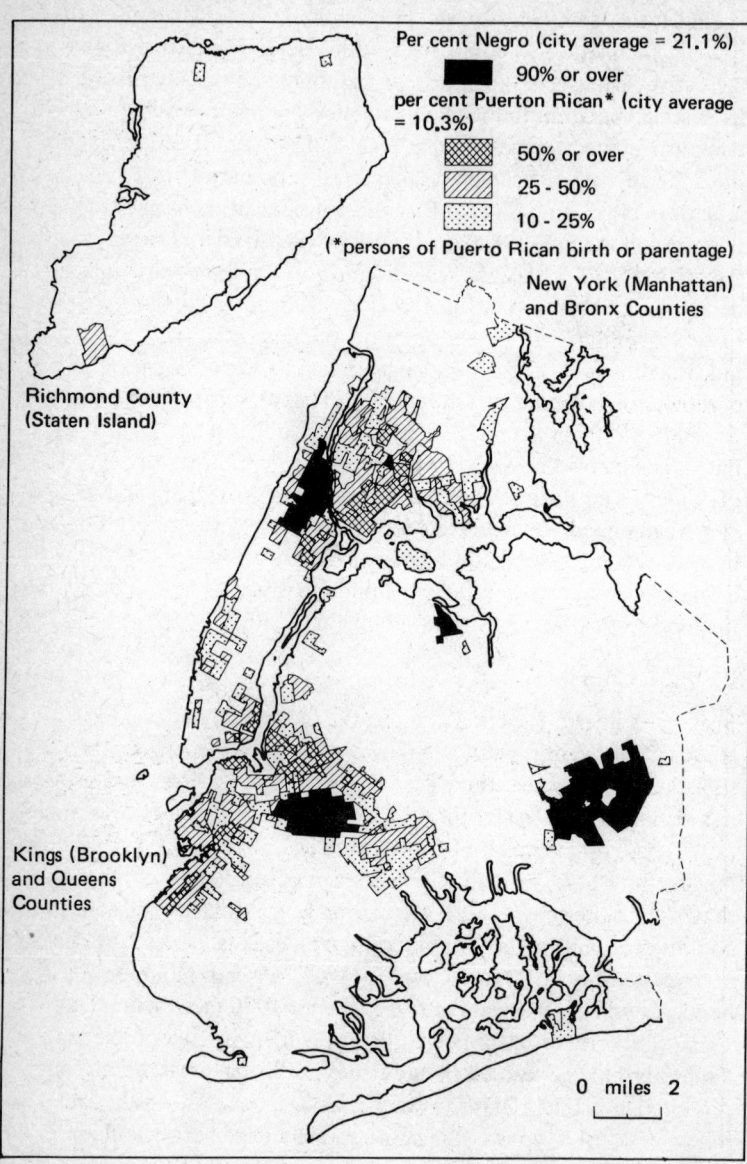

Source: US Bureau of the Census, Census of Population and Housing, PHC (1)-145 (1970), Tables P-1 and P-2.

**Figure 5.2: Distribution of Black Puerto Ricans in New York City, 1970**

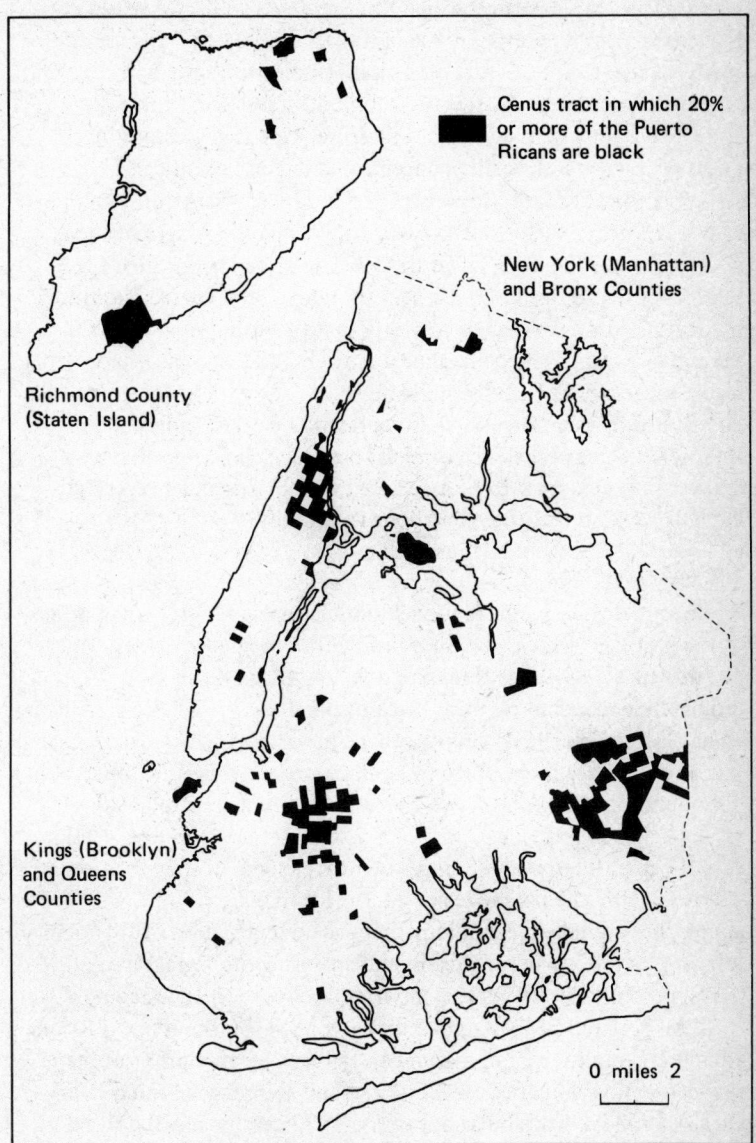

Source: NYC Planning Department, special tabulations from the 1970 Census.

'pulled apart' spatially, with their darker-skinned members residing more with blacks than with other Puerto Ricans or with non-Hispanic whites. The simple pattern which Kantrowitz (1969b) describes no longer seems to hold even in Manhattan. Black Puerto Ricans are scattered throughout Central and East Harlem with only a suggestion of a linear distribution along the interstice. In Brooklyn and Queens, however, a different interpretation is suggested: black Puerto Ricans are especially concentrated in areas of intense black settlement (in Bedford-Stuyvesant and in Jamaica-St Albans) and not in areas of high Puerto Rican concentration, on the fringes of those areas (compare Figure 5.1). Of the 170 census tracts in which black Puerto Ricans comprise 20 per cent or more of the Puerto Rican population, only two have a majority Puerto Rican population. Seventy are tracts which are almost entirely (90 per cent or more) black, especially in Queens and Manhattan. The experience of black Puerto Ricans therefore seems to represent a marked indication of the strength and persistence of racial prejudice, as Puerto Ricans are generally reluctant to be associated with blacks and are very un-likely to have sought these locations voluntarily.

*Trailblazers or Followers*

Static spatial analysis tends to yield rather contradictory explanations of the processes which were responsible for observed patterns. Thus Kantrowitz (1969b) has argued that Puerto Rican dispersal is ultimately dependent on prior black dispersal (as in Jamaica-St Albans), while Gottmann (1961), among others, has argued the contrary: that Puerto Ricans are more likely to be the pioneers in opening up neighbourhoods to minority settlement, gaining access to housing which is denied to blacks because of race prejudice. The final section of this paper, then, is an attempt to uncover some of the processes which underlie the paradoxes of Puerto Rican segregation. Two approaches are taken, examining the relative segregation of first- and second-generation Puerto Ricans, and analysing the segregation of socially mobile Puerto Ricans, in terms of education and income.

Rosenberg (1974) has argued that second-generation Puerto Ricans are more likely to live in predominantly black neighbourhoods than first-generation migrants. Data on first- and second-generation Puerto Ricans, from special tabulations of the 1970 census, reveal a slight tendency in the opposite direction (see Table 5.6). Second-generation Puerto Ricans (born in the United States) are marginally less segregated from blacks, as they are too from whites and from the

**Table 5.6: Indices of Dissimilarity and Segregation for First and Second Generation Puerto Ricans, Negro and White in New York City: 1970**

New York City: 1970

|  | 1. | 2. | 3. | 4. | 5. |
|---|---|---|---|---|---|
| 1. Total population* | – | 61.3 | 59.5 | 70.5 | 66.8 |
| 2. Puerto Ricans born in Puerto Rico |  | – | 11.9 | 53.9 | 64.5 |
| 3. Puerto Ricans born in United States |  |  | – | 52.4 | 64.1 |
| 4. Negro |  |  |  | – | 71.0 |
| 5. White |  |  |  |  | – |

* Index of segregation.
Source: Special tabulation by New York Department of City Planning, from US Census of Population and Housing, 1970.

total population, than first-generation migrants (born in Puerto Rico), though the low index of dissimilarity between the generations indicates the inferential problem posed by the high proportion of second-generation Puerto Rican children who live with first-generation parents.

Static analysis of the segregation of blacks, whites and Puerto Ricans, using actual cross-tabulations of 'race' and income by census tracts for the period 1950–60, led Kantrowitz (1973: Chapter 3) to conclude that more affluent blacks show the same tendency to separate themselves spatially from their own poor as rich whites separate themselves from poor whites. This tendency was even more marked among rich Puerto Ricans who were yet more spatially segregated from their own poor than was the case among non-whites. Each group acts towards its poor, and the poor of other groups, in roughly the same way and distances itself if it can.

Research on racial neighbourhood transition has argued per-suasively that, at least in the early stages of 'succession', black families entering previously all-white neighbourhoods tend to have similar or superior socio-economic profiles to the white families they replace. In crude terms, upper-income blacks pioneer the 'invasion' of middle-income white suburbs. But it has been argued that this 'circulation of elites' model breaks down when a third group — the Puerto Ricans — is introduced; among them, the more poorly educated move independently of the better educated into areas previously dominated by a non-Puerto Rican population (Kantrowitz, 1973: 59).

Detailed socio-economic data on the Puerto Rican population in New York City in 1970 are available at census tract level only for those tracts with 400 or more Puerto Ricans present, thus excluding 5 per cent of the city's (most assimilated?) Puerto Ricans. Analysis of median Puerto Rican family incomes and education levels in these tracts, however, gives further confirmation to Kantrowitz's paradoxical findings.

Puerto Rican median family incomes are substantially higher (average $7,039) in tracts with a low concentration of Puerto Ricans (10 per cent or less; n = 51) than for the total city tracts for which Puerto Rican income data are available (average $5,701; n = 444). Similarly, Puerto Rican education levels are much higher in tracts with low Puerto Rican concentrations (10 per cent or less; average 9.2 years) than city-wide (average 8.4 years). Tracts with low Puerto Rican concentrations thus appear to be substantially more 'elite' in terms of education and income than the average.

Those census tracts with high Puerto Rican median family incomes ($8,000 or above), moreover, have lower average concentrations of both Puerto Ricans (17.6 per cent) and blacks (20.4 per cent) than the total population of census tracts for which Puerto Rican income data are available city-wide (29.4 per cent and 32.3 per cent respectively). This suggests that, to the extent that rich Puerto Ricans separate themselves spatially from poorer Puerto Ricans, they do this by moving to white neighbourhoods rather than living with economically advantaged blacks. Similar data for education reveal that those tracts with the most highly educated Puerto Ricans (with a median of ten or more school years completed) also tend to have a much less concentrated Puerto Rican population (16.6 per cent) than the average for the city (29.4 per cent) and a much lower concentration of blacks (25.6 per cent compared to 32.3 per cent city-wide).

Table 5.7 is based on the census tracts for which socio-economic data were available for the Puerto Rican population in New York City in the 1970 census. Table 5.7(a) presents a cross-tabulation of tracts by the median school years completed by the Puerto Ricans in those tracts, classified by the concentration of blacks (per cent Negro) and Puerto Ricans (per cent Puerto Ricans). Table 5.7(b) presents data in the same format for the median family incomes of the Puerto

**Table 5.7: Classification of Census Tracts with 400 or more Puerto Ricans (1970) by**

**(a) Median school years completed by the Puerto Rican population, and by per cent Negro and per cent Puerto Rican, 1970**

| (a) Median school years completed (Puerto Ricans) | No. tracts | Per cent Negro | Per cent Puerto Rican |
|---|---|---|---|
| 5.7 and below | 4 | 50.0 | 25.5 |
| 5.8 – 7.0 | 64 | 31.1 | 34.7 |
| 7.1 – 8.3 | 150 | 34.4 | 36.3 |
| 8.4 – 9.6 | 162 | 33.2 | 26.0 |
| 9.7 – 10.8 | 51 | 28.4 | 17.3 |
| 10.9 and above | 15 | 20.9 | 17.6 |
| | n = 446 | | |

Mean (median school years completed) = 8.4
Standard deviation = 1.27

**(b) Median family income of the Puerto Rican population (1969), and by per cent Negro and per cent Puerto Rican, 1970**

| (b) Median family income (Puerto Ricans) | No. tracts | Per cent Negro | Per cent Puerto Rican |
|---|---|---|---|
| $4,111 and below | 56 | 36.2 | 32.8 |
| $4,112 – 5,700 | 191 | 36.3 | 36.1 |
| $5,701 – 7,289 | 138 | 30.3 | 22.9 |
| $7,290 – 8,878 | 40 | 19.1 | 19.3 |
| $8,879 – 10,467 | 10 | 22.5 | 20.5 |
| $10,468 and above | 9 | 19.3 | 20.5 |
| | n = 444 | | |

Mean (median family income) = $5,701
Standard deviation = $1,588

Source: US Census of Population and Housing, 1970.

Rican population and by per cent black and Puerto Rican in those tracts. Class intervals of education and income correspond to standard deviations from the mean. The data permit a number of generalisations about the characteristics of 'elite' Puerto Rican tracts. Table 5.7(a) shows that poorly educated Puerto Ricans live in tracts with higher proportions of blacks than better educated Puerto Ricans. The tracts in which the most highly educated Puerto Ricans reside also seem to have low concentrations of Puerto Ricans, although the tracts with lowest education levels paradoxically show the same tendency. Table 5.7(b) is analogous: high-income Puerto Rican tracts have low proportions of blacks, and low proportions of Puerto Ricans generally.

As far as the data and this kind of ecological analysis permit us to generalise, in both cases (for education and income), the Puerto Rican 'elite' seems reluctant to share with less advantaged Puerto Ricans or with blacks.

## Conclusion

The primary paradox of Puerto Rican segregation — that they are less segregated than blacks despite being of lower socio-economic status and recent migrants to New York — is underlain by a number of other paradoxes arising from the ambiguities of Puerto Rican ethnicity. The relationship between black and Puerto Rican segregation, which has been abundantly demonstrated, suggests an alternative explanation of recent trends in residential segregation which existing models of ethnic 'assimilation' fail to provide. As a possible 'control group' for the racial component in residential segregation, the Puerto Ricans seem to provide further evidence for a cultural basis to the persistence of ethnic segregation.

## Notes

1. For a discussion of the index of dissimilarity and related measures, see Duncan and Duncan (1955), Taeuber and Taeuber (1965: Appendix A), and Timms (1965).
2. No explanation has been found for the differences between the values in Kantrowitz's matrix of 1960 dissimilarity indices and my own. The latter are presented here as they are known to be directly comparable with the 1970 figures and as they are available for a larger number of ethnic groups.
3. Ethnic group totals are based on first and second generation 'foreign stock' totals, as are data for those of 'Puerto Rican birth or parentage'. Blacks

were enumerated on a different basis, including all those claiming a 'Negro' racial origin. There may therefore be some overlap between 'Negro' and ethnic group totals.

4. There is a large literature on the Puerto Rican migration. See, for example, Chenault (1938), Mills *et al.* (1950), Padilla (1958), Handlin (1959), Fitzpatrick (1971) and Nieves Falcón (1975).

## Bibliography

Chenault, L. (1938) *The Puerto Rican Migrant in New York City*, Columbia University Press, New York

Duncan, O.D. and Duncan, B. (1955) 'A Methodological Analysis of Segregation Indexes', *American Sociological Review*, 20, 210–17

Duncan, O.D. and Lieberson, S. (1959) 'Ethnic Segregation and Assimilation', *American Journal of Sociology*, 64, 364–74

Fitzpatrick, J.P. (1971) *Puerto Rican Americans: the Meaning of Migration to the Mainland*, Prentice-Hall, Englewood Cliffs, New Jersey

Gottmann, J. (1961) *Megalopolis: the Urbanized Northeastern Seaboard of the United States*, Twentieth Century Fund, New York

Guest, A.M. and Weed, J.A. (1976) 'Ethnic Residential Segregation: Patterns of Change', *American Journal of Sociology*, 81, 1088–111

Handlin, O. (1959) *The Newcomers: Negroes and Puerto Ricans in a Changing Metropolis*, Harvard University Press, Cambridge, Massachusetts

Kantrowitz, N. (1969a) 'Ethnic and Racial Segregation in the New York Metropolis', *American Journal of Sociology*, 74, 685–95

Kantrowitz, N. (1969b) *Negro and Puerto Rican Populations of New York City in the Twentieth Century*, American Geographical Society, New York

Kantrowitz, N. (1973) *Ethnic and Racial Segregation in the New York Metropolis: Residential Patterns Among White Ethnic Groups, Blacks and Puerto Ricans*, Praeger, New York

Lieberson, S. (1961) 'The Impact of Residential Segregation on Ethnic Assimilation', *Social Forces*, 40, 52–7

Mills, C. Wright, Senior, C. and Goldsen, R. (1950) *Puerto Rican Journey*, Harper and Row, New York

New York Times, The (1972) 'Puerto Ricans Say Census Cuts Political Power Here', 2 October

Nieves Falcón, L. (1975) *El emigrante puertorriqueño*, Ediciones Edil, Riô Piedras, Puerto Rico

Padilla, E. (1958) *Up From Puerto Rico*, Columbia University Press, New York

Rosenberg, T.J. (1974) *Residence, Employment and Mobility of Puerto Ricans in New York City*, Department of Geography, Research Paper No. 151, University of Chicago, Chicago

Rosenberg, T.J. and Lake, R.W. (1976) 'Toward a Revised Model of Residential Segregation and Succession: Puerto Ricans in New York', *American Journal of Sociology*, 81, 1142–150

Taeuber, K.E. and Taeuber, A.F. (1964) 'The Negro as an Immigrant Group', *American Journal of Sociology*, 69, 374–82

Taeuber, K.E. and Taeuber, A.F. (1965) *Negroes in Cities: Residential Segregation and Neighborhood Change*, Aldine, Chicago

Timms, D. (1965) 'Quantitative Techniques in Urban Social Geography', pp. 239–65 in Chorley, Richard J. and Haggett, Peter (eds.), *Frontiers in*

*Geographical Teaching*, Methuen, London
Torruellas, Luz M. and Vázquez, José L. (1976) *Labor Force Characteristics and Migration Experience of the Puerto Ricans* (Part II): *a Cross-Sectional Analysis of Return Migration to Puerto Rico Using 1970 Census Data* (Final Report), Fordham University, New York
Van Valey, T.L., Roof, W.C. and Wilcox, J.E. (1977) 'Trends in Residential Segregation: 1960–1970', *American Journal of Sociology*, 82, 826–44

## Acknowledgements

This paper was written during the course of doctoral research financed principally by the Social Science Research Council and by a Fulbright-Hays Award. I am also indebted to Dr Ceri Peach, who supervised the research, and to Professor Nathan Kantrowitz, for his generous interest and encouragement. The computations were made with the assistance of Mr Frank Pettit and Dr Paul Griffiths. Miss Sue Smith made valuable comments on an earlier draft of the paper. The maps were drawn in the Drawing Office of the Department of Geography, University College London.

# 6 THE BLACK PROFESSIONAL AND RESIDENTIAL SEGREGATION IN THE AMERICAN CITY

Harold M. Rose

## Introduction

Black populations in American cities continue to be more highly segregated than any other large ethnic group. The Hispanic population, which represents the most rapidly growing, major new ethnic minority, was recently found to be much less segregated from the other white population than was true of blacks (Massey, 1979: 555–7). It has been noted, however, that the intensity of black residential segregation in the nation's larger central cities declined slightly between 1960 and 1970 (Roof, 1978: 454). But changes in the reduction of levels of residential segregation continue to lag behind changes in socio-economic mobility. The incongruence between rates of status change and residential change does much to weaken the argument that the existing pattern of racial residential segregation is basically tied to differences in social class. On the other hand, the role of ethnic solidarity has been employed to illustrate the desire of a number of European ethnic groups to continue to occupy ethnic enclaves even though characterised by a level of economic progress that would permit the abandonment of these enclaves (Bleda, 1978: 99).

## Housing Submarkets and Black Professionals

Acknowledging that changes are occurring in the level of central city residential segregation, albeit slowly, the question becomes who are the participants in the change and what represents the preferred environment, in terms of racial composition, of those persons possessing the broadest options for participating in a variety of residential environments. It is assumed that black professionals possess a greater potential for residential mobility than any other segment of the black population. Between 1960 and 1970 young blacks between the ages of 25–34 were shown to have made the greatest socio-economic advances. They were thus in an improved position to establish residence in a variety of housing submarkets, provided that racial barriers to entry were being lowered. There was some evidence that this was the case as a number of attitudinal surveys show that opposition to the presence of black neighbours of equal socio-economic status was declining (Pettigrew, 1980), although there is some recent evidence which shows that young whites are becoming somewhat less liberal in their housing attitudes (Condran, 1979: 74).

The principal objective of this paper, however, is to examine the pattern of residential choice and the preferred racial residential environment of a sample of black professionals drawn from four metropolitan areas. These include: Houston, Texas; Los Angeles, Cal.; Milwaukee, Wis.; and Philadelphia, Pa. In no way does this sample purport to be representative of all black professionals as it was basically drawn from a narrow cross-section of the professional class. But nevertheless it should provide some insight into the kind of housing markets that high-status blacks participate in and demonstrate whether they perceive race to be a continuing barrier to the exercise of free choice.[1]

## Data Collection Method

The sample of black professionals chosen for inclusion in this study was selected purposively rather than randomly. There are drawbacks associated with this procedure, but for the type of study being conducted the initial advantages are thought to outweigh the disadvantages. The problem comes with attempting to operationalise the category, black professional. The method chosen to operationalise black professionals is a very narrow one and does not embrace a broad cross-section of persons generally thought to represent professionals. Black professionals in this instance were persons who held faculty or academic staff positions in three large public universities and one large private university.

This selection procedure was augmented by the inclusion of the members of a professional men's organisation in one of the cities, which did include a diversity of occupational types, as a means of comparing a less specialised group of black professionals with those whose professional status is associated with academia. The black faculty and academic staff persons were identified through the use of both formal and informal mechanisms for this purpose. Once the universe of subjects had been identified they were mailed a questionnaire and requested to participate in a study designed to tap their perceptions regarding system openness. The response to this request varied among institutions, but produced an average yield of 42 per cent with an n of 165.

## Primary Focus of Study

The system openness questionnaire focused primarily on two sets of concerns. One set was related to the presence of barriers in employment-related activity and the other to barriers interfering with the exercise of choice in housing markets. It is on the latter question that this paper will focus. The decision to investigate the preferences and perceived barriers confronted by black professionals was motivated in part by our general lack of knowledge of the changes that might be taking place in the residential location behaviour of this population and the implications it has for the nature of black residential configurations in large urban settings in general.

One would suppose that black professionals would demonstrate a greater propensity to participate in non-black markets if the status model of residential choice is an accurate predictor of housing market behaviour. This conjecture is predicated upon the supposition that higher status persons seek residential environments that provide a diverse display of specific amenities. Thus for black professionals whose housing needs cannot be satisfied within the black-white border of the existing ghetto, one would assume a willingness to seek housing in markets remote from the location of the central ghetto.

## Housing Market Segregation and Status Attainment

The growth of a black professional class during the sixties and its continued growth during the seventies should be expected to lead to a demand for a greater variety of housing options than were available to a smaller black professional class in the past. Farley demonstrated, using 1970 census data, that residential segregation persisted both in terms of status attainment as well as race, but status attainment was essentially associated with in-group segregation (1977: 510—14). That is to say that high-status blacks were segregated from low-status blacks, but that they were even more highly segregated from high-status whites. The latter conclusion was derived using educational attainment as an effective measure of status.

Employing a smaller sample of places than Farley, Simkus indicated some limited reduction in the intensity of residential segregation between blacks and whites in the highest occupational categories

(1978: 90). But the evidence is quite weak when one considers that the level of segregation between black professionals and white professionals was more than double that of white professionals and white labourers (Simkus, 1978: 86). Thus prior to the seventies blacks, regardless of status attainment, could largely be shown to participate in housing markets that were identified as black or in markets on the black-white border. The latter markets are seldom stable, in terms of racial composition, and are almost inevitably scheduled to become part of the black submarket.

Many professional blacks may be negatively inclined to seek housing in markets perceived to be centres of racial hostility, alien behaviour and aloof neighbours. Others may exhibit little concern with these potential attributes of the neighbourhood of entry. A variety of questions are likely to be addressed by the prospective mover and the decision arrived at is likely to reflect the personal orientation of the individual on the issue of the role of race on one's personal identity, social network and the context in which one performs his or her professional role. For some blacks, the retention of a black identity is likely to be very important and the threat of loss of the support associated with residence in black ethnic neighbourhoods might lead to rejecting the notion of seeking housing in a non-black market.

Seldom were non-black markets perceived to represent integrated neighbourhoods by our respondents. It has been demonstrated that blacks perceive residential integration to represent a near equal presence of blacks and whites in a neighbourhood (Farley, Bianchi and Colosanto, 1979: 104—5). Yet we are uncertain how black professionals might perceive the desirability of neighbourhoods in which blacks constitute fewer than 10 per cent of the population,[2] for often it is neighbourhoods with this racial composition that offer the most complete range of amenities. Thus blacks who have attained a professional status and who wish to have access to a diversity of residential amenities will often be required to extend their housing search to submarkets which are distant from the primary black spatial community.

## Black Professionals and the Questions of Ethnic Identity

Black professionals who perceive themselves as ethnic blacks might also be less inclined to seek accommodation in non-black submarkets than non-ethnic blacks, although there is little hard data to support that contention. The issue of black ethnicity is one around which much uncertainty abounds. The question becomes how important is an involuntarily acquired ethnic status on participation in non-ethnic housing markets, holding other factors constant. It is assumed that an attachment to subgroup values, norms and behaviours is likely to vary as a function of the variety of kinds of experiences that individual members of the group have encountered in their contacts with non-group members and institutions. Where contacts between blacks and others have been limited to unequal status contacts and where blacks have been rejected by institutions over which they have no control, one should logically expect a previously involuntary ethnicity to have evolved into a state of voluntary ethnic solidarity. This solidarity has been attributed to efforts designed to overcome discrimination, but with the weakening of discrimination a corresponding weakening of ethnic bonds should result.

The question becomes, for the purpose of attempting to ascertain the willingness of blacks to become members of residential communities in which members of their ethnic group are seldom represented, what percentage of the black population would be willing to establish residence in a non-ethnic environment? The inability to participate in the reward structure of the larger society is likely to act as a constraint against one's willingness to display a lower commitment to ethnic values and social networks. Yet, according to Taylor, it is possible for blacks to display a variety of kinds of identification with spatial and socio-psychological communities (1979, pp. 1416–18), such that a socio-psychological identification does not preclude residence outside of the black spatial community. One of the concerns that will be evaluated here is the role of the strength of identification with the socio-psychological community on the decision to reside in non-black environments. For it is the latter decision that is likely to have the greatest impact on altering the segregation index in American cities.

The strength of black ethnicity is simply one independent variable among a number of variables, however, that enter the decision to search for housing in specific residential submarkets. The housing requirements of the prospective home-seeker; the financial strength; life-style orientation; knowledge of housing availability; and perceived barriers to submarket entry are all likely to influence one's spatial search sphere. It is assumed that black professionals who choose to seek housing in the spatial black community or the black-white border zone are more strongly committed to an ethnic orientation than those who choose to participate in non-black submarkets.

One would expect the intensity of ethnic affiliation to reflect itself in the importance of race in choosing a residential environment. It is well known that non-black ethnic and specific status attainment groups are non-reluctant to express a preference for persons holding membership in groups with which they are affiliated and to reject the presence of those with whom they have only limited affinity. A recent study of Jewish residential behaviour in Chicago illustrates this point. Jaret found a continuing inclination of Jewish movers to settle on blocks that were frequently more intensively Jewish than the blocks on which they had previously resided, although it appears that the tendency to cluster is partially conditioned by Orthodox or Reform status. According to Jaret, 'These findings suggest that among Jews the desire to live in close proximity to group members is still strong' (1979: 240).

### The Importance of Race in Choosing a Residential Environment

To test operationally the receptivity of blacks to choose residence in environments where blacks constitute only a small share of the persons at the neighbourhood scale, the respondents were asked how important race was in choosing a residential environment. Those responding that race was unimportant were thought to represent persons whose attachment to an ethnic identification was weak, while those responding that race was very important were thought to represent persons who perceived themselves in highly ethnic terms. Thus it is hypothesised that the more strongly one specifies the importance of race in choosing a residential environment the lower the probability that one will choose to satisfy one's housing needs in non-black submarkets. This reasoning suggests a strong association between membership in the socio-psychological community and the spatial community. It is quite possible, however, that the strength of ethnic identification is not strongly related to the racial residential character of the chosen environment of residence.

The hypothesis that no differences exist in the importance of race on the choice of neighbourhood of residence by racial make-up of the neighbourhood in which one presently resides was rejected in only one instance. In Philadelphia the null hypothesis was rejected at the 0.02 level of significance. In the latter city respondents in black and mixed markets overwhelmingly reported race to be an important consideration in choosing a neighbourhood of residence and was of no importance to those who primarily resided in non-black markets. In both Houston and Los Angeles more than 70 per cent of the respondents indicated that race was an important consideration, but differences among residents based on the racial make-up of their existing neighbourhood were not statistically distinguishable at the level of significance. The Milwaukee (B)[3] respondents differed from the others in that the majority reported that race would not be an important variable influencing their choice of a residential environment. If our assumption about the influence of ethnicity on residential choice is correct, then Milwaukee (B) residents seem to be almost equally divided between ethnics and non-ethnics, and in neither instances are these identities a function of the racial composition of the neighbourhood of residence.

To be sure that what was being measured was in accord with the previously stated assumptions respondents were asked to express the degree of importance of race on residential choice. When the null hypothesis was cast in this framework the results were the same, on a city-by-city basis, as they were in the previous instance. But while not statistically significant, it can be shown that differences in the strength of the importance of race does show an association with the racial make-up of the neighbourhood of residence. In general, persons indicating race to be a very important variable are more likely to reside in black submarkets, although this is not universally the case. It is possible that neighbourhood racial preference rather than the perceived racial make-up of the existing neighbourhood is a more sensitive index of strength of ethnic identity.

When neighbourhood preference was substituted for perceived racial composition the results were found to change only slightly. A larger chi-square was observed in the Houston case, but in all others the value of chi-square declined. The magnitude of change in the value of chi-square no doubt represents the level of discordance between preferred racial composition and what was believed to be the actual composition. The change in Philadelphia and Los Angeles was minor, indicating a congruence between the ideal and the actual. In Houston and Milwaukee, however, an inverse relationship was observed in the direction of change in chi-square. Fewer persons expressed a desire to live in predominantly black areas in Houston than actually resided there. But for those who did prefer majority black neighbourhoods, race was viewed as very important. Race was also very important for those persons preferring residence in non-majority black neighbourhoods, but its importance declined as a function of residence in neighbourhoods where blacks were only nominally present. Incongruence, however, was often exhibited between neighbourhood preference and actual racial composition.

No Houston respondent viewed race as being of only limited importance in choosing a residential environment. The Milwaukee (B) respondents differed from those in Houston by expressing a preference for neighbourhoods that were 10—29 per cent black. Yet more than half of the persons from Milwaukee were residents of neighbourhoods that were less than 10 per cent black. In the latter instance it does not appear that the degree of importance of race is associated with the desire to reside in predominantly black neighbourhoods. 'Mildly important' represented the modal category for Milwaukee respondents. But even in a population that is only mildly ethnic in terms of neighbourhood preference, given a choice one would prefer residence in environments that fall outside those limits which define non-black submarkets. While the latter group had frequently participated in those markets, these were not the environments of first choice. In the Milwaukee case ethnic identity and spatial propinquity are not found to be strongly associated.

In Philadelphia persons expressing the strongest ethnic identities prefer to reside in fringe neighbourhoods, whereas those who indicate that race is only mildly important show a preference for neighbourhoods that are 10—29 per cent black. The latter neighbourhood type is the one preferred by most Philadelphia residents, followed closely by a preference for fringe neighbourhoods. Los Angeles respondents, who were most often found to reside in non-black submarkets, also expressed a preference for neighbourhoods that were 10—29 per cent black and secondarily for fringe zones. These were persons for whom race was very important in its influence on neighbourhood choice. Those who viewed race as only mildly important generally showed a preference for non-black submarkets.

## Neighbourhood of Residence and Neighbourhood Preference

It is clear that neighbourhood preference on the basis of race is a more sensitive index of ethnic identity than is neighbourhood of residence. In all cities, with the exception of Houston, respondents expressed a preference for residence in neighbourhoods that were 10—29 per cent black, regardless of actual racial make-up of their present neighbourhood of residence. It appears that one can manifest strong ethnic feelings without specifying a preference for residence within the black community. Although a sizeable share of persons expressing a strong ethnic identity in Houston and Philadelphia would prefer residence in black-white border markets. These findings indicate that ethnic identity is strong among most black professionals, but that feelings of ethnicity do not hamper persons from seeking residence in non-black housing markets. Yet it is also apparent that the weaker one's ethnic identity the higher the probability that one will express preference for residence in non-black markets. But a weak ethnic identity is manifested by only a small proportion of all residents.

## Housing Needs

The housing needs of our respondent population are strongly influenced by a number of demographic characteristics. Among those traits which are generally considered more important are stage in the life-cycle, family status, family size and family income. The latter variable generally dictates in which submarkets the housing search activity will take place. In three of the cities in our sample the modal age group of respondent membership was 35–49. In one city the modal group was 50–64. The respondents represented in this survey can best be described as mature adults whose status as professionals ranges from a small percentage who are newcomers to their fields to the majority who have practised their professions for an extended period of time. These are persons who were most often found to be married and whose families were small, seldom exceeding two children. They most often indicated that a three-bedroom single-family structure represented the kind of unit best required to satisfy their needs. While this general description of our respondent population is a valid one, some notable variations from city to city were observed in relationship to one or more variables.

Home ownership among this population was found to be high, ranging from a low ownership level of 59.4 per cent in Los Angeles to a high of 95.7 per cent among the male social service organisation members in Milwaukee. The latter group was older and included many persons who held high-status jobs in public administration. Other respondents holding academic positions were likely to be home-owners in 70 per cent of the cases. Younger persons who were un-married or persons regardless of age who were divorced or living in some other arrangement were generally found to be apartment or condominium occupants.

There is little question that most black professionals are seeking housing in the owner occupancy market and are primarily oriented to the purchase of three-bedroom structures with one or more baths. Once the basic housing needs of the group have been established, the next question is where within the respective metropolitan areas will one attempt to satisfy these needs. To what extent is the search behaviour for housing based on requirements largely associated with life-cycle stage likely to be constrained by barriers perceived to operate in markets with few or no black residents? And to what extent does income act as a constraint to narrow the field of search? These are questions that we will attempt to address with one or more of our respondent groups.

### Barriers to Housing Access: Actual and Perceived

There is continuing widespread evidence that racial discrimination in the sale and renting of housing still abounds. Today's discrimination is much less blatant than that practised in earlier periods, but continues to form a persistent barrier that limits the submarkets in which blacks may be expected to participate. The preliminary results of a recent HUD study can be used to document the extent of continuing discrimination in a number of American cities (Wilson, 1979: 106). A policy of racial steering is thought to represent the most widespread tactic employed by real estate brokers today to effect the racial composition of submarkets (Pearce, 1979: 325–41). Yinger cites other practices which are also used. They include stating the unavailability of housing meeting the buyer's specification; showing housing to blacks only in the black-white border zone; misrepresenting the selling price; and failing to provide assistance in securing mortgage financing (Yinger, 1977: 11–12). In order to negotiate selected housing submarkets, blacks will be required to demonstrate a determination to confront obstacles designed to keep them out of the market or to limit their entry. This determination is becoming increasingly apparent. Yet Perin advises 'Although many more whites and blacks are living as neighbors today, there are no significantly large-scale trends toward the breakdown of rigid institutional barriers for blacks in their quests for access to jobs and housing' (1977: 172–3).

The black professionals responding to our question asking if they perceived race to be a continuing barrier restricting access to housing submarkets provided a mixed response. The largest percentage of persons in each city sample indicated that race was a barrier to submarket entry.

**Table 6.1: Perception of Race as a Barrier by Strength of Barrier**

|  | Strong per cent | Mild per cent | Weak per cent | Unreported per cent |
|---|---|---|---|---|
| Houston | 60.5 | 15.4 | 23.1 | |
| Philadelphia | 70.2 | 23.4 | 4.3 | |
| Los Angeles | 55.0 | 40.0 | 5.0 | |
| Milwaukee (A) | | | | |
| Milwaukee (B) | 26.3 | 31.6 | 5.3 | 36.8 |

Almost three-quarters of the Philadelphia respondents stated that race was a barrier, while fewer than half shared this belief in the Los Angeles and Milwaukee (B) sample. Uncertainty was expressed in almost one-quarter of the cases in Los Angeles, Houston and the Milwaukee (B) groups. Only persons from the Los Angeles group and the Milwaukee (B) group perceived racial barriers to be non-existent and in both instances approximately three-tenths of the respondents held these perceptions. If these perceptions are an accurate indicator of the actual persistence of barriers in our sample cities, one should expect more widespread participation in non-border markets in Los Angeles and Milwaukee than elsewhere.

It is uncertain if the perceived role of barriers on residential access is directly related to the individual's housing market experiences or to secondarily derived evidence. It is expected that those persons who reside in what they perceive to represent integrated neighbourhoods would differ from those residing in non-integrated neighbourhoods on the role of barriers. The direction of the expected difference is not easy to specify. But generally it will be assumed that persons living in integrated neighbourhoods will be less inclined to indicate that race is a barrier than persons who perceive themselves as residing in non-integrated environments. When this hypothesis was tested, it was rejected in all city samples with the exception of Milwaukee (B).

The weakest support for the presence of barriers to residence integrated neighbourhoods was observed in Houston. In neither Philadelphia nor Los Angeles were there significant differences in the belief that race served as a barrier to access and residence in integrated v. non-integrated environments. However, Los Angeles residents in integrated neighbourhoods were more likely to indicate that race was a barrier than persons living in non-integrated environments. This attitude may partially be attributed to the subjective manner in which an integrated neighbourhood has been derived. It was observed that some respondents who indicated that they resided in neighbourhoods where blacks constituted less than 10 per cent of the population did not view those neighbourhoods as integrated. In the Milwaukee (B) sample persons residing in non-integrated neighbourhoods were most often persons who thought barriers existed, but a large share of those reporting residence in an integrated neighbourhood reported uncertainty about the role of race.

## Psychological Barriers Hampering Access

A major goal of this paper is to determine the willingness of black professionals to establish residence in housing submarkets that are only minimally black. It is evident that willingness is only one of many variables operating which will impact on the decision to search for housing in non-black markets, but an important one nevertheless. Bullough reported more than a decade ago that willingness to search for housing in non-black markets was related to feelings of anomie, even among middle-class blacks (1969: 51–62). One would expect, however, that such feelings would have diminished somewhat during the most recent decade.

The extent to which barriers might be expected to have diminished will be associated principally with the success that individuals in the sample have had in attempts to negotiate the system. That is to say, to what extent do individual respondents still encounter barriers to goal achievement which are racially motivated. In those cities where barriers are known to be more prevalent, generally, residence in non-black submarkets is expected to be less extensive. In such communities residence in the zone of quality housing within a black submarket or on the black-white border should be expected to predominate.

## Residence in Non-Black Submarkets

Residence in non-black submarkets varies considerably among cities. Non-black submarkets are operationally defined, for this study, as submarkets where blacks constitute 10 per cent or less of all households and possess locations which are non-contiguous to the black-white border zone. The smallest participation in non-black housing markets reported by our respondents was that from Philadelphia (23.8 per cent), followed by Houston with almost 30 per cent participation. One would have assumed logically that the lowest

participation would have occurred in Houston, solely on the basis of
the regional effect. The most widespread participation in non-black
markets was found to occur in Los Angeles (66.7 per cent), followed
by the two Milwaukee groups, both of which reported more than half
of the respondents resided in submarkets where only a nominal black
presence was observed.

A variety of factors obviously entered into the decisions which led
to the patterns just described. Among them are housing needs, the
desire for their children to attend integrated schools, easy access to
place of employment and the absence of ties to the local black
community. The latter variable might be more important than all
others, but unfortunately no attempt was made to assess directly the
contribution of that variable. There is some evidence indicating that
middle-income black movers from outside of SMSAs are more likely
to choose residence in non-black submarkets than are locals. The
percentage of respondents residing outside of the SMSA prior to
assuming their present job varied from a high of 55 per cent for
Milwaukee (A) to a low of 33 per cent for Milwaukee (B) respondents.
Philadelphia, Houston and Los Angeles respondents reported that
35—40 per cent had moved directly from another community to
assume their present employment. With such a limited range of
variation in persons previously residing elsewhere one would expect
this variable to account for only limited differences among cities.

## The Housing Market Behaviour of Migrants Compared to Non-migrants

It is possible that persons who did not reside in their respective cities
prior to taking their present job were operating under a different set of
constraints than persons who had always lived in these cities. Certainly
the inertia associated with local ties would be less likely to influence
one's decision regarding a satisfactory residential location. Likewise real
estate agents who assist employers to locate appropriate residences for
their employees may have represented an intervening variable. These
and other factors could act in such a way as to lead to a different
pattern of residential distribution among migrant and non-migrant
employees. A review of the contingency tables describing the racial
mix of neighbourhoods occupied by migrants and non-migrants shows
mixed results.

Houston migrants were found to reside in predominantly non-black
submarkets, whereas locals were found to reside in black submarkets.
In Philadelphia, both migrants and non-migrants were most often found
in predominantly black neighbourhoods or border markets. There was,

however, a slightly greater tendency for migrants to move after establishing residence to non-black submarkets than was true of residents. But this did not alter the predominant pattern where neither group was found to participate extensively in non-black markets. Los Angeles differed from each of the others by displaying a high level of non-black submarket participation on the part of both migrants and non-migrants. Yet there was a slightly stronger inclination for natives to choose to live in the black community. But only a minority of the Los Angeles respondents lived in black neighbourhoods regardless of migrant status.

There is some weak evidence that persons coming into the city from outside will more often select housing in non-black markets. If ties in the black community impede the search for housing in markets beyond the fringe of the black community, then migrants would logically be expected to exhibit a greater willingness to participate in a more expansive search space. In those cities where both actual and perceived barriers are thought to be at a minimum, then the submarkets chosen by black members of the academic community should not differ significantly from that of migrant white academics holding constant income and stage in the life-cycle. Where barriers are perceived to be more widespread the pattern of neighbourhood racial mix is not likely to distinguish migrants from non-migrants.

## A Comparison of Submarket of Residence by City

Seldom did the majority of respondents indicate that they had chosen residence in non-black submarkets; nor did the majority of respondents indicate that they resided in predominantly black neighbourhoods. The largest percentage residing in predominantly black neighbourhoods were residents of Houston (44.4 per cent) and the smallest percentage were represented by respondents from Milwaukee (A), where only 12 per cent lived in such neighbourhoods. The remaining respondents lived in neighbourhoods where blacks comprised 10 to 49 per cent of the neighbourhood's residents (Table 6.2). Most respondents lived in neighbourhoods which were less than 30 per cent black. Philadelphia respondents, however, were found primarily in what have been described as ghetto fringe areas. The quality, design and price of housing in ghetto fringe areas are often a strong inducement to participate in the black-white border market, although some writers have demonstrated that price discrimination in these markets is often encountered by the early entrants.

**Table 6.2: Black Professional Participation in Housing Submarkets on the Basis of Racial Composition of the Neighbourhood of Residence**

|  | Non-black market (0–9% black) per cent | Mixed market (10–29% black) per cent | Black market (30–49% black) per cent | (50% black) per cent |
|---|---|---|---|---|
| Houston | 27.8 | 16.7 | 11.1 | 44.4 |
| Los Angeles | 66.7 | 3.0 | 9.1 | 21.2 |
| Milwaukee (A) | 57.6 | 12.1 | 18.2 | 12.1 |
| Milwaukee (B) | 50.0 | 18.2 | 4.5 | 27.3 |
| Philadelphia | 21.7 | 18.3 | 30.0 | 30.0 |

## Housing Amenities and Sub-market Identification

Black professionals regardless of strength of ethnic identity also manifest an interest in upgrading their housing package, and in order to do this often find it necessary to move great distances from the territorial black community. Those who are only able to satisfy their housing demand in non-black submarkets do not appear hesitant to participate in those markets, even though they frequently specify a preference for residence in submarkets where blacks are found in larger numbers.

There are persons, however, who appear to be committed to residing in integrated environments. Among our respondents, the modal neighbourhood preference based on racial composition was 10–29 per cent black, although a minority expressed preference for neighbourhoods that were 30–49 per cent black. The demographic structure of the population, however, was less important in defining integration than were feelings of social isolation. Blacks residing in non-black markets were less often inclined to view themselves as living in integrated neighbourhoods than were persons living in mixed markets. Thus integration as perceived by our sample of black professionals was more often associated with residence in mixed markets than in non-black markets.

Housing costs are employed here as a surrogate for the quality of the housing package, although considerable discrepancy in cost is likely to occur between cities. Nevertheless it is assumed that persons most interested in acquiring the maximum housing amenities will be found in the highest housing cost group in each city, constrained only by ability to purchase. In each city, family income appears to be strongly related to stage in the life-cycle. Thus one would expect mature and older families to dominate the market for housing possessing the most complete set of amenities. The extent to which variations occur in the structure of life-cycle status should be expected to produce a corresponding variation in the extent of participation in high-cost housing markets. As a rule the highest housing category ($\geqslant$\$75,000) employed in this assessment was most often confined to non-black submarkets. Los Angeles, however, represented the exception with housing in this category occurring in all submarkets.

Family income was found to be highest in Milwaukee (B) group and lowest in the Philadelphia sample. If family income is a critical variable in influencing housing choice and maximum amenity housing is found in non-black submarkets, then participation in non-black submarkets should vary as a function of family income. This relationship holds in each city group with the exception of Los Angeles. In Los Angeles, persons with somewhat lower family incomes also participate in higher cost markets. Thus stage in the life-cycle should prove to be an important contributor to the decision to seek housing in non-black markets. Young families will often be confined to border markets and mixed markets when seeking to purchase homes. But mature families, who generally have higher incomes, more often have greater financial ability to seek housing in high-cost markets. Among older families the financial potential exists but a variety of non-financial factors might impede overt decisions to seek housing in the non-black market, i.e. ties to an ethnic community, absence of school-age children, etc.

## The Spatial Distribution of Black Professionals by City

The previous discussion of the residential preference of black professionals and the racial composition of neighbourhoods of residence has primarily left untouched the actual spatial pattern of residence of the population of interest. While an improved understanding of the potential for residence in non-black markets might have been derived from this discussion it is still very important for these housing market preferences and patterns to be converted to positions in geographic space. It is only then that additional meaning can be provided which will aid in bolstering our earlier findings. The spatial pattern of residence of this population varies from city to city.

Some of the major issues involved in the location of this population in real space are those which highlight the distribution of this population in relationship to the territorial black community: nearness to place of employment; in submarkets based on housing cost; and city versus suburban residence. The extent to which of these attributes will be given some attention will vary as a function of data availability. The most complete treatment of these attributes is available from the information appearing in the map describing the pattern of Milwaukee. Housing price descriptions at the submarket level were also derived for Houston, but the submarkets employed are so large that their validity is of doubtful value.[4]

Black professionals in Milwaukee tend to cluster in several locations, but three of these clusters are located near the boundary of the 1970 black community or within the zone of middle-income housing found inside that community. Secondary clusters are also shown to exist in two suburban communities. The Milwaukee (A) group shows a strong affinity for residence in the East-side rental markets in which academics are found in large numbers. This stands in contrast to the pattern displayed by the Milwaukee (B) group who tend to be attracted to markets on the northern margin of the city and adjacent suburbs (see Figure 6.1). The latter group has a stronger affinity for residence in the suburban markets, but likewise has a larger share of members residing in the black territorial community. The pull of the university itself is matched in strength by participation in two other submarkets, one of which is in the black community and the other in the black-white border. Participation in submarkets beyond the central county of the SMAS is limited. Most persons seem to have confined their search to submarkets in which housing costs are moderate (see Figure 6.2).

A clustering of locations was observed in both Houston and Philadelphia. Yet a more dispersed pattern of residential location can be observed in Houston than in Philadelphia. In the latter city a larger percentage of blacks were found within the territorial black community. The Germantown-Mt Airy community in Philadelphia is the community which tends to attract the largest share of the persons in the sample. This represents a zone of attractive homes where racial turnover has been described as slow, but occurring nevertheless (Muller, Meyer and Cybriwsky, 1976: 18). Residence in black residential markets appears to be more nearly complete in Philadelphia than elsewhere. Likewise,

**Figure 6.1: Milwaukee – Residential Location of Selected Black Professionals**

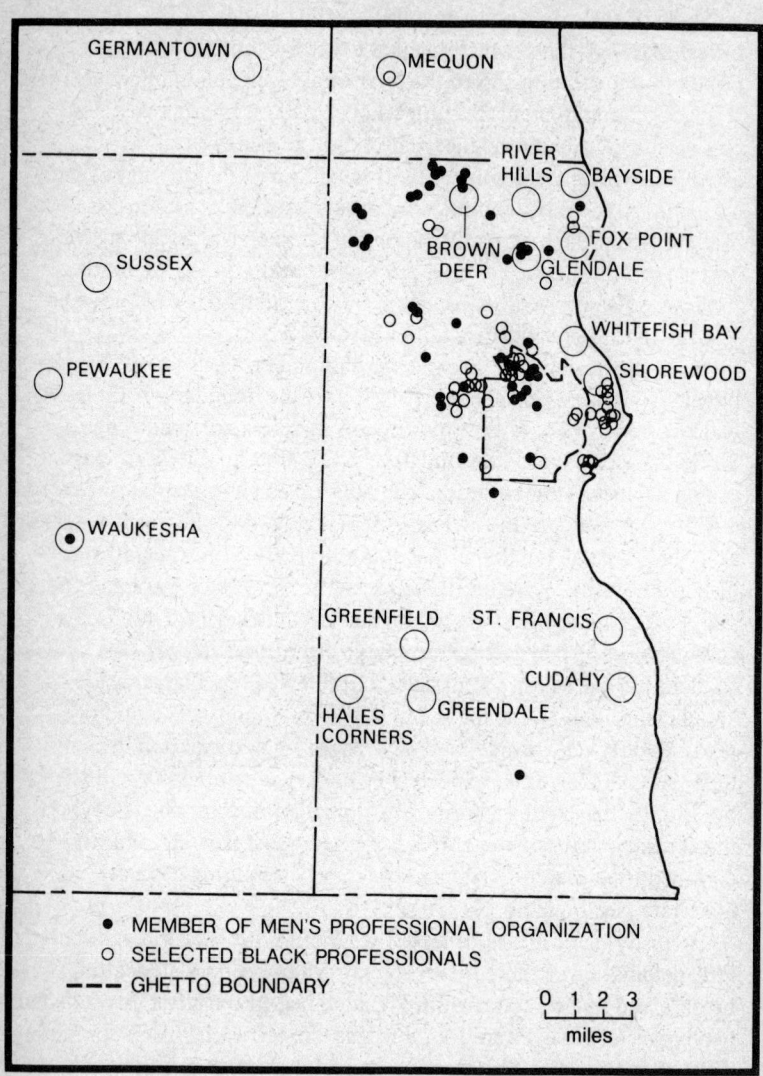

**Figure 6.2: Milwaukee — Mean Cost of Single Family Housing by Submarket**

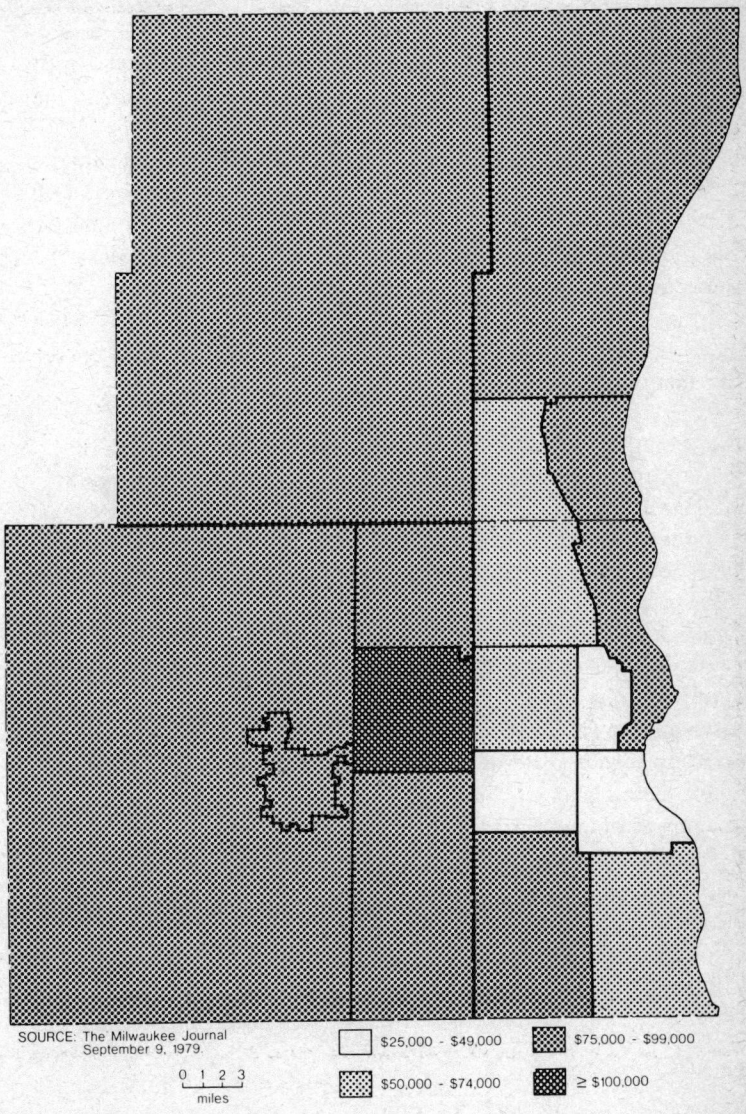

SOURCE: The Milwaukee Journal
September 9, 1979.

0 1 2 3
miles

$25,000 - $49,000          $75,000 - $99,000

$50,000 - $74,000          ≥ $100,000

black professionals do not appear to be attracted to the market in close proximity to the university as was the case in Milwaukee.

Only in Los Angeles are black professionals dispersed and largely absent from the black community. The university itself does exert some influence on the pull of black professionals into markets which are the sites of general faculty residence. The sprawling nature of the city and an absence of ethnic solidarity might have impacted differently on housing availability based on housing cost segmentation. A more complete explanation of the Los Angeles pattern must await the availability of housing cost information within specific submarkets. But the Los Angeles pattern of black professional residence does show major differences from the patterns observed in other cities.

## Summary and Conclusions

Based on the results from a small non-randomly-drawn sample of black professionals in four large regional metropolises, housing submarkets beyond the black-white border are being entered. More than half our respondents resided outside of the central black community with most having established residence in non-black submarkets. But those participating in non-black submarkets show a wide range of variation from city to city.

As we enter a new decade in the American housing experience, the question of the extent to which traditional patterns of spatial residence based on race are likely to persist looms large. How long will it take blacks to acquire patterns of residence that resemble those of other ethnic groups who entered the American city at a slightly earlier time? The rate at which this change occurs will be partially conditioned by the continued perception of barriers to participation in non-black markets, as well as the persistence of real barriers; group economic progress; and the strength of ethnic identity among both blacks and non-blacks. While signs of change are apparent, the inertia associated with the past is not expected to lead to major breakthroughs in the pattern of intra-urban population distribution during this decade.

## Notes

1. The housing market participation of that class of black professionals that we have chosen to investigate was investigated previously by Winsberg. That author's work served as the impetus which stimulated this study. His investigation,

however, was confined to a small, but growing, southern university town and as such makes it somewhat difficult to generalise his findings to settings in which most blacks currently reside.

2. Non-black submarkets are defined in this study as those constituting fewer than 10 per cent black households. Strazheim (1974) previously identified non-black (white) submarkets as those that were less than 15 per cent black. Since whites generally show a high level of sensitivity to the presence of blacks at the neighbourhood scale the lower value was employed in this study as the critical level defining non-black housing submarkets.

3. In Milwaukee two groups were requested to respond to the system openness questionnaire. Persons holding membership in the professional service organisation are identified as the Milwaukee (B) group and those affiliated with the institution of higher education as the Milwaukee (A) group.

4. In both Milwaukee and Houston the mean housing values by submarket were derived by drawing a 20 per cent random sample of units for sale which were advertised in one of the communities' local newspapers. Thus the submarkets identified are those which were derived by the real estate department of the newspapers. The sample data were drawn from the record of a single day in September 1979.

# Bibliography

Bleda, Sharon E. (1978) 'Intergenerational Differences in Patterns and Bases of Ethnic Residential Dissimilarity', *Ethnicity*, 5, 91–107

Bullough, Bonnie (1969) *Social-Psychological Barriers to Housing Desegregation*, Special Report no. 2, University of California, Berkeley

Condran, John G. (1979) 'Changes in White Attitudes Toward Blacks: 1963–1977', *Public Opinion Quarterly*, 43, 463–76

Farley, Reynolds (1977) 'Residential Segregation in Urbanized Areas of the United States in 1970: An Analysis of Social Class and Racial Differences', *Demography*, 14, 497–518

Farley, Reynolds, Bianchi, S. and Colosanto, D. (1979) 'Barriers to Racial Integration of Neighborhoods: the Detroit Case', *The Annals*, 441, 97–113

Jaret, Charles (1979) 'Recent Patterns of Chicago Jewish Residential Mobility', *Ethnicity*, 6, 235–48

Massey, Douglas S. (1979) 'Residential Segregation of Spanish Americans in United States Urbanized Areas', *Demography*, 16, 553–64

Muller, Peter O., Meyer, K.C. and Cybriwsky, F.A. (1976) *Philadelphia, A Study of Conflicts and Social Cleavages*, Ballinger Publishing Company, Cambridge, Massachusetts

Pearce, Diana M. (1979) 'Gatekeepers and Homeseekers: Institutional Pattern on Racial Steering', *Social Problems*, 26, 325–41

Perin, Constance (1977) *Everything In Its Place, Social Orders and Land Use in America*, Princeton University Press, Princeton, N.J.

Pettigrew, Thomas F. (1980) 'Racial Change and the Intrametropolitan Distribution of Black Americans' in Arthur P. Solomon (ed.), *The Prospective City*, MIT Press, Cambridge, Mass., 52–79

Roof, Wade C. (1978) 'The Negro as an Immigrant Group – A Research Note on Chicago's Racial Trends', *Ethnic and Racial Studies*, 1, 452–64

Simkus, Albert A. (1978) 'Residential Segregation By Occupation and Race in Ten Urbanized Areas, 1950–1970', *American Sociological Review*, 43, 81–93

Strazheim, Mahlow R. (1974) 'Housing Market Discrimination and Black Housing Consumption', *Quarterly Journal of Economics*, 19–43

Taylor, Ronald L. (1979) 'Black Ethnicity and the Persistence of Ethnogenesis', *American Journal of Sociology*, 84, 6, 1401–23

Wilson, Franklin O. (1979) *Residential Consumption, Economic Opportunity, and Race*, Academic Press, New York

Winsberg, Morton D. (1979) 'Residential Integration Among Professional Blacks in Tallahassee, Florida', *Research Bulletin, Florida A. & M. Univ.*, 23, 11–18

Yinger, John (1977) 'Prejudice and Discrimination in the Urban Housing Market', Department of City and Regional Planning, Harvard University, Discussion Paper D77-9, Cambridge, Massachusetts

# 7 THE DEVELOPMENT OF SOUTH ASIAN SETTLEMENT IN BRITAIN AND THE MYTH OF RETURN

Vaughan Robinson

The Ballards (1977) have proposed a four-stage development cycle for South Asian settlement in Britain. The movement of South Asian groups through such a cycle may be thought to demonstrate increasing permanence, steady erosion of cultural values, and a rejection of the economic reasoning behind the initial migration. In the assimilationist tradition, spatial and temporal changes in Asian settlement would be seen as outward manifestations of the adoption of the values and norms of the receiving society.

This paper builds upon the early foundations of the Ballards' work by extending their chronology to take in both an explicit consideration of spatial patterns of residential location through time and, in addition, more recent changes in Asian housing preference. Consideration is then given as to whether movement through such a development cycle can really be viewed as being symptomatic of change internal to the groups concerned, or whether it demonstrates alternative strategies to achieve the same objective under changing external conditions.

## The Early Pioneer Phase

The earliest phase of Asian settlement in Britain was characterised by the small-scale migration of single males. In many cases the migration was spontaneous and motivated by a search for adventure and economic success. Many of the early migrants were employed aboard British ships, either as stokers, e.g. the Gujeratis (Dahya, 1974) and Mirpuris (Anwar, 1979) or as galley-hands, e.g. the Sylhetis (Ballard and Ballard, 1977). Crew members would occasionally jump ship whilst in British ports either to take up jobs as unskilled labourers or to exploit more specialised niches; the Sylhetis, for instance, established tea rooms, whilst some Punjabis become door-to-door pedlars (Ballard and Ballard, 1977; Faux, 1980).

For all these groups, barring the Mirpuris, similar 'push' factors had

149

operated to encourage overseas migration. In all cases, pressure on the land was severe in the sending areas (Brooks and Singh, 1979) because of increasing population density and the fragmentation of holdings. Employment on British ships, or direct migration to the UK was seen as a way of reducing this pressure and providing an additional source of income. In many cases, early settlers remained in Britain only for a short period before being replaced by other close relatives who had worked their passage to the UK. This system of rotation was the forerunner of more concentrated chain migration through the sponsorship of passages.

The small scale of early pioneer settlement prevented the development of unique or coherent ethnic areas in British cities. Rose (1969) suggests that the Indian population of Birmingham numbered less than 100 in 1939, for example, whilst Dahya (1974) estimates that the South Asian population of Bradford was as small as 30 in 1944. The temporary nature of residence in Britain, and the economic motives behind migration discouraged the purchase of housing by the pioneers who opted instead for renting rooms from private landlords. The concentration of that housing sector in the twilight zone ensured a loose ecological succession, with the Asians renting property vacated by earlier immigrant groups, such as the East Europeans. Of all the early studies only Little (1948) draws attention to the existence of a truly segregated community in the form of the Muslim area north of Loudon Square in Bute Town. Even here, though, sharing of ethnic space with other groups prevented complete encapsulation.

## The Lodging-house Era

In time, both push and pull factors united to encourage a period of mass migration. In India and Pakistan general conditions and specific factors both combined to provide unusually strong push factors. The need to maintain landholdings was a major factor which necessitated the search for alternative sources of income (Brooks and Singh, 1979; John, 1969; Desai, 1963). Moreover the social importance placed upon land-ownership (Pettigrew, 1972) and the fear of loss of status (*izzet*) if the members of the family had to become landless labourers (Aurora, 1967), provided an additional spur to the search for extra income. In parallel, the 1950s witnessed a major boom in the British economy and the beginnings of a shift to tertiary rather than secondary employment. The social stigma and lack of financial inducement to working in the less attractive sectors of industry created a vacuum at the base of the employment hierarchy which was filled by both West Indian and Asian immigrants (Peach, 1968; Robinson, 1980a). The combination of these economic opportunities and the social and economic push factors in the sending society thus coincided to stimulate much more widespread migration. The economic motivation behind migration and therefore a belief that it represented only a short-term expedient coincided to produce a 'myth of return'. It was important that the Asian migrant minimised expenditure whilst in Britain to allow maximum investment in the village of origin, and hence create the concomitant economic security which would allow an earlier retirement to India or Pakistan. Great stress was thus placed on maximising remittances from Britain by restraining expenditure and encouraging shift work or overtime (Robinson, forthcoming). In parallel, the growing economic investment and the continuing emotional investment in the sending society encouraged social encapsulation and boundary maintenance whilst in the UK. Restricted extra-community interaction guarded against cultural contamination which might prevent an eventual return to the village. In short, Asian workers in Britain regarded themselves as economic transients. Consequently the migration maintained its all male character.

Several factors encouraged the concentration of new Asian migrants in existing locations. First, the impermanence and economic orientation of migration was reflected in the continued demand for privately rented accommodation. Such accommodation was only available in the zone in transition. Secondly, chain migration and sponsored passages ensured that new arrivals entered existing areas of settlement near kin and friends. Thirdly, the desire to maintain social encapsulation encouraged voluntary clustering; propinquity allowed regular interaction between fellow migrants and facilitated the construction of new pseudo-traditional social networks (Jeffery, 1976). Increasingly then, Asians became concentrated in inner-city areas, first in lodging-houses owned by whites and latterly in the all-male Asian household.

The pattern of life in such 'immigrant colonies' has perhaps best been described by Rex and Moore (1967) in their study of Sparkbrook, although P.N. Jones (1967) has also studied aspects of residential segregation during this period. His analysis of 1961 census data for the city of Birmingham pointed to the concentration of Asians in the larger Edwardian and Victorian terraces of the middle ring, and their relative absence from the small terraces of the inner areas. Similar preferences and patterns were found in other towns during this period by Kearsley and Srivastava (1974) in Glasgow, Jones and McEvoy (1974) in Huddersfield, Husain (1975) in Nottingham, and Werbner in Manchester (1979).

## Consolidation or Family Reunion

Several reasons may be suggested as to why the lodging-house era gave way to that of family reunion during the 1960s: first, the need to have the father present to discipline children; secondly, the fear that un-accompanied residence in Britain might encourage the husband to leave his wife for an English woman (Desai, 1963); and thirdly, that the increasing complexity and completeness of the social networks of Asian males in Britain encouraged status competition solely within the arena of the British settlement (Ballard and Ballard, 1977). As hospitality and the entertainment of guests was a crucial factor in determining *izzet* within the British arena, the presence of womenfolk became much more important.

Despite the administrative obstacles to family reunion and the fear of cultural contamination of wives and daughters, the migration of dependants gathered momentum during the late 1960s and early 1970s.

The creation of the Asian nuclear family in Britain, or exceptionally a limited extended family, altered the housing requirements of the settlement. As a result the characteristic lodging-house gave way to the single-family dwelling, often in the shape of by-law terraces near the city centre. Goodall (1966) thus noted that by 1966 this was the characteristic type of Asian housing in Huddersfield, whilst similar housing patterns have been observed during this period of settlement by other authors; Kearsley and Srivastava (1974) for Glasgow, Jones and McEvoy (1974) and Duncan (1977) for Huddersfield, Husain (1975) for Nottingham, Jeffery (1976) for Bristol, Robinson (1979a) for Blackburn, and Werbner (1979) for Manchester.

The demographic restructuring of the Asian minority in Britain, and its movement into the owner-occupied sector have also been paralleled by a physical relocation of the settlement. This has been accomplished in some cases by the expansion of existing ethnic space into contiguous owner-occupied areas. Examples of this trend are Birmingham (Jones, 1970; Woods, 1979), Coventry (Thompson, 1970), London (Lee, 1973), Nottingham (Husain, 1975) and Rochdale

(Anwar, 1979). In other cases, the movement to single-family dwellings has seen the development of newly-pioneered ethnic space. Glasgow provides an excellent example of such relocation (Kearsley and Srivastava, 1974), whilst Werbner (1979) details the parallel relocation of Pakistanis in Manchester to the smaller terraces of West Longsight in the south. In the case of secondary Asian settlements in Britain, the question of physical relocation did not arise since the lodging-house era had been absent. Dundee provides an example of a settlement which began with single-family dwellings in the 1960s (Jones and Davenport, 1972).

## Suburbanisation or Municipalisation

At present, the fourth stage in the development of Asian settlement is still nascent. It is characterised by suburbanisation to better quality residences. Nowikowski and Ward (1978) have warned against confusing the two groups who take part in this movement; their study of the suburbs of South Manchester revealed the presence of Asian professionals whose mobility patterns were characterised by moves between the suburbs of different cities. This group had not experienced residence in existing core areas. Kearsley and Srivastava (1974) noted a similar group of professionals in Glasgow in more substantial property north of the Clyde. This, they suggested, resulted from a desire for social distancing from the increasingly crowded core areas. However, in addition, to this group, Nowikowski and Ward (1978) also discovered the presence of an Asian *petite bourgeoisie* in South Manchester who had 'made good' through small businesses (Werbner, 1980). This group had decentralised from the inner city in their search for middle-class status. Such a move did not indicate a rejection of the ethnic community or a lack of ethnic commitment. Ballard and Ballard (1977) drew a similar conclusion from their findings about the suburbanisation of Sikhs in Leeds. Husain (1975) has also recognised a dispersal of Sikhs and East African Asians in Nottingham during the 1960s to peripheral private estates in the urban district. However Werbner (1979) has provided the most detailed description of the process of decentralisation. She comments upon a three-pronged suburbanisation of Pakistanis in South Manchester.

The alternative although not mutually exclusive course of settlement development is towards municipalisation. Although evidence for such a phase is at present small, it is nevertheless growing.

Robinson's (1980b) study of Blackburn has shown that council housing applications from Asians have increased dramatically since 1973. This was also true of allocations to Asians. Flett (1977) has shown similar trends at work in Manchester, as have the Open University in Bedford.

## The Development of Asian Settlement: Integration?

The movement of the Asian population away from the austerity and impermanence of the lodging-house era could be seen as a concomitant of greater integration to, and more active participation in, British society. The period of family reunion necessitated greater household expenditure both in terms of day-to-day running expenses and long-term housing costs. The movement into single-family dwellings could be seen as a diversion of funds which would ordinarily have been invested in improved housing conditions or extended landholdings in the village of origin. In short, family reunion sees a reorientation of expenditure and investment patterns away from the sending society towards the receiving society. This increased economic investment in Britain could be said to parallel similar trends in emotional attachments. Certain authors have thus used the differential movement into family dwellings as an indicator of differential rejection of traditional values by subgroups within the Asian minority. The Ballards (1977), for instance, note that the Sikhs in Leeds have been particularly keen to move out of the lodging-houses: in 1971 there remained in the city few Sikh families which had not been reunited. In contrast the Mirpuris were still maintaining the all-male household. In a similar fashion, Jeffery (1976) notes that Christian Pakistanis in Bristol have often encouraged their aged relatives to join them in Britain, since they now regard the UK as their permanent home. Conversely, Muslim Pakistanis in Bristol rarely bring other than immediate relatives to Britain since they still believe in the myth of return. Family reunion has thus been seen as an indicator of social and cultural reorientation away from the sending society and towards British society. In a similar vein, the shift towards council tenancy demonstrates increased adoption of the housing norms of the indigenous working class; it also represents the rejection of the traditional predilection for ownership of property which is greatly stressed in most studies of Asian housing preference. It marks a movement towards a situation where income passes out of the community in the form of rent; and finally, it demonstrates a rejection of traditional housing standards previously determined by pre-migration experience (Dahya, 1974) in favour of demands for better quality housing within the context of the British stock. Such factors suggest a growing involvement by Asians in British society and an abandonment of the concept of return migration. Under such circum-stances, increased competition for scarce resources by an active Asian population could well herald the escalation of latent hostility.

## The Development of Asian Settlement: Encapsulation?

### The Single-family Dwelling and Family Reunion

*Social and Economic Considerations.*    In contrast to the explanation provided above, several authors have suggested that the period of family reunion acts not to weaken but to strengthen, social and economic ties with the sending society. Jeffery's (1976) study of Pakistanis in Bristol has shown the numerous obligations that tie a migrant to his kin group in the sending society. Jeffery has also shown how many of these obligations are tightened after family reunion. The movement of a migrant's sons and wife to Britain forces him to rely upon his brothers or more distant kin to oversee property left in the village. These relations are entrusted with the task of rent collection and the profitable investment of this capital. They are also responsible for ensuring that property is well maintained regardless of whether the migrant rents it out in his absence. In a similar way, although migrants might be relieved of the need to send money to Pakistan to maintain their wives after reunion, this obligation is often replaced by remittances to help parents or younger brothers and sisters. In essence whilst family reunion removes some of the short-term economic and social obligations that bind the migrant to the sending society, these are often replaced by similar or more stringent obligations in a broader context.

More importantly though one can also view the period of family reunion as one of economic gain. Thompson (1970) has shown how family reunion may increase total household income despite the greater costs involved. His study of Punjabi youths in Coventry shows how child migrants begin to contribute to family income and remittances at an early age. Similar factors operate for the female members of the reunited family since although few older Asian women officially work or register as unemployed, many accept work within the community. Shah (1975) has noted this feature of the

East End rag trade, and Maw (1974) and Anwar (1979) have commented upon similar situations elsewhere. Home-working is also common
among Asian teenage girls prior to marriage. Anwar (1979) estimates
that the average home-worker earns between £10–£20 per week,
whilst he also comments upon the regular employment of school
children. It would seem that, despite higher housing costs and
additional household expenditure, the reunited family is capable of
earning a greater amount of disposable income which would allow an
earlier return migration. Analysis of individual family histories tends
to bear this out. The case of Mr. A, a Gujerati who is now resident in
Blackburn, exemplifies the economic advantages of family reunion.
Mr. A came to Britain in 1962 at the age of 37. He came alone direct
from India and took up employment in the textile industry. His wife
and two married sons joined him later, and he now considers his
family complete. In 1977 Mr A earned only £37 per week as a
labourer in the mills, a job which bears little relation to his pre-
migration experience as a farmer. Family reunion has considerably
augmented joint family income though. Mr A's two sons, aged 30
and 23, are both employed, one as a weaver in the textiles industry,
the other in the electronics industry. They both live in the home of
the joint family and give their wages to Mr A. Total income was £163
per week in 1977 as a result. In the case of Mr A, then, the income
from the head of household accounts for only 23 per cent of total
family income, the rest being provided by members of the family
who have migrated to Britain during the 1970s.

*Housing Considerations.*    The movement to single-family dwellings
from lodging-houses can also be seen as being economically and
socially motivated. Lodging-house residence was not cheap and has
become less so as the privately rented sector has been squeezed more
tightly. A random sample of some 365 households drawn from the
Electoral Register of Blackburn in 1978 provided information that
demonstrates this. Only 3 per cent of the sample lived in
privately rented accommodation, and these tenants paid an average
weekly rent, in 1978, of £6.50 per head. This compares with the
average derived from the PEP sample of £6.39 per head per week
(Smith, 1976). The Blackburn figure is, however, slightly ambiguous
since some 'renters' were recent migrants temporarily lodging with
fellow villagers; hospitality of this kind was not paid for in cash but
would later be repaid in terms of factional support or material
obligations. The true cost of privately rented accommodation is

therefore nearer £9 per week per head when such cases are excluded. In general then, rent represented about one-fifth of net income.

The Blackburn example demonstrates that movement into a terraced owner-occupied property actually decreased expenditure on housing both absolutely and in per capita terms. 130 respondents were willing to declare both income and mortgage repayments. Average total household income in 1978 was £230.37 per month whilst average monthly mortgage repayments were £34.45. Average expenditure per household on owner-occupied property was thus £8.61 per week or £1.65 per head per week. These figures represent approximately 15 per cent of total household income. In absolute terms then, the movement into owner-occupation represented a slight reduction in actual housing costs, a substantial decrease in per capita housing costs and a worthwhile reduction in housing costs as a per-centage of net household income. The shift to single-family dwellings did not raise expenditure in such a way as to postpone or prevent return migration.

Owner-occupation also provides a remunerative long-term invest-ment for the Asian migrant. Property can be sold prior to return migration to provide working capital and a lump sum for investment by the migrant on his arrival in the village. According to those 313 Asian owner-occupiers who were asked to value their property in the 1978 sample in Blackburn, the average investment in property was £3,957. This sum is likely to be increasing rapidly with the general upward trend in property values, and with the existence of a 'community centrality premium' for houses located within core areas near ethnic services, kin and friends (Robinson, 1979b; 1981). Werbner (1979) goes so far as to suggest that property speculation parallels going into business as a route to financial success.

*Spatial Sorting.*    The movement from the lodging-house also allowed the minority to re-establish patterns of social distancing. The lodging-house was often a multi-ethnic unit both in terms of Asian and European groups, and in terms of different Asian groups themselves. Many of the ethnic mixes tolerated by individuals in the lodging-houses did, in fact, contradict accepted preferences and prejudices. Desai (1963) and Rex and Moore (1967) point to the cultural con-cessions and conflicts that such arrangements enforced on lodgers. Desai noted how the 'Indian houses' acted as sources of accommodation for Pakistanis, Irish, West Indians and English. He also showed how arguments between these groups often involved violence and recrimination.

The constant fear of cultural contamination, which might ultimately prevent a return to the village of origin, encouraged the Asian lodgers to seek a culturally more secure environment. The move to single-family dwellings, and the attendant processes of sorting, allowed the creation of considerably more homogeneous ethnic areas in British cities. Because of the myth of return, such homogeneity may be seen as a social and cultural imperative.

Analysis of residential segregation within the Asian settlement in Blackburn demonstrates this process of sorting at work. Whilst early studies of Asian lodging-houses in British cities showed some degree of spatial sorting, the situation in Blackburn in 1977 was one of intra-community polarisation (Robinson, 1979c). Between 1971 and 1977 the degree of residential segregation between the combined Asian population and the indigenous population remained remarkably constant. Analysis of IDs at several spatial scales revealed segregation to be consistent, or registering a slight decrease (see Table 7.1); this trend contrasts markedly with that of the 1960s when segregation between Asians and the indigenous population increased significantly (Peach, Winchester and Woods, 1975).

**Table 7.1: Trends in Segregation between the Asian and Indigenous Population: Blackburn CB, 1971—7**

|        | Indices of dissimilarity | |
| ------ | ----- | ----- |
| Scale  | 1971  | 1977  |
| Ward   | 53.6[a] | 51.0[b] |
| ED     | 73.1[a] | 73.3[b] |
| Street | 85.3[c] | 75.3[c] |

Source:  [a]1971 Census Small Area Statistics. Calculated for individuals.
[b]Electoral Register plus additions by snowball interviewing calculated for individuals.
[c]Electoral Register. Calculated for households.

However, it is possible that the decrease in segregation between 1971 and 1977 stems not from the weakening of spatial encapsulation, but from the spatial expansion of the settlement to allow internal social distancing. In order to provide separate ethnic areas for each of the groups within the Asian settlement, new white areas had to be pioneered. The pioneering would result in a greater degree of spatial mixing between the Asian population in total and the indigenous population. In reality, the decline in spatial segregation between the indigenous and combined Asian populations could thus mask a process of greater intra-settlement polarisation. Data difficulties prevent temporal comparisons of polarisation except on the grounds of birth-place, a variable which is not the most important axis of differentiation (Robinson, 1979c). However, comparison of census- and survey-derived IDs on this criterion reveal a remarkably constant pattern of polarisation disturbed largely by the use of differently defined 'African' populations (see Table 7.2).

**Table 7.2: Ward and Enumeration District-level Indices of Dissimilarity: Blackburn CB, 1971 to 1977**

| Ward level | | 1971 | | |
|---|---|---|---|---|
| | | India | Pakistan | Africa |
| | India | – | 37.7 | 24.9 |
| 1977 | Pakistan | 35.8 | – | 43.4 |
| | Africa | 21.1 | 43.0 | – |
| ED level | | 1971 | | |
| | | India | Pakistan | Africa |
| | India | – | 51.9 | 34.2 |
| 1977 | Pakistan | 51.0 | – | 54.4 |
| | Africa | 27.1 | 51.1 | – |

Note: 1971 'Africa' category follows census. 1977 'Africa' category includes only East and South African Asians. 1977 'Pakistan' category excludes Bangladesh. All 1977 categories include children of English and non-English birth.
Source: 1971 Census Small Area Statistics, 1977 Survey of 8,862 Asians drawn from the Electoral Register and augmented by snowball interviewing.

There appears to be little evidence for a significant decline in community polarisation during the 1970s. But, as Lieberson (1981) has pointed out, the ID fails to take account of the absolute size of groups and their differing growth rates. Use of the P* index (see Robinson, 1980c) circumvents this problem and allows more accurate temporal comparisons. Table 7.3 thus contrasts the degree of community polarisation found in 1971 with that found in 1977, as measured by P*. When group size is introduced, clear evidence exists for the increasing isolation of different birth-place groups within Asian

**Table 7.3: Ward Level P\* Indices: Blackburn CB, 1971 and 1977**

|  | 1971 | | 1977 | |
|  | P* | Expected P* | P* | Expected P* |
|---|---|---|---|---|
| India | 0.08 | 0.02 | 0.25 | 0.09 |
| Pakistan | 0.04 | 0.02 | 0.13 | 0.03 |
| Africa | 0.02 | 0.005 | 0.08 | 0.02 |

Source: 1971 Census Small Area Statistics and 1977 Survey.

residential space.

However the synchronic analysis of polarisation found in Blackburn in 1977 reveals an even more detailed pattern of fission, quantified in Table 7.4. The table presents enumeration district level indices of dissimilarity on the combined criteria of religion, language and birthplace. The six groups listed in the table account for 94.5 per cent of all Asian adults in the town.

Despite the fact that some of these groups contain a relatively small number of individuals (see Woods (1976) for a discussion of the relationship between group size and the ID), the data show that intrasettlement polarisation within Blackburn is substantial, the minimum

**Table 7.4: Intra-settlement Polarisation: Blackburn CB, 1977**

| ID[a] | 1 | 2 | 3 | 4 | 5 | 6 |
|---|---|---|---|---|---|---|
| 1 | – | 58.4 | 65.0 | 42.7 | 53.8 | 70.2 |
| 2 |  | – | 38.4 | 52.3 | 50.5 | 68.0 |
| 3 |  |  | – | 56.5 | 52.5 | 64.4 |
| 4 |  |  |  | – | 42.4 | 65.9 |
| 5 |  |  |  |  | – | 68.7 |
| 6 |  |  |  |  |  | – |

[a] IDs calculated for 4,232 individuals at ED level over those 85 EDs with Asian residents.

| 1 | = | Indian | Muslim | Urdu |
|---|---|---|---|---|
| 2 | = | Pakistani | Muslim | Urdu |
| 3 | = | All | Muslim | Punjabi |
| 4 | = | Indian | Muslim | Gujerati |
|  |  | E. African | Muslim | Gujerati |
| 5 | = | Indian | Muslim | Kutchi |
|  |  | E. African | Muslim | Kutchi |
| 6 | = | Indian | Hindu | Gujerati |
|  |  | E. African | Hindu | Gujerati |

ID being 38.4, the maximum 70.2, and the mean 56.6. Family reunion and the movement into single-family dwellings has allowed a marked socio-spatial sorting of the Asian population into its constituent groups. Spatial segregation thus retains social and cultural cleavages prior to a return migration. This confirms that different subgroups within the Asian minority become polarised into sharply delineated spatial clusters which are homogeneous (Robinson, 1979c).

## Municipalisation

*Social and Economic Considerations.*    The extant literature on the housing preference of Asians in Britain stresses a predilection for the ownership of land and property. Renting is equated with the loss of income, often to individuals or groups outside the minority; it provides neither the short- nor long-term security which allows Asians to visit friends and kin in India or Pakistan; it is relatively expensive; and it could be said to contradict religious and cultural objections to profiteering by the privileged. Because of these factors, council tenancy has not been favoured by Asians in the early phases of settlement development. However, evidence suggests that public renting has recently increased in popularity with the Asian population. Such a change in preference and behaviour patterns could be viewed as a movement towards more permanent settlement on the part of the Asians. It would also be seen as a rejection of cultural values and a movement towards a less economically orientated existence. More detailed analysis reveals this thesis to be misjudged.

Robinson (1980b) has already indicated the pioneer role of the East African Asians in the shift towards council housing. Their decision to reject owner-occupation stemmed from a desire for better housing standards and more importantly from economic motives. The Asians from East Africa were never likely to return there because of the conditions of their expulsion. They consequently possessed no myth of return and no desire to defer material gratification to a later date. Conversely, on their arrival in Britain, many were penniless (although others had made prior arrangements) and most held a desire to enter business as soon as possible. The desire for better quality housing and for capital to set up a business placed contradictory demands upon the East African's limited resources. Council housing provided a way out of this impasse. It did not need a large sum of initial capital yet it provided modern, high-amenity dwellings. In the case of Blackburn, East African Asians have thus pioneered the movement into council housing whilst in many other large Asian settlements they have also become involved in retailing and manufacturing. Although the shift to council housing was begun by East Africans, it was maintained by other more traditional Asian groups who did believe in return migration. This could not have happened unless municipalisation made economic sense. Rent rebates ensured that local authority housing was considerably cheaper than either private renting or owner-occupation of a tunnel-back. In December 1978 an average Asian family living in Blackburn might pay as little as 68 pence rent per week, after rebates. Moreover, this would be for a three-bedroomed house built in 1977 and possessing a high level of amenities. In economic terms then, council housing freed a lump sum which could be remitted immediately for investment in India or Pakistan, and additionally reduced weekly commitments to about 10 per cent of average mortgage payments. Council housing supported rather than challenged the economic orientation of migration, and the myth of return.

*Spatial Considerations.*    Despite the economic advantage of council housing, municipalisation could still be regarded as a rejection of ethnic orientation since it necessitates movement out of the security of ethnic space. Again, however the situation in Blackburn reveals this to be only partly true.

An analysis of the location of Asian families in council housing in Blackburn shows marked spatial concentration in estates near the centre of the city (see Figure 7.1). Estates which contain a large number of Asian families are located contiguous to existing owner-occupied core areas. It would appear that community centrality is still a desired feature for Asians who have moved into council housing. However, as the Runnymede Trust (1975) and Parker and Dugmore (1977) have pointed out, residence in a particular type of council house or a particular council estate does not necessarily imply a pre-ference on the part of the resident. In order to obviate this analytic difficulty, data were collected on the expressed preferences of Asians as revealed by application forms from the period 1967–78. Mapped preferences closely followed the patterns of allocations, thereby underlining the desire for centrally located estates proximate to existing core areas.

When Asians on one of the popular central estates were asked about their reasons for living there, they provided answers which confirmed the continued importance of community centrality. Spatial proximity to established core areas was the most frequent answer. Within this

**Figure 7.1: The Location of Asian Families in Council Housing in Blackburn, 1978**

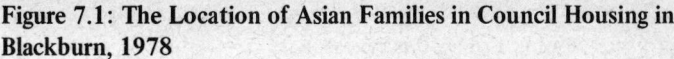

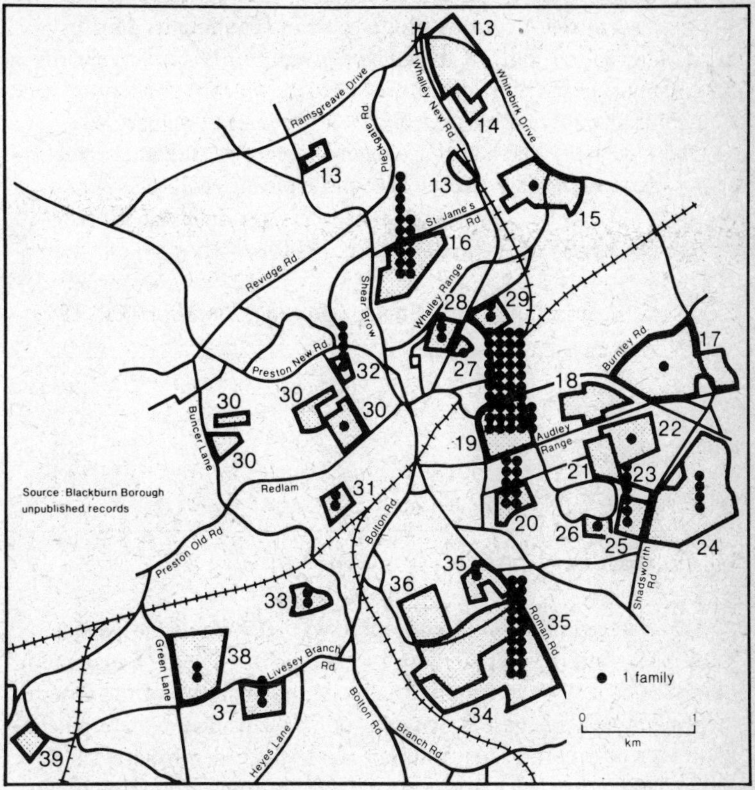

group of factors, nearness to the mosque was dominant, followed by residence near relatives, and finally near friends, and Asian shops and services. None of the interviewees commented upon the superiority of the houses or their amenities.

The importance of community centrality is additionally borne out by the attitude of Asians to offers of alternative accommodation to that of their first choice. Asians in Blackburn hold out for offers on their selected estates only, and are willing to wait a considerable length of time until vacancies become available. The case of an Asian household who turned down six offers of accommodation (without even inspecting the properties), in order to obtain a house on a particular estate, is not atypical. Asians seem to desire community central council houses as much as they desire community central owner-occupied houses. Moreover, they do not appear keen to accept council housing which does not meet this criterion.

Further evidence to suggest that Asians regard the shift into council housing as a move to cheaper property within community territory rather than a move outside it, can be derived from a study of polarisation between estates. The number of Asians who are publicly housed in Blackburn is still small (516 individuals in January 1979), yet there are signs that social distancing is being created in the public sector in the same way that it exists in the private sector. This is apparent from Table 7.5 which lists IDs between linguistic subgroups for the five largest council estates in Blackburn.

**Table 7.5: Polarisation within Council Housing: Blackburn CB, 1979**

|          | Gujerati | Urdu | Punjabi | Kutchi |
|----------|----------|------|---------|--------|
| Gujerati | –        | 31.4 | 29.1    | 35.7   |
| Urdu     |          | –    | 26.3    | 28.6   |
| Punjabi  |          |      | –       | 33.1   |
| Kutchi   |          |      |         | –      |

Note: IDs calculated for the five most important estates.

The average index, on this criterion, was 30.7 whilst the average for birth-place groups was 32.0, with a minimum of 19.4 and a maximum of 42.8. The lack of comparable data and the small size of the groups involved prevents precise statements, but it seems that nascent polarisation may be present. Calculation of location quotients indicates a similar conclusion, with overrepresentation of some groups in certain estates (e.g. the location quotient for Kenyan Asians in estate 28 = 4.22) and underrepresentation in others (e.g. the location quotient for Kenyan Asians in estate 19 = 0.57).

Moreover a study of patterns of intra-urban mobility occasioned by the shift from owner-occupation to council tenancy indicate that a re-shuffling process may be at work. Council estates are often 'colonised' by the Asian subgroup which occupies contiguous owner-occupied areas. The council housing provides a means of community expansion for the subgroup, which adopts the area as its own. The estate then acts as a pole of attraction to members of the subgroup who reside in more distant outliers of the group's ethnic territory. The Bennington Street estate (no. 20) demonstrates this pattern clearly. Location quotients reveal it to be a Gujerati Indian/East

African estate, sharing these characteristics with the contiguous privately-owned dwellings. Of the ten Asian residents on the estate, all moved from what could be termed Gujerati Indian/East African areas (as defined in Robinson, 1979c). However, within this overall pattern, individuals moved to the estate both from nearby core areas and from more isolated areas to the west, north and north-east of the city which were of importance to the Indians or East African Gujerati groups. Council housing is therefore aiding polarisation by providing housing adjacent to the existing ethnic space of a sub-group.

## Suburbanisation

Suburbanisation, as such, is still nascent within the Asian settlement in Blackburn. The settlement demonstrates little tendency for outward migration through the increasing status of an emergent *petite bourgeoisie*. The bulk of the Asian population in Blackburn who could be classified as suburbanised fall firmly into the other half of Nowikowski and Ward's (1978) dichotomy. They are professionals who took up suburban residence upon arriving in the city. They have few ties with, or experience of, the inner city. Evidence does suggest, though, that the settlement is undergoing a degree of decentralisation. However, this could result more from the need to expand ethnic space than from a desire for better housing conditions or a rejection of community links. With the expansion of the minority, and the development of polarisation, each subgroup has located a favourable area to regard as community territory. The rapid increase in child-births which followed family reunion has also added impetus to the need for greater overall ethnic space and specific subgroup territory. In view of this, decentralisation was inevitable. St Paul's Ward provides an example of the way in which less central areas are pioneered by particular sub-groups in Blackburn. According to the Electoral Register, St Paul's Ward had an Asian population which was slightly overrepresented in 1968 (LQ = 1.3). Steady growth of the community through in-migration from other wards ensured that the Asian population was considerably overrepresented (LQ = 2.3) by 1976. The 14 per cent growth in the adult Asian population in the ward between 1968 and 1974 occurred despite the fact that the ward contained better quality housing and was less central. In parallel to this decentralisation, existing core areas did not grow in relative terms during the same period. The wards with the largest Asian populations recorded LQs in 1976 which were in many cases only marginally higher than those recorded in 1968 (e.g. St Michael's Ward 1968 LQ = 1.5, 1975 LQ = 1.6). Closer scrutiny reveals the movement into St Paul's Ward to be a function of polarisation. The ward now contains one of the major Hindu core areas of the settlement, within which 56 per cent of the total Hindu population can be found. In this case, decentralisation resulted not from a desire for better housing nor from the anglicisation of the population, but from the need to pioneer space to allow social distancing.

Analysis of residential segregation within the settlement on the criterion of social class provides little support for the existence of centrifugal mobility. As Table 7.6 demonstrates, social classes 3, 4 and 5 are relatively undifferentiated spatially, with average IDs of 25.4 at enumeration district level. Conversely, social class 2 is markedly residentially isolated from all other classes, recording an average index of 53.5. This suggests the presence of a static, suburban, white-collar group and a relatively undifferentiated, static, central group. There is little evidence to support the development of an emergent upper working class with tendencies towards centrifugal mobility.

**Table 7.6: Social Class Segregation within the Asian Settlement: Blackburn, 1977**

| Social class[a] | 2 | 3 | 4 | 5 |
|---|---|---|---|---|
| 2 | – | 53.1 | 46.2 | 61.1 |
| 3 | | – | 19.6 | 26.2 |
| 4 | | | – | 30.3 |
| 5 | | | | – |
| n = | 73 | 741 | 1210 | 305 |

[a] IDs calculated at enumeration district level.

Whilst there appears to be little evidence for suburbanisation in real terms within Blackburn, this may result from the socio-economic structure of the minority within this city. Evidence from elsewhere does, however, demonstrate that suburbanisation cannot simply be equated with a weakening of the cultural or ethnic community. Nowikowski and Ward (1978) proved that even after suburbanisation, work, leisure and family life took place within an ethnic context. Jeffery (1976) has also stated that suburbanisation should be seen as part of a general process of 'Westernisation' begun after migration.

## Conclusion

Study of national trends has allowed the validation of the Ballards' (1977) cycle which described changes in the structure and location of Asian settlement within British cities. This cycle contains three major phases, those of the early pioneer, the lodging-house and a family re-union. Two alternative, but not mutually exclusive phases can be added to this cycle; those of municipalisation and suburbanisation.

Study of these five phases at one level would indicate an increasing degree of social and residential permanence, a gradual rejection of the economic motive behind residence in Britain, and the persistent weakening of the desire for social and spatial encapsulation.

This paper has argued that there are strong economic motives behind the movement into single-family dwellings and later into council housing. Both reduce regular expenditure on housing, and additionally provide superior accommodation. The timing and economic advantages of these two trends suggest that they were motivated not by a growing desire for permanent settlement, but by the continued belief in a myth of return.

Moreover, phases in the development of Asian settlement in British cities cannot only be seen as economic strategies towards a long-term goal, but also as conferring substantial short-term advantages. Foremost amongst these is the need to create systems of social distancing. The movement into single-family dwellings and council properties provided an opportunity to recreate the spatial distance and social distance which had been missing in the lodging-houses. Maintenance of social cleavages by residential polarisation reinforces the myth of return, and avoids possible sources of cultural contamination which might ultimately prevent a successful return to the village of origin. Whilst *vilayati* (returning migrants) are expected to show signs of substantial 'Westernisation', they are not expected to indicate any 'anglicisation'.

The later phases of Asian settlement in British cities, therefore, are not discontinuous, either in terms of motives or in terms of values, with the austere early phases dominated by the lodging-house. The dynamics of Asian settlement reflect the strategies adopted by the minority in response to changing *external* circumstances. They cannot be taken as being necessarily symptomatic of any changes in the *internal* orientation of the Asian minority which continues to maintain a passive stance with regard to British urban society.

## Bibliography

Anwar, M. (1979) *The Myth of Return; Pakistanis in Britain*, Heinemann, London

Aurora, G.S. (1967) *The New Frontiersmen*, Popular Prakastan, Bombay

Ballard, R. and Ballard, C. (1977) 'The Sikhs; The Development of South Asian Settlement in Britain', in J.L. Watson (ed.), *Between Two Cultures*, Blackwell, Oxford

Brooks, D. and Singh, K. (1979) 'Ethnic Commitment versus Structural Reality; South Asian Immigrant Workers in Britain', *New Community*, 7, 19–31

Dahya, B. (1974) 'The Nature of Pakistani Ethnicity in Industrial Cities in Britain', in A. Cohen (ed.), *Urban Ethnicity*, Tavistock, London

Desai, R. (1963) *Indian Immigrants in Britain*, Oxford University Press, London

Duncan, S. (1977) *Housing Disadvantage and Residential Mobility: Immigrants and Institutions in a Northern Town*, University of Sussex Dept. of Urban and Regional Studies Working Paper No. 5, Brighton

Faux, R. (1980) 'From the Punjab to the Western Isles', *The Times*, 28 October

Flett, H. (1977) *Council Housing and the Location of Ethnic Minorities*, SSRC/RUER, Bristol

Goodall, J. (1966) *IRR Newsletter* supplement on Huddersfield, IRR, London

Husain, M.S. (1975) 'The Increase and Distribution of New Commonwealth Immigrants in Greater Nottingham', *East Midlands Geographer*, 6, 105–29

Jeffery, P. (1976) *Migrants and Refugees, Muslim and Christian Pakistani Families in Bristol*, Cambridge University Press, Cambridge

John, D.W. (1969) *Indian Workers' Associations in Great Britain*, Oxford University Press, London

Jones, H.R. and Davenport, M. (1972) 'The Pakistani Community in Dundee. A Study of its Growth and Demographic Structure', *Scott. Geogrl. Mag.*, 88, 74–85

Jones, P.N. (1967) *The Segregation of Immigrant Communities in the City of Birmingham, 1961*, University of Hull Dept. of Geography Occasional Paper No. 7, Hull

Jones, P.N. (1970) 'Some Aspects of the Changing Distribution of Coloured Immigrants in Birmingham, 1961–66', *Trans. Inst. Br. Geogr.*, 50, 199–219

Jones, T.P. and McEvoy, D. (1974) 'Residential Segregation of Asians in Huddersfield', paper delivered to Inst. Br. Geogr. Conference at Norwich

Kearsley, G.W. and Srivastava, S.R. (1974) 'The Spatial Evolution of Glasgow's Asian Community', *Scott. Geogrl. Mag.*, 90, 110–24

Lee, T.R. (1973) 'Immigrants in London: Trends in Distribution and Concentration, 1961–71', *New Community*, 2, 145–59

Lieberson, S. (1981) 'An Asymmetrical Approach to Segregation', Chapter 3 of this volume

Little, K. (1948) *Negroes in Britain. A Study of Racial Relations in English Society*, Routledge and Kegan Paul, London

Maw, L. (1974) *Immigrants and Employment in the Clothing Industry: The Rochdale Case*, Runnymede Trust, London

Nowikowski, S. and Ward, R. (1978) 'Middle Class and British? An Analysis of South Asians in Suburbia', *New Community*, 7, 1–11

Parker, J. and Dugmore, K. (1977) 'Race and Allocation of Public Housing – a GLC Survey', *New Community*, 6, 27–41

Peach, C. (1968) *West Indian Migration to Britain: A Social Geography*, Oxford

University Press, London

Peach, C., Winchester, S.W.C. and Woods, R.I. (1975) 'The Distribution of Coloured Immigrants in Britain', *Urban Affairs Annual Review*, 9, 395–419

Pettigrew, J. (1972) 'Some Observations on the Social System of the Sikh Jats', *New Community*, 1, 354–64

Rex, J.A. and Moore, R. (1967) *Race, Community and Conflict: A Study of Sparkbrook*, Oxford University Press, London

Robinson, V. (1979a) 'Contrasts between Asian and White Housing Choice', *New Community*, 7, 195–201

Robinson, V. (1979b) 'Choice and Constraint in Asian Housing in Blackburn', *New Community*, 7, 390–7

Robinson, V. (1979c) *The Segregation of Asians within a British City; Theory and Practice*, Oxford University School of Geography Research Paper No. 22, Oxford

Robinson, V. (1980a) 'Correlates of Asian Immigration to Britain, 1959–74', *New Community*, 8, 115–23

Robinson, V. (1980b) 'Asians and Council Housing', *Urban Studies*, 17, 323–31

Robinson, V. (1980c) 'Lieberson's P* Index; a Case-Study Evaluation', *Area*, 12, 307–12

Robinson, V. (1981) *The Dynamics of Ethnic Succession; A British Case-Study*, Oxford University School of Geography Working Paper No. 2, Oxford

Robinson, V. (forthcoming) 'Asians in Britain; a Study in Encapsulation and Marginality', in D. Ley, C. Peach and C. Clarke (eds.), *The Geography of Plural Societies*, Allen and Unwin, London

Rose, E.J.B. (1969) *Colour and Citizenship*, Oxford University Press, London

Runnymede Trust (1975) *Race and Council Housing in London*, Runnymede Trust, London

Shah, S. (1975) *Immigrants and Employment in the Clothing Industry: The Rag Trade in London's East End*, Runnymede Trust, London

Smith, D.J. (1976) *The Facts of Racial Disadvantage: A National Survey*, PEP, London

Thompson, M.A. (1970) 'A Study of Generation Differences Amongst Sikhs', Unpublished MPhil thesis, University of London

Werbner, P. (1979) 'Avoiding the Ghetto: Pakistani Migrants and Settlement Shifts in Manchester', *New Community*, 7, 376–89

Werbner, P. (1980) 'From Rags to Riches: Manchester Pakistanis in the Textile Trade', *New Community*, 8, 84–96

Woods, R.I. (1976) 'Aspects of the Scale Problem in the Calculation of Segregation Indices: London and Birmingham, 1961 and 1971', *Tijdschrift voor Econ, en Soc. Geografie*, 67, 169–74

Woods, R.I. (1979) 'Ethnic Segregation in Birmingham in the 1960s and 1970s', *Ethnic and Racial Studies*, 2, 455–77

# 8 BUSINESS DEVELOPMENT AND SELF-SEGREGATION: ASIAN ENTERPRISE IN THREE BRITISH CITIES

Howard E. Aldrich, John C. Cater, Trevor P. Jones
and David McEvoy

The rapid rise of an Asian-owned small business sector in Britain has as
yet received no more than scanty documentation. Treatment of the
topic is usually to be found embedded in works of a more general
nature such as Allen, Bentley and Bornat (1977). This neglect is surprising in that minority business development may generally be taken
as an indicator of the economic and social standing of an ethnic or
racial minority. In the USA, for example, the ownership and control
of small businesses by groups such as the Chinese, Japanese and Jews
has been shown to be a vital instrument of social mobility, a starting
block from which these minorities have propelled themselves towards a
measure of economic parity with majority society (Light, 1972).
Conversely, an underrepresentation in business (as in the case of the
black American community) has been seen as a serious handicap to
minority social advancement (Foley, 1966).

The Chinese in America appear to have followed a sequence of
business development followed in outline by many successful
minorities. Initially the Chinese were concentrated in arduous tasks
such as domestic service and construction. Discrimination ensured that
self-employment in retailing was seen by ambitious Chinese as perhaps
the only route to self-advancement (Saxton, 1971). At first Chinese
businesses concentrated on the provision of specialist services to the
Chinese community, but by the 1930s the majority had come to cater
for the population at large, albeit in low-status arduous trades such
as laundries, restaurants and groceries. This was an important step
since the initial ethnic market was clearly limited in size whereas
penetration of the white market in effect created an 'export' sector
for the Chinese community. Resources thus gained were used to
finance education and thereby opened alternative routes to occupational
mobility for succeeding generations. The Chinese are now viewed as
having achieved virtual parity with majority society (Newman, 1973).

In contrast black capitalism in the USA has failed to provide a
social ladder for all but a fraction of the black population. Even

federal funding in the late 1960s has failed to achieve anticipated growth rates. Black business is viewed with suspicion by many blacks and suffers from high failure rates and low profits (Foley, 1968; Frazier, 1957; Tabb, 1970).

If the principle that business success acts as a catalyst for social advance has general applicability, then the Asian communities of Britain appear to possess enormous potential for upward mobility. Their ownership of a large and growing number of retail and service establishments and their gradual penetration of sectors such as manufacturing and banking seem to afford a sure means of escape from their current economic disadvantage (Cater, Jones and McEvoy, 1978). Yet, although superficial evidence suggests a kind of transatlantic parallel with Jews or Chinese Americans, careful scrutiny reveals a less sanguine picture. It is therefore the intention of this paper to examine the validity of the minority business-social development hypothesis and its application to Asian business activity in three British urban areas.

## Asian Business Development in Britain

Our study is derived from a survey financed by SSRC (McEvoy, 1980). Attention was focused on five wards in each of three areas: Bradford, Ealing and Leicester. The five wards were those which had the highest proportion of immigrants from India and Pakistan in 1971 (Table 8.1).

A complete inventory of all retail and service businesses in these areas was made in the spring of 1978. Samples of Asian and white businesses were then drawn and interviews conducted in the summer of 1978. Approximately 100 Asian businesses and 100 white businesses were interviwed in each city. Interviews with Asian shopkeepers were conducted mainly by bi-lingual and multi-lingual students of Asian origin. Interviews with white shopkeepers were conducted mainly by the authors with the assistance of white students.

In keeping with popular stereotypes, our findings initially suggest that the Asian business community in Britain represents a case of true entrepreneurial vigour. The insignificant handful of cafes and corner grocers which heralded its birth in the late 1950s has been replaced by a great profusion of outlets offering a wide variety of goods and services. Measured in numbers of shops owned (though not in volume

**Table 8.1: Ethnic Structure of Population and Retail Establishments**

| Ward | Per cent pop. Asian 1971 | Per cent electorate Asian 1977[a] | No. of shops 1978 | Per cent shops Asian 1978 |
|---|---|---|---|---|
| *Bradford* | | | | |
| Bradford Moor | 11.18 | 19.96 | 188 | 23.40 |
| Laisterdyke | 12.78 | 16.25 | 211 | 19.43 |
| Little Horton | 9.92 | 14.82 | 197 | 19.28 |
| Manningham | 24.82 | 33.94 | 481 | 35.76 |
| University | 26.38 | 45.92 | 387[b] | 31.78 |
| | | | | |
| *Leicester* | | | | |
| Charnwood | 8.97 | 26.74 | 259 | 21.62 |
| Latimer | 8.81 | 32.28 | 172 | 37.80 |
| St Margaret's | 7.32 | 22.13 | 276 | 18.84 |
| Spinney Hills | 14.45 | 41.37 | 279 | 36.20 |
| Wycliffe | 18.18 | 41.91 | 172 | 41.86 |
| | | | | |
| *Ealing* | | | | |
| Dormers Wells | 6.39 | 22.05 | 132 | 34.85 |
| Glebe | 21.59 | 53.55 | 196 | 46.43 |
| Northcote | 35.74 | 65.63 | 172 | 55.13 |
| Springfield | 2.92 | 8.08 | 110 | 20.00 |
| Walpole | 4.86 | 10.81 | 289 | 7.61 |

Notes:

[a] The percentage of the electorate with Asian names is likely to be an under-estimate of the Asian share of the population, because much of the Asian population is too young to vote. It is likely to be a much better reflection of the Asian share of economically active age groups, especially since few Asians are of retirement age.

[b] The shop figures for University Ward, Bradford, omit the central business district which was excluded from the survey because it contains few Asian shops and serves a dispersed rather than a local population.

Sources:

| | |
|---|---|
| 1971 population: | percentage of population born in India and Pakistan, 1971 census |
| 1977 electorate: | percentage of electorate with Asian names, 1978 Electoral Registers |
| 1978 shops: | field work by authors |

of business) Asians had captured a considerable share of the retail economy of all three areas by the late 1970s (Table 8.1). As might be expected, the contribution of minority retailing is most striking — both visually and statistically — in areas of the greatest Asian residential concentration, as for example in Manningham Ward, Bradford, or Northcote Ward, Ealing.

When it is considered that the first Asian businesses were established

only a little over two decades ago, it is evident that the present high
volume of retailing is the result of very rapid growth. In the absence
of longitudinal surveys, this is difficult to gauge accurately: in the
case of Bradford, however, an approximation of past growth rates can
be arrived at by comparing the survey figures with estimates made for
earlier years by other workers. Estimates for 1966 put the number of
Asian retail and service outlets at 152 and comparison with our 1975
field survey indicates a tripling of this number in under a decade
(Dahya, 1974; Cater and Jones, 1979). Although 1978 survey figures
indicate a reduced growth rate, there has nevertheless been an increase
of over a quarter over the 1975 figure, an addition of no less than 110
outlets to 560. Although the period of explosive growth now seems
at an end, current expansion remains impressive especially in the
context of a general decline in non-Asian inner-city business.

In all three cities, rapid growth has been linked to diversification, a
notable increase in the range of goods and services sold, with a per-
ceptible shift in emphasis from low to higher order retailing activities.
Initial development centred upon very low order shops with a preponderance of general stores, grocers and butchers but, while these
activities are still significantly overrepresented in the Asian business
spectrum, their proportion has fallen as diversification into more
specialised activities has occured. Table 8.2 demonstrates the range of
activity in one sample area. Although no systematic enumeration of
non-retailing enterprises was undertaken, it is clear that retail growth
has helped to generate linked activities such as wholesaling and that
Asian entrepreneurial activity extends to manufacturing, banking and
a variety of service industries. Even so, it would be unwise to lose
sight of the fact that the typical entrepreneur is still the small corner
shop retailer. A 1980 survey by the city authorities (City of Bradford,
1980) estimates that there are 793 Asian-owned firms in Bradford,
of which exactly 500 are in the distribution sector. Many of the
remainder are in related service sectors.

Perhaps the most noteworthy feature of this expansion is that, in
Bradford and Leicester at least, it is occurring amid the physical and
economic decay of the inner city, cheek-by-jowl with declining
activity, employment and population. As in other cities, Asian
success seems to be filling the vacuum created by others' failure and
it is tempting to concur with the view that Asian commercial vigour
is a vital regenerating force for the British inner city (Hall, 1977).
Virtually independent of official urban aid policies, Asian enterprise
seems to have succeeded in the face of all the classic commercial

**Table 8.2: The Retail Structure of Wycliffe**

| Type of outlet | No. non-Asian shops | Asian shops | Asian per cent of total |
|---|---|---|---|
| Grocer | 9 | 27 | 75 |
| Butcher | 5 | 3 | 38 |
| Fish/Poultry | – | – | – |
| Greengrocer | 2 | 0 | 0 |
| Bread and cakes | 3 | 1 | 25 |
| Off-licence | 2 | 1 | 33 |
| Other food | – | – | – |
| Confectionery, news and tobacco | 9 | 4 | 31 |
| Boots and shoes | 2 | 1 | 33 |
| Menswear | 1 | 1 | 50 |
| Women's and general clothing | 10 | 12 | 55 |
| Furniture | 1 | 1 | 50 |
| Electrical goods | 6 | 1 | 14 |
| Cycles and perambulators | 1 | 0 | 0 |
| Hardware | 7 | 2 | 22 |
| Books and stationery | 4 | 1 | 20 |
| Chemists and photographic dealers | 5 | 1 | 17 |
| Jewellery, leather and sports goods | 2 | 2 | 50 |
| Other non-food | 0 | 4 | 100 |
| Banks | 5 | 1 | 17 |
| Estate agents | 1 | 1 | 50 |
| Cafes and restaurants | 10 | 3 | 23 |
| Hairdressers | 4 | 2 | 33 |
| Dry cleaners and launderettes | 1 | 2 | 67 |
| Other services | 10 | 1 | 9 |
| Totals | 100 | 72 | 42 |

Source: field work by authors, 1978.

disadvantages of the inner city and in spite of all the handicaps associated with immigrant and racial minority status.

## Business and Voluntary Segregation

This picture of Asian entrepreneurs busily working towards their own self-defined goals and seemingly immune from the constraints imposed by the surrounding social environment is entirely consistent with a view which frequently underpins studies of Asian communities in Britain. In explaining Asian relationships with white society and especially the acute segregation of the two groups (Cater and Jones, 1979), many writers emphasise what might be termed the 'principle of minority group autonomy'. Segregation from the white majority, it is argued (or implied), should be seen not so much as a consequence of white rejection but as an expression of minority free choice. A key factor in Asian social behaviour in Britain has been the wish to preserve ethnic identity, a wish which has operated to maintain divisions both between the distinctive Asian linguistic and religious groups and between Asians as a whole and white society (Dahya, 1974).

Cultural isolationism has been bolstered by adherence to language and religion and by the device of self-segregation, both social and spatial. Important surveys of Bradford (Dahya, 1974) and Glasgow (Kearsley and Srivastava, 1974) stress minority choice rather than majority-imposed constraints as the prime cause of residential segregation. Segregated and tightly clustered ethnic neighbourhoods support cultural exclusiveness by fostering close social contact between group members and by acting as protective spaces within which an Asian need rarely be exposed to non-Asian contact (Brooks and Singh, 1978–9). Residential location within the oldest and least desirable urban areas is linked to the wish to economise on housing in order to divert savings into business investment or remittances. It is therefore rational utility-maximising behaviour coupled with non-European housing norms which attracts Asians to slum neighbourhoods and cultural isolationism which promotes geographical isolation.

In many respects the nature of business activity in the three study areas supports this picture of Asian minorities standing largely outside mainstream British society and working towards autonomously defined goals. Both from the individual and collective viewpoints, commercial activity seems to be operating on the terms of the minority rather than the majority population. For a growing number of individuals it provides an ideal opportunity to by-pass the barriers imposed by a white-dominated job market. Indeed, for most proprietors, participation in commerce offers the only means by which aspirations and previous experience may be matched with present reality.

The proposition that Asian self-employment is at least partly motivated by a desire to avoid low-status jobs in the white labour market seems to be supported by the large number of well-qualified Asian shopkeepers in sharp contrast to the more typical pattern of small shopkeepers being poorly educated and of humble social origins. In the current study it was found that educational qualifications differ sharply between the Asian and white samples, chiefly due to the high proportion of graduates among the former (Table 8.3). These findings are consistent with an earlier study of Bradford which showed that, in 1965, over half of a sample of small proprietors had been self-employed businessmen, managers or professionals before migrating to Britain. On arrival, many had been forced into menial wage-earning tasks before being able to enter (or re-enter) business. Self-employment, apart from conferring the usual rewards of personal satisfaction and social status, is clearly one of the few escape routes from the discrimination customarily faced by non-white job-seekers (Allen *et al.*, 1977).

While self-employment is still attainable only by a comparatively few individuals, nevertheless the success of commercial enterprise has vital collective significance. On the simplest level, the very existence of diverse ethnic business means that the ethnic consumer's special tastes are adequately met. In Bradford for example, with one shop for every 68 potential customers, Asians have a theoretically greater choice than the city's whites, with one outlet to every 114 people. More pertinently, however, commercial strength is a force in maintaining ethnic identity in an alien environment. The preservation of minority identity depends first on isolation from the dominant culture and secondly on the ready availability of goods and services which form an integral part of that identity. In both respects business plays an essential role. By removing the need for customers to venture into white-owned shops in white areas, it reinforces the insulating effect of residential segregation and, by supplying special food, clothing and personal services, it ensures that dietary habits and other customs essential to traditional Muslim, Sikh and Hindu cultures can be maintained without inconvenience. It is arguable whether even the mosques and Sikh temples now established in the three cities play a greater part in the preservation of cultural exclusiveness. If institutional completeness is an index of cultural separation, then the profusion and variety of the Asian small business sector in Britain implies an extreme degree of independence from the wider society (Kahn, 1976).

Almost by definition, cultural independence is linked with some degree of economic independence. Through ownership of the bulk of shops patronised by Asians together with certain wholesaling and manufacturing firms, the minority has to some extent gained control of its own subeconomy. Their condition appears in sharp contrast to the ghetto economy of black America which is largely dominated

**Table 8.3: Ethnicity and Socio-economic Background**

| | Ethnicity of owner/manager and city | | | | | | | |
|---|---|---|---|---|---|---|---|---|
| | Bradford | | Leicester | | Ealing | | All cities | |
| | Asian | White | Asian | White | Asian | White | Asian | White |
| Age | 39 | 47** | 38 | 49** | 38 | 48* | 38 | 48** |
| Years of education | 10.2 | 10.1 | 10.2 | 9.9 | 10.2 | 8.9+ | 10.2 | 9.7+ |
| Educational qualifications: | | | | | | | | |
| (0) None | 51 | 60** | 65 | 38** | 15 | 40** | 43 | 45** |
| (1) 'O' Levels | 4 | 3 | 10 | 9 | 3 | 9 | 6 | 7 |
| (2) Secondary school | 30 | 11 | 6 | 34 | 28 | 23 | 22 | 23 |
| (3) 'A' Levels | 1 | 1 | 3 | 4 | 7 | 3 | 4 | 3 |
| (4) Apprenticeship | 0 | 17 | 4 | 6 | 1 | 17 | 2 | 14 |
| (5) Tech. training | 3 | 7 | 2 | 5 | 7 | 4 | 4 | 5 |
| (6) Poly/Un. grad. | 12 | 0 | 10 | 4 | 39 | 4 | 20 | 3 |
| Total per cent | 101 | 99 | 100 | 100 | 100 | 100 | 101 | 100 |
| Per cent father self-employed | 21 | 29 | 75 | 29** | 58 | 28** | 49 | 28** |
| Per cent who inherited business | 1 | 8+ | 1 | 8+ | 2 | 8 | 2 | 8** |

Note on significance of differences between whites and Asians in each city and across all cities: The significance of differences was tested by an analysis of variance on interval variables and chi-square on the other variables. Significance levels are noted by the following symbols: **0.01; *0.05; +0.10. Usually if there is no symbol next to a column for a particular city, the between group difference is *not* significant at the 0.10 level.

by whites (Aldrich, 1973). British Asians have apparently avoided this form of exploitation by controlling a sub-economy sufficiently large and far-reaching to re-circulate much Asian income within the group. The pattern is one of income earned in the white economy and spent in the Asian sub-economy.

## Market Orientation

Up to this point, we have a picture of a burgeoning small business community providing both individual job satisfaction and collective freedom from external cultural and economic domination. There is however an acute conflict between individual and collective goals. The inward orientation of Asian business, its overwhelming dependence upon its own ethnic market, is clearly consistent with the collective goal of minority cultural independence but is seriously at variance with the goal of individual commercial success. The effectiveness of small business as a social ladder and as a means of personal enrichment is greatly inhibited by a market whose limited purchasing power imposes severe restrictions upon participation rates and expansion. As demonstrated by the Chinese American case, the key to expansion lies in entry into the white market with its larger size and per capita income. but, as yet, comparatively few Asian shopkeepers have been willing to tap this potential. Up to now, commercial expansion has been tied closely to the growth of Asian population, with shops and services proliferating in response to the upsurge in the number of Asian customers. Table 8.1 shows the dramatic increase in the Asian population in recent years, an increase which has provided extensive but far from unlimited scope for retailing.

The strength of reliance upon the ethnic submarket may be gauged from Table 8.4 which shows the ethnic composition of customers using both Asian and white shops in the sample. It is evident that Asian business is concerned primarily — though not exclusively — to serve its own ethnic clientele. To a considerable extent, shopkeepers benefit from a protected market, from the presence of a group of consumers whose requirements can only be met by shopkeepers of the same ethnicity. The degree of exclusiveness varies by industry, being most pronounced for clothing shops and restaurants and least in trades such as newspapers, grocery and confectionery, where few special products are involved and little personal contact required. Moreover, substantial penetration of the white market is confined to

**Table 8.4: Racial Composition of Customers**

| | Bradford White | Bradford Asian | Leicester White | Leicester Asian | Ealing White | Ealing Asian | All cities White | All cities Asian |
|---|---|---|---|---|---|---|---|---|
| | | | | City and race of owner | | | | |
| Number of customers per day | 183 | 154** | 132 | 104** | 143 | 140** | 152 | 133** |
| *Per cent of customers who are:* | | | | | | | | |
| White | 70 | 29** | 71 | 33** | 68 | 28** | 70 | 30** |
| Asian | 27 | 67 | 22 | 58 | 23 | 66 | 24 | 64 |
| West Indian | 2 | 3 | 5 | 5 | 6 | 4 | 4 | 4 |
| *Grocery Businesses* | | | | | | | | |
| *Per cent of customers who are:* | | | | | | | | |
| White | 76 | 38** | 72 | 49** | 87 | 36** | 76 | 42** |
| Asian | 22 | 57 | 19 | 41 | 8 | 57 | 19 | 50 |
| West Indian | 1 | 5 | 6 | 6 | 3 | 6 | 4 | 5 |
| *Confectioners, Tobacconists and Newsagents* | | | | | | | | |
| *Per cent of customers who are:* | | | | | | | | |
| White | 67 | 61 | 69 | 44 | 60 | 58 | 66 | 56 |
| Asian | 28 | 38 | 26 | 53 | 30 | 33 | 28 | 40 |
| West Indian | 3 | 7 | 3 | 2 | 6 | 8 | 4 | 6 |
| *Clothing Shops* | | | | | | | | |
| *Per cent of customers who are:* | | | | | | | | |
| White | 69 | 10** | 75 | 19** | 64 | 17** | 70 | 16** |
| Asian | 30 | 84 | 20 | 71 | 24 | 74 | 24 | 76 |
| West Indian | 1 | 0 | 3 | 4 | 7 | 2 | 4 | 2 |
| *Restaurants* | | | | | | | | |
| *Per cent of customers who are:* | | | | | | | | |
| White | 94 | 31** | 96 | 27** | 83 | 30** | 90 | 30** |
| Asian | 1 | 67 | 2 | 72 | 12 | 67 | 5 | 68 |
| West Indian | 4 | 1 | 1 | 2 | 6 | 2 | 4 | 2 |

Note: for significance levels see Table 8.3.

low-order unspecialised trades where there is least competition from white retailers. Conversely higher-order activities are almost entirely dependent upon the protected market. Specialised consumer needs support such exclusive activities as Asian language bookshops, travel agents selling trips to the sub-continent and clothing stores dealing in traditional Asian dress. The general rule seems to be that ethnic exclusiveness increases with the level of specialisation and that diversification into higher orders has relied heavily upon the growth of an ethnic clientele.

Lest it be supposed that these findings are representative of all Asian retailers throughout Britain, it should be emphasised that independent surveys conducted in Croydon (Mullins, 1980) and Wandsworth (Aldrich, 1979) identify Asian business communities for whom the minority market is comparatively insignificant. These areas differ from those currently under review in having experienced a lower rate of immigration, and therefore a lower level of Asian population. Operating as they are in areas where whites form a substantial population majority, Asian entrepreneurs perform a largely middleman-minority function and their ability to survive in such circumstances demonstrates that ethnic protection is not a necessary precondition for Asian business activity. In the three study areas, however, it is certainly a sufficient precondition. Here there can be no doubt that business development is a direct function of population

**Table 8.5: Regression of Per cent Asian-owned Shops on Per cent Asian Population, for Three Cities**

| City | Per cent Asian residents | | Adjusted $R^2$ | N |
|---|---|---|---|---|
|  | b | b* |  |  |
| A. 300 by 300 metre square areas | | | | |
| Bradford | 0.455 | 0.414 | 0.17 ** | 204 |
| Leicester | 0.676 | 0.600 | 0.35 ** | 136 |
| Ealing | 0.336 | 0.355 | 0.12 ** | 135 |
| B. 500 by 500 metre square areas | | | | |
| Bradford | 0.604 | 0.565 | 0.31** | 85 |
| Leicester | 0.766 | 0.682 | 0.46** | 61 |
| Ealing | 0.635 | 0.671 | 0.44** | 85 |

Notes:   b = unstandardised regression coefficient
b* = standardised regression coefficient
** $p < 0.001$

size, a relationship confirmed by the close locational ties between numbers of Asian shops and size of Asian residential population (Table 8.5). Within each area, the number of Asian shops is greatest in neighbourhoods of maximum Asian population concentration, indicating that the pattern of retail succession has followed closely that of residential succession.

## Market Limitations

The restricted purchasing power of the protected market imposes two principal limits on the effectiveness of business as a means of social mobility: first it limits the number of entrants to business and secondly it reduces the profitability to those who do enter. With regard to entry, it is evident that the minority market alone can support comparatively few firms. Opportunities for advancement through self-employment are rare and, although Asian businesses are numerous in relation to population size, these firms are too few to absorb the entrepreneurial and managerial aspirations of more than a fraction of the active population. In the Bradford case, even if it is assumed that each of the 560 shops supports one proprietor, self-employed persons would make up only 2—3 per cent of the active population. The significance of this point is heightened by the limited opportunities for other than menial work offered by the white job market and the realisation that small business provides one of the few ladders for the ambitious. Indeed, if business is to be regarded as a social ladder, then it is an extremely narrow one with footholds for but a small fraction of the would-be climbers.

Overreliance on a restricted market also reduces the profitability and growth of firms. In all three areas Asian firms are overconcentrated in the least profitable and most marginal sectors of retailing, characterised by (i) a preponderance of very small firms; (ii) a preponderance of low-order activities; (iii) poor physical fabric; (iv) high failure rate.

*Scale*

If the average number of customers per day is taken as an approximate index of business scale, then there is a significant difference between white and Asian shops in the sample. Table 8.4 shows that the average number of customers attracted by Asian shops is much lower than that of white shops, a reflection of the fact that the former are concentrated at the lower end of the size range. Even in comparison with other inner-city retailers, whose scale is generally small and living precarious, Asian shopkeepers appear particularly diminutive. In Bradford especially it would seem that many of the smallest outlets are patronised by so few clients as to indicate a mismatch between supply and demand. Certainly the Bradford Asian shop-customer ratio of 1:68 would suggest that the market is already groaning under more outlets than it can comfortably bear (Cater *et al.*, 1978).

## Type of Business

Despite the emphasis placed earlier upon the diversification of retailing and its shift towards higher order (and usually more profitable) lines of goods or services, it should be underlined that this change has involved only a minority of traders. A prime distinction between low- and high-order retailing is of course that the latter is subject to far higher customer thresholds than the former and is thus more likely to be stunted by a low market potential. In consequence the trend towards upward diversification is a slow one with the retail sector still typified by the corner grocer or newsagent (Table 8.2).

## Physical Fabric

Asian shops are rarely located in purpose-built accommodation, the vast majority of outlets combining retail activity with residential accommodation for their occupants. In Bradford especially these outlets are often located in deteriorating buildings in obscure and in-accessible sites away from recognised shopping thoroughfares. Although Asians appear to be the worst placed in this respect, it must be recognised that these disadvantages apply in some degree to the small independent white retailer, with central and prime suburban sites increasingly falling into the hands of the large multiple concern (Cater, 1979).

## Failure Rates

Irrespective of ethnicity, small retail business is characterised by high failure rates and rapid turnover. This is reflected in national trends which show a marked decline in the number of retail outlets since 1951, part of a trend towards a growing scale of retail activity. High death rates of retail businesses are particularly pronounced in inner-city areas, where low incomes, rapid population turnover and environmental and social decay add up to an insecure business environment (Dawson and Kirby, 1979). Although again not a specifically ethnic problem, the Asian minority in Bradford and Leicester are by their very location destined to suffer disproportionately. Such problems are reflected in the high vacancy rates evidenced in areas like Manningham in Bradford, which has one-sixth of its shop premises lying vacant compared with a city-wide figure of 11 per cent.

The cumulative weight of evidence would suggest that Asian shop-keepers are underrewarded and likely to be more preoccupied with survival than with expansion or personal enrichment. In effect, the Asian shopkeeper has exchanged the status of second-class worker for that of second-class proprietor and the visible gloss of self-employment simply acts to conceal the continuing presence of racial disadvantage. The growth of self-employment has generally functioned to absorb surplus labour rather than to increase the economic status of Asians and should thus be seen as a process of involution rather than as a genuine case of development.

## 'Export Orientation'

Many of these considerations apply even to that section of the business community who have succeeded in enlarging their market potential by attracting a high level of white patronage. As yet, this 'export' strategy has provided no sure formula for self-enrichment. Breaking into the white market usually requires the Asian shopkeeper to adopt one or both of the following strategies:

1. Entry into branches of retailing which are being steadily abandoned by the white shopkeepers on account of their low return.
2. Adopting highly competitive practices, such as opening at unsocial hours, which increases the real costs incurred.

Our survey indicates that many Asian shopkeepers have adopted highly competitive practices. Long hours of opening are common (especially early mornings, evenings and Sundays) (Table 8.6). Extensive use of family labour is also made (Table 8.7). However, the figures should go some way to dispelling the myth that Asian business practices involve unfair competition. Asians are no more likely to offer credit than whites and fewer Asians make deliveries. Differences between the three cities are sometimes larger than differences between the ethnic groups, for example in the number of hours worked by the shop owner (Table 8.6). In general the figures indicate that, while Asian shopkeeping is an arduous way of life, white shopkeeping is only marginally less

**Table 8.6: Ethnicity and Competitive Behaviour**

| | Ethnicity of owner/manager and city | | | | | | | |
| | Bradford | | Leicester | | Ealing | | All cities | |
| | Asian | White | Asian | White | Asian | White | Asian | White |
|---|---|---|---|---|---|---|---|---|
| Days open per week | 6.4 | 5.8** | 6.1 | 5.6** | 6.2 | 5.6** | 6.2 | 5.6** |
| Hours open per day | 11.1 | 9.6** | 9.2 | 8.8 | 9.9 | 8.6*** | 10.1 | 8.9*** |
| Per cent open Sundays | 66 | 22** | 41 | 19** | 48 | 11** | 52 | 17** |
| Per cent make deliveries to customers | 42 | 51 | 31 | 37 | 36 | 46 | 36 | 44 |
| Per cent belong to merchant's co-operative | 22 | 31 | 10 | 2 | 10 | 7 | 14 | 13 |
| Per cent with savings from business | 26 | 60** | 21 | 46** | 27 | 44* | 25 | 50** |
| Per cent sell on credit | 39 | 38 | 41 | 42 | 30 | 35 | 37 | 38 |
| Per cent grossing £750 or more per week | 27 | 34 | 44 | 15** | 55 | 39+ | 41 | 29** |
| Hours worked per week | 68 | 61* | 60 | 56 | 54 | 54 | 61 | 57* |
| Asians only: | | | | | | | | |
| Per cent offering special services to Asian customers | 29 | – | 8 | – | 7 | – | 15** | – |
| Per cent feeling pressure to offer special services | 34 | – | 34 | – | 18 | – | 29** | – |

Note: for significance levels see Table 8.3.

**Table 8.7: Ethnicity and Business Size**

| | Ethnicity of owner/manager and city | | | | | | | |
| | Bradford | | Leicester | | Ealing | | All cities | |
| | Asian | White | Asian | White | Asian | White | Asian | White |
|---|---|---|---|---|---|---|---|---|
| Total number of employees | 1.70 | 1.62 | 1.90 | 2.03 | 2.56 | 2.50 | 2.05 | 2.06 |
| Full-time employees | 1.21 | 0.39** | 1.18 | 0.90 | 1.73 | 1.26 | 1.37 | 0.86** |
| Part-time employees | 0.50 | 1.45** | 0.96 | 1.04 | 1.01 | 1.22 | 0.82 | 1.23** |
| Family and relatives employed | 1.22 | 0.46** | 1.33 | 0.61** | 1.49 | 0.73** | 1.35 | 0.61*** |
| Number who work without pay | 0.94 | 0.20** | 0.69 | 0.28** | 0.84 | 0.22** | 0.82 | 0.23*** |
| Number of children working in business | 1.7 | 1.3 | 1.4 | 1.4 | 1.6 | 1.3 | 1.6 | 1.3+ |
| White employees (excludes family) | 0.02 | 0.88** | 0.06 | 1.30** | 0.11 | 1.44** | 0.06 | 1.22** |
| Non-white employees (excludes family) | 1.20 | 0.01** | 0.36 | 0.0** | 0.95 | 0.20* | 0.84 | 0.08* |

Note: for significance levels see Table 8.3.

arduous.

As noted by several writers, a keynote of Asian social behaviour in Britain has been the wish to avoid overt conflict with majority society and to 'expose themselves only minimally to situations where they might be discriminated against' (Hiro, 1971). Self-segregation in business is entirely consistent with this view and, while a preoccupation with the ethnic market may be seen as an assertion of cultural independence, it is equally important to stress its conflict avoidance function. Asian businessmen have frequently limited themselves to markets where they cannot be perceived as a threat by non-Asians and it is noteworthy that significant inroads into the white market have usually been achieved in spheres generally considered to be undesirable by white traders. In all three cities, the most white-oriented Asian enterprises are concentrated in trades such as groceries, newsagents, taxi-hire and off-licences where long hours, low returns and arduous conditions apply and where white entre-preneurs have long been in retreat. As in the housing and employment spheres, Asians are acquiring residual resources willingly abandoned by their former owners. Conflict remains latent because Asians are willing to acquiesce in the role appointed for them by the dominant group.

## Emergent Capitalism

It may be objected that rather than suffering from the constraints of racism, Asian business is facing problems inherent in any form of emergent capitalism. Disadvantage stems not from externally imposed barriers but from internal weaknesses related to commercial infancy. Could it not be that the infant's discomfort is caused by teething troubles rather than by maternal ill-treatment? In terms of a stages of growth model (and at the risk of an intolerable mixture of metaphors), Asian business is engaged in a phase of consolidation preparatory to take-off. Their situation may well be highly reminiscent of Chinese American business in, say, the 1920s, when 'export' penetration was being achieved at the cost of short-term sacrifice and initial hard-won gains formed the basis for progress into more rewarding spheres.

This line of reasoning cannot be answered on the basis of available empirical evidence. Arguing from known information about Asian retail growth trends and extrapolating these into the future, it is plausible to suggest that Asian capitalism is about to launch into an expansion large enough to provide every aspiring entrepreneur with a viable business of his own. Such projections can be neither justified nor refuted since we do not know any of the parameters. We do not know how many 'aspiring entrepreneurs' live in the Asian communities of the three cities nor is there any reliable method by which this could be ascertained. Nor do we know what constitutes a viable business. The criteria of viability may differ not only between whites and Asians but also between different sectors of the broad ethnic groups. The levels of aspiration and satisfaction may be very different for a white pensioner, a white family man, a Kashmiri peasant and a refugee Asian businessman from East Africa. At least some of the differences between cities that we have observed may be the result of the varied origins of the Asian population. Bradford Asians are pre-dominantly Pakistanis, whereas Ealing has a high proportion of Sikhs and Leicester has experienced substantial inflows from East Africa. (Compare for example the proportions of Asians with self-employed fathers in Table 8.3.)

We do know, however, that commercial self-employment is one of the few options open to an ambitious Asian and that, because of market size, it is open only to a small fraction of the Asian population. We also know that many of the existing firms are very low yielding and cannot give a qualified Asian the sort of returns he could earn in white industry were he himself white. In addition we can assume continued growth of Asian population and job demands and rising aspirations on the part of new generations. Although unable to quantify our predictions, we may nevertheless safely conclude that, if business is to be the sole means by which Asians achieve parity with whites, then there would need to be a truly astonishing expansion and diversification of business activity. Such expansion could take place only through the wholesale displacement of white business by Asians: such a scenario is of course totally lacking in credibility, involving as it does a wholly unprecedented displacement of a dominant majority by a subordinate racial minority.

## Cultural Values and Commercial Yardsticks

Our interpretation of the evidence has up to this point emphasised a view of Asians as losers in a one-sided conflict over commercial resources. A principal objection to this view may be that it tends to attribute Western urban values to non-Western rural people (Dahya,

1974). It may be argued that the Asian businessman is not primarily motivated by capitalist goals such as profit and enrichment and that in these circumstances it is surely misguided to measure business success by conventional business criteria. Success may be equated with the satisfaction derived variously from a sense of independence, an ability to fulfil social obligations, prestige as a community leader and participation in a total way of life as opposed to a job of work. This however would be a one-sided and short-sighted view. Apart from its implicit support for the unequal status of a minority, it implies that Asian values are uniform, will not change over time and that the Asian communities will maintain a state of insulation from mainstream society for an indefinite period. It must be highly unlikely however that British-born children of Asian parentage, socialised in English schools, will continue unswervingly to maintain traditional ethnic beliefs while absorbing no values whatsoever from the dominant culture. It seems more likely that material ambitions may rise to the point where the business sector, narrow as it is, will no longer provide a remotely adequate social ladder.

## Conclusion

On a superficial level, the findings of the current survey lend support to the idea that Asian social behaviour in Britain is largely governed by the group's own autonomously defined goals. The vigour of commercial expansion suggests that Asians are able successfully to overcome the disadvantages attached to minority status by developing self-contained social structures largely insulated from external pressures. Closer examination, however, reveals that these pressures may well be operating at one remove. Commercial growth is not necessarily to be equated with commercial success and high levels of rewards are confined to a small fraction of the community and won at extremely high cost. Paradoxically, their very success in shielding themselves from white competition is the root cause of their commercial disadvantage. As long as this reliance upon segregated markets continues, then commercial self-employment will fail to provide the ladder necessary for Asians to achieve a measure of economic and social equality in Britain.

# Bibliography

Aldrich, H.E. (1973) 'Employment Opportunities for Blacks in the Black Ghetto', *American Journal of Sociology*, 78, 1403–25

Aldrich, H.E. (1979) 'Asian Shopkeepers as a Middleman Minority: A Study of Small Businesses in Wandsworth', in D. Eversley and A. Evans (eds.), *Inner City Employment*, Heinemann, London

Allen, S., Bentley, S. and Bornat, J. (1977) *Work, Race and Immigration*, University of Bradford, pp. 244–70

Brooks, D. and Singh, K. (1978–9) 'Ethnic Commitment versus Structural Reality: South Asian Immigrant Workers in Britain', *New Community*, 7, 19–30

Cater, J.C. (1979) 'Asian and non-Asian Retailing in three British Cities', unpublished paper delivered to Institute of British Geographers Annual Conference, Manchester

Cater, J.C., Jones, T.P. and McEvoy, D. (1978) 'The Institutional Ghetto: the Case of Asians in Bradford', unpublished paper delivered to Institute of British Geographers Annual Conference, Hull

Cater, J.C. and Jones, T.P. (1979) 'Ethnic Residential Space: The Case of Asians in Bradford', *Tijdschrift voor Economische en Sociale Geografie*, 70, 86–97

City of Bradford (1980) unpublished analysis of Rates Masterfile, Bradford

Dahya, B. (1974) 'The Nature of Pakistani Ethnicity in Industrial Cities in Britain', in A. Cohen (ed.), *Urban Ethnicity*, Tavistock Press, London, pp. 77–118

Dawson, J.A. and Kirby, D.A. (1979) *Small Scale Retailing in the UK*, Saxon House, Farnborough

Foley, E.P. (1966) 'Limitations of the Black Businessman', *Daedalus*, 95, 425–8

Foley, E.P. (1968) *The Achieving Ghetto*, Washington National Press, Washington, DC

Frazier, E.F. (1957) *Black Bourgeoisie*, Free Press, New York

Hall, P. (1977) 'The Inner Cities Dilemma', *New Society*, 3 February, 223–5

Hiro, D. (1971) *Black British: White British*, Eyre and Spottiswood, London, p. 126

Kahn, V.S. (1976) 'Pakistanis in Britain: Perceptions of a Population', *New Community*, 5, 222–9

Kearsley, G.W. and Srivastava, S. (1974) 'The Spatial Evolution of Glasgow's Asian Community', *Scottish Geographical Magazine*, 90, 110–24

Light, I.H. (1972) *Ethnic Enterprise in America*, University of California Press, Berkeley

McEvoy, D. (1980) *Retail and Service Business and the Immigrant Community*, SSRC Final Report HR 5520

Mullins, D. (1980) 'Race and Retailing: The Asian-owned Retail Sector in Croydon', unpublished paper delivered to Institute of British Geographers Annual Conference, Lancaster

Newman, W.M. (1973) *American Pluralism: A Study of Minority Groups and Social Theory*, Harper and Row, New York

Saxton, A. (1971) *The Indispensable Enemy*, University of California Press, Berkeley

Tabb, W.K. (1970) *The Political Economy of the Black Ghetto*, Norton, New York

## Acknowledgement

This work was carried out under SSRC grant HR 5520: *Retail and Service Business and the Immigrant Community* (McEvoy, 1980).

PART FOUR:

SOCIAL AND SPATIAL DISTANCE

# 9 ETHNIC SEGREGATION AND ETHNIC INTERMARRIAGE: A RE-EXAMINATION OF KENNEDY'S TRIPLE MELTING POT IN NEW HAVEN, 1900–1950

Ceri Peach

## Introduction

The origin of this paper is an implicit but unnoticed conflict in the models of ethnic assimilation in American society proposed by Kennedy (1944; 1952) and Duncan and Lieberson (1959). If the patterns of ethnic segregation reported by Duncan and Lieberson were typical of American cities and if the correlations which they established between measures of spatial segregation and social assimilation were also generally applicable, then there exists a strong *a priori* reason for doubting the existence of the triple melting pot, as proposed by Kennedy.

### Kennedy's Thesis

Kennedy argued from analysis of New Haven, Connecticut, marriages in 1870, 1900, 1930, 1940 and 1950 that while ethnic and national origin differences were diminishing, they did so within continuing religious divides:

> the different nationalities are merging, but within three religious compartments rather than indiscriminately: with Protestant British-Americans, Germans, and Scandinavians intermarrying mutually; Catholic, Irish, Italians, and Poles forming a separate intermarrying group; and Jews remaining almost completely endogamous. A triple religious cleavage rather than a multilinear national cleavage, therefore, seems likely to characterize American society in the future. (Kennedy, 1944: 331)

Although its proponents outnumber its detractors, Kennedy's hypothesis has been attacked. Thomas (1951) demonstrated from a much wider survey of Catholic marriages, that the proportion of mixed marriages was much higher than that suggested by Kennedy's New Haven data. Besanceney (1965) directly and indirectly attacked

Kennedy's methodology and thesis. There was a failure to state whether rates were based on couples or on individuals; a failure to take the size of the group into account and to distinguish actual rates from mathematically expected rates; and finally a failure to distinguish between ethnic and religious rates in proposing her thesis.

Nevertheless, Kennedy's analysis attracted distinguished support (Hollingshead, 1950; Herberg, 1960). Its argument seems taken for granted and as a point of departure by Glazer and Moynihan (1963) and even though Thomas's (1951) arguments led Gordon (1964: 130) to a cautious and sensitive handling of the idea, the thesis was clearly influential. In a perceptive survey of the literature (Yancey, Ericksen and Juliani, 1976), Kennedy's melting pot papers are referred to as classics. In short, Kennedy's thesis on assimilation was itself well assimilated into the literature.

## Implicit Conflicts in the Literature

The objections to Kennedy's thesis that seem implicit from Duncan and Lieberson's (1959) study of assimilation are different from those proposed by Thomas and Besanceney. They concern the relationship between segregation and intermarriage which Duncan and Lieberson established from Chicago data for 1930 and 1950.

From the point of view of the present paper, two of Duncan and Lieberson's findings are of central importance. The first is their demonstration of an inverse relationship between segregation and exogamy: high rates of segregation correlated with low rates of exogamy. Duncan and Lieberson did not employ direct marriage data, but had to infer the rate of intermarriage from the percentage that second-generation immigrants with one native-born parent formed of the total second-generation group with foreign and mixed parentage. 'Other things being equal, the higher the percentage of the second generation with one native born parent, the greater the amount of intermarriage between the first generation and the native population' (Duncan and Lieberson, 1959). Although their data were not ideal, their demonstration was of fundamental importance. Lieberson (1961) replicated this finding on a large number of US cities; confirmation of the observation has also been made elsewhere on more directly applicable marriage data (Jones, 1967; Timms, 1969; Peach, 1974).

The second matter contained in Duncan and Lieberson's paper, which is of critical importance to the present argument, is their demonstration of the levels of spatial residential segregation exhibited by different national origin groups. Duncan and Lieberson showed relatively low rates of segregation between the various 'old' European groups, including the Irish. The rates for many of the 'new' groups, notably the Poles and Italians, however, were much higher, not only from the 'old' groups but from each other. Subsequent work by Lieberson (1961; 1963) and by Kantrowitz (1969) has shown consistent patterns of spatial segregation for the same group in different US cities.

Thus, since it can be shown that Duncan and Lieberson's findings on ethnic segregation were more generally applicable to US cities and not confined to Chicago, and since the relationship, which they demonstrated, of segregation to exogamy is also more generally applicable, it follows that there is a strong *a priori* reason for doubting the existence of an intermarrying group containing relatively highly segregated Italians and Poles and relatively dispersed Irish. Indeed, following Beshers (1962: 135) or, more accurately, reversing his argument, it should be possible to predict low Irish rates of intermarriage with Italians and Poles from a knowledge of the rates of segregation which separate them. Correspondingly higher degrees of intermarriage would be predicted for the Irish with the British-Americans, Germans and Scandinavians with whom they would be assumed to share higher degrees of social mixing. Thus, if New Haven conformed to the patterns reported for other American cities, Kennedy's proposed melting pot of Irish, Italians and Poles, in turn separated from a melting pot of British-Americans, Germans and Scandinavians, would be highly improbable. The expectation from Duncan and Lieberson's work would be of 'old' European groups (including the Irish) coalescing to form a marriage pool, while the segregated Italians and Poles remained separate from it and also from each other.

## The Alternative Hypothesis

The implicit conflict of Kennedy's thesis with that of Duncan and Lieberson has led to the present paper which re-examines the data for ethnic intermarriage in New Haven upon which the triple melting pot hypothesis was based. The analysis is confined to national origin or ethnic groups and does not consider the religion of individual members of those groups. In other words, this paper examines whether the mixture of nationalities, hypothesised by Kennedy, took place, not whether all members of a given national group belong to its purported, corresponding religious group.[1] Although the term 'Protestant' and 'Catholic' are employed in this paper, they are shorthand terms for the national groupings proposed by Kennedy.

## The Data

Certificates of all marriages taking place in the City of New Haven are filed in the New Haven Hall of Records. Records are also received from other New England states and other Connecticut centres, of marriages in which any partner is a resident of the New Haven recording area. These records are kept in bound volumes. This study uses all records in the bound volumes. The marriage certificate population therefore includes all marriages by occurrence plus marriages occurring elsewhere in New England to New Haven residents.

There are, however, substantial differences in the number of marriages reported for each of the years by the present study and by Kennedy. For 1870, 1900 and 1930, Kennedy's figures are roughly double those of the present study. The first possibility seems that Kennedy used county rather than township figures, but reflection shows this to be unlikely. Kennedy does not explicitly describe her data source, but it is clear from footnote three of her 1944 paper that she is referring to the town and not the county. Calculating the county figures would mean dealing separately with 27 townships and then aggregating figures. Figures for marriage, by occurrence, for New Haven town and for New Haven county are given for comparison. The figures for the present study being by occurrence and by residence are somewhat larger than the figures for the town by occurrence only (Table 9.1).

It seems that Kennedy used the same data source as the present

**Table 9.1: Comparison of Marriage Occurrences in New Haven**

|      | Kennedy   | Present study | County | Town  |
|------|-----------|---------------|--------|-------|
| 1870 | 920       | 484           | 1,177  | 547   |
| 1900 | 1,770     | 901           | 2,143  | 917   |
| 1930 | 2,358     | 1,448         | 3,032  | 1,335 |
| 1940 | 3,816     | 2,406         | 4,977  | 1,986 |
| 1950 | not given | 2,275         |        |       |

Source: New Haven Hall of Records and Kennedy (1944; 1952), State of Connecticut annual reports on vital statistics (see bibliography, p. 216).

study but counted marriages for each partner rather than for each couple in 1870, 1900 and 1930. However, on this basis, her figure for 1940 would be expected to be about 4,800 instead of 3,800. It is possible that an arithmetical error on her part explains this difference.

Data for names, age, race, marital status, parental names and type of ceremony were abstracted for each partner and each marriage in 1900, 1930 and 1950 and for 10 per cent of the 1940 marriages. Additionally, data on occupations, addresses and birth-places were collected for all of the 1900 marriages, for systematic 20 per cent samples of the 1930 and 1950 marriages and for a systematic 10 per cent sample of all 1940 marriages. The address data were used for the analysis of segregation between groups. Parental nationality was also abstracted from the 1900 records, but this information ceased to be given on Connecticut licences after June 1906. Each record was numbered serially for each year and an evaluation was made at the time of transcription of the ethnic origin of each parent of each partner. This study is therefore based on detailed records of 4,865 marriages, 9,730 individual partners and 19,460 parents of couples.

For 1900, the combination of the names of each partner, the nationality of both parents, the birth-place of each partner and the type of ceremony (as well as ancillary information on occupations of grooms and addresses) makes the definition of the ethnic group of each partner relatively uncomplicated. For subsequent years, however, the proportion of foreign-born decreases, making birth-place a less useful indicator; parental nationality disappears from the records and ethnicity has to be inferred from names of partners and their parents, race, type of ceremony and so forth. The few cases where identification was not practicable were assigned to an 'other' category. The difficulties facing this study were no greater than those facing the original Kennedy investigation, but they should be recognised rather than ignored.

In the compilation of marriages within and between each ethnic group, separate tabulations were kept of each category of mixed parentage. As the amount of intermarriage increased over time, the number of mixed categories and the proportion of the marrying population with mixed parentage also increased. The matrix for 1950 grooms' ethnicity by brides' ethnicity is an array of 60 by 55 categories. This has advantages for analysis in that it is possible to separate, for example, in the outmarriage of British-American grooms to Irish brides, the contribution made by grooms with British-American fathers and Irish mothers marrying brides with Irish fathers

Table 9.2: Marriage Within and Between Selected Ethnic Groups, New Haven, 1900

| Ethnic group of grooms | Total | Ethnic group of brides | | | | | | | | | | | |
|---|---|---|---|---|---|---|---|---|---|---|---|---|---|
| | | 1 | 2 | 3 | 4 | 5 | 6 | 7 | 8 | 9 | 10 | 11 | 12 |
| Total | 901 | 248 | 114 | 30 | 1 | 278 | 9 | 122 | 9 | 6 | 3 | 44 | 37 |
| 1 British-American | 272 | 196 | 28 | 2 | – | 39 | 4 | 1 | 2 | – | – | – | – |
| 2 German | 111 | 14 | 63 | 3 | – | 26 | 3 | – | 2 | – | – | – | – |
| 3 Scandinavian | 28 | 2 | 2 | 23 | – | 1 | – | – | – | – | – | – | – |
| 4 Dutch | 1 | 1 | – | – | – | – | – | – | – | – | – | – | – |
| 5 Irish | 253 | 27 | 16 | 2 | – | 205 | 1 | 1 | – | 1 | – | – | – |
| 6 French | 10 | 3 | 1 | – | – | 5 | 1 | – | – | – | – | – | – |
| 7 Italian | 124 | 2 | 2 | – | – | – | – | 120 | – | – | – | – | – |
| 8 Polish | 8 | 1 | 1 | – | – | 1 | – | – | 5 | – | – | – | – |
| 9 Other Catholic | 5 | – | 1 | – | – | 1 | – | – | – | 4 | – | – | – |
| 10 Other | 4 | 1 | – | – | – | – | – | – | – | – | 3 | – | – |
| 11 Jewish | 46 | 1 | – | – | – | – | – | – | – | 1 | – | 44 | – |
| 12 Black | 39 | 1 | – | – | 1 | – | – | – | – | – | – | – | 37 |

Note: For column headings see corresponding number row heading.
Source: See text.

**Table 9.3: Marriage Within and Between Selected Ethnic Groups, New Haven, 1930**

| Ethnic group of grooms | Total | Ethnic group of brides | | | | | | | | | | | |
|---|---|---|---|---|---|---|---|---|---|---|---|---|---|
| | | 1 | 2 | 3 | 4 | 5 | 6 | 7 | 8 | 9 | 10 | 11 | 12 |
| Total | 1,448 | 376 | 126 | 48 | 4 | 236 | 35 | 307 | 96 | 11 | 7 | 154 | 48 |
| 1 British-American | 413 | 229 | 45 | 11 | 1 | 82 | 15 | 14 | 14 | – | – | 2 | – |
| 2 German | 143 | 45 | 47 | 11 | 1 | 24 | 4 | 5 | 5 | 1 | – | 1 | – |
| 3 Scandinavian | 49 | 17 | 6 | 16 | – | 8 | – | – | 1 | 1 | – | – | – |
| 4 Dutch | 7 | 3 | 2 | – | – | 1 | – | – | 1 | – | – | 1 | – |
| 5 Irish | 182 | 47 | 17 | 5 | 2 | 93 | 6 | 7 | 4 | – | – | – | – |
| 6 French | 33 | 7 | 3 | 2 | – | 10 | 7 | 2 | 2 | 1 | – | 2 | – |
| 7 Italian | 322 | 15 | 4 | 2 | – | 13 | 2 | 274 | 9 | 1 | – | 2 | – |
| 8 Polish | 78 | 7 | – | 1 | – | 4 | 1 | 4 | 58 | 8 | – | – | – |
| 9 Other Catholic | 12 | 1 | 1 | – | – | 1 | – | – | 1 | – | – | – | – |
| 10 Other | 8 | 1 | – | – | – | – | – | – | – | – | 7 | – | – |
| 11 Jewish | 153 | 4 | 1 | – | – | – | – | 1 | 1 | – | – | 146 | – |
| 12 Black | 48 | – | – | – | – | – | – | – | – | – | – | – | 48 |

Note: For column headings see corresponding number row heading.
Source: See text.

**Table 9.4: Marriage Within and Between Selected Ethnic Groups, New Haven, 1950**

| Ethnic group of grooms | | Ethnic group of brides | | | | | | | | | | | |
|---|---|---|---|---|---|---|---|---|---|---|---|---|---|
| | | 1 | 2 | 3 | 4 | 5 | 6 | 7 | 8 | 9 | 10 | 11 | 12 |
| Total | 2,275 | 515 | 168 | 50 | 5 | 255 | 65 | 666 | 174 | 16 | 15 | 202 | 144 |
| 1 British-American | 499 | 234 | 51 | 13 | 3 | 74 | 18 | 70 | 27 | 5 | – | 4 | – |
| 2 German | 137 | 45 | 33 | 5 | 1 | 21 | 4 | 17 | 11 | – | – | 1 | – |
| 3 Scandinavian | 58 | 17 | 9 | 11 | – | 10 | 1 | 6 | 3 | – | – | 1 | – |
| 4 Dutch | 7 | 3 | 1 | – | – | – | – | 2 | 1 | – | – | – | – |
| 5 Irish | 250 | 67 | 28 | 8 | – | 89 | 9 | 31 | 15 | – | – | 3 | – |
| 6 French | 45 | 10 | 8 | 3 | – | 8 | 5 | 9 | 2 | – | – | – | – |
| 7 Italian | 692 | 86 | 24 | 6 | 1 | 29 | 20 | 487 | 35 | 2 | 1 | 2 | – |
| 8 Polish | 185 | 42 | 10 | 2 | 1 | 16 | 5 | 33 | 75 | – | 1 | – | – |
| 9 Other Catholic | 21 | 2 | – | 2 | – | 2 | 2 | 4 | 1 | 9 | – | – | – |
| 10 Other | 23 | 2 | – | 2 | – | 1 | – | 4 | – | – | 13 | – | – |
| 11 Jewish | 214 | 7 | 4 | – | – | 5 | 1 | 3 | 2 | – | – | 192 | – |
| 12 Black | 144 | – | – | – | – | – | – | – | – | – | – | – | 144 |

Note: For column headings see corresponding number row heading.
Source: See text.

and British-American mothers.

For the purpose of publication, however, ethnicity is assigned in the marriage tables according to the ethnic group of the father of each partner. Calculations, not published here, were made on the basis of assigning all those with British-American fathers, but mothers of a different ethnic group, to the mother's ethnic group. This has no significant effect on the results reported below.

Tables 9.2, 9.3 and 9.4 give absolute figures for marriage within and between the various ethnic groups in 1900, 1930 and 1950. The table for 1940 is omitted since it was based on a 10 per cent sample rather than the 100 per cent coverage, and in general trends lies midway between the 1930 and 1950 figures. All marriages are included in these tables so that the list of ethnic groupings is more extensive than that reported by Kennedy. The French (largely of French-Canadian origin), for instance, have been given a separate listing and are regarded as part of the Catholic pool. Lithuanians, Hungarians, Ukrainian Roman Catholics, Czechs, Portuguese and Spanish are included in the 'other Catholic' category. Greeks, Russian Orthodox, Armenians and Latvians are included in the 'other' category.

## Analysis

### Ethnic Intermarriage

In order to demonstrate the presence or absence of a marrying pool, criteria and standards of expectation must be defined. Following Besanceney (1965) and Ramsøy (1966), rates of observed to expected marriages are given in Tables 9.5, 9.6 and 9.7. However, in view of criticism by Goodman (1965) and Tyree (1973) of standard observed to expected tables, a modification of the calculation has been employed.[2] Thus the range of all values presented in the tables is from zero to two with one representing the coincidence of the observed with randomly expected values, and two the maximum possible excess of observed over expected. The main criterion for an intermarrying pool proposed here is that the amount of inter-marriage between two groups should be equal to or greater than that based on random expectation.

It is important to note that the method for judging intermarriage proposed here depends not on how that number of grooms and brides that marries exogamously is divided between different ethnicities, but on whether marriage between two groups is greater or less than 'expected' values. Expected figures, for all tables, were calculated on

Table 9.5: Ratio of Observed to Expected Number of Marriages (Revised Calculations) Between Ethnic Groups, New Haven, 1900

| Ethnic group Grooms | 1 | 2 | 3 | 4 | 5 | Brides 6 | 7 | 8 | 9 | 10 | 11 |
|---|---|---|---|---|---|---|---|---|---|---|---|
| 1 British-American | 1.70 | 0.81 | 0.22 | 0.46 | 1.20 | 0.03 | 0.74 | – | – | 0.69 | 0.36 |
| 2 German | 0.46 | 1.50 | 0.81 | 0.76 | 1.24 | – | 1.11 | – | – | 0.49 | 0.59 |
| 3 Scandinavian | 0.26 | 0.56 | 1.82 | 0.12 | – | – | – | – | – | 0.35 | 0.08 |
| 4 Irish | 0.39 | 0.50 | 0.24 | 1.73 | 0.40 | 0.03 | – | – | – | 0.41 | 0.07 |
| 5 French | 1.03 | 0.79 | – | 1.28 | 1.10 | – | – | – | – | 0.92 | 1.07 |
| 6 Italian | 0.06 | 0.13 | – | – | – | 1.98 | – | – | – | 0.07 | – |
| 7 Polish | 0.45 | 0.99 | – | 0.41 | – | – | 1.62 | – | – | 0.57 | 0.27 |
| 8 Jewish | 0.08 | – | – | – | – | – | – | 2.00 | – | 0.05 | – |
| 9 Black | 0.09 | – | – | – | – | – | – | – | 2.00 | – | – |
| 10 Protestant Pool | 0.44 | 0.79 | 0.39 | 0.52 | 1.59 | 0.02 | 0.97 | – | – | – | – |
| 11 Catholic Pool | 0.30 | 0.41 | – | 0.13 | 0.26 | 0.03 | – | – | – | – | – |

Note: For column headings see corresponding number row heading. For calculation of values above 1, see text. For definition of the Protestant and Catholic Pools, see p. 205.

**Table 9.6: Ratio of Observed to Expected Number of Marriages (Revised Calculation) Between Ethnic Groups, New Haven, 1930**

| Ethnic group Grooms | Brides | | | | | | | | | | |
|---|---|---|---|---|---|---|---|---|---|---|---|
| | 1 | 2 | 3 | 4 | 5 | 6 | 7 | 8 | 9 | 10 | 11 |
| 1 British-American | 1.45 | 1.10 | 0.80 | 1.09 | 1.20 | 0.16 | 0.51 | 0.05 | — | 1.05 | 0.64 |
| 2 German | 1.07 | 1.30 | 1.15 | 1.01 | 1.02 | 0.16 | 0.53 | 0.07 | — | 1.14 | 0.56 |
| 3 Scandinavian | 1.12 | 1.04 | 1.31 | 1.00 | — | — | 0.31 | — | — | 1.19 | 0.43 |
| 4 Irish | 0.99 | 1.01 | 0.83 | 1.42 | 1.05 | 0.18 | 0.33 | 0.05 | — | 1.00 | 0.30 |
| 5 French | 0.82 | 1.00 | 1.03 | 1.17 | 1.19 | 0.29 | 0.91 | — | — | 0.96 | 0.95 |
| 6 Italian | 0.18 | 0.14 | 0.19 | 0.25 | 0.26 | 1.86 | 0.42 | 0.06 | — | 0.17 | 0.30 |
| 7 Polish | 0.35 | — | 0.39 | 0.31 | 0.53 | 0.24 | 1.73 | 0.24 | — | 0.27 | 0.32 |
| 8 Jewish | 0.10 | 0.08 | — | — | — | 0.03 | 0.10 | 1.95 | — | 0.09 | 0.03 |
| 9 Black | — | — | — | — | — | — | — | — | 2.00 | — | — |
| 10 Protestant Pool | 1.09 | 1.13 | 1.12 | 1.11 | 1.21 | 0.15 | 0.50 | 0.05 | — | — | — |
| 11 Catholic Pool | 0.47 | 0.46 | 0.48 | 0.39 | 0.63 | 0.20 | 0.44 | 0.07 | — | — | — |

Note: For column headings, see corresponding number row heading. For calculation of values above 1, see text.

**Table 9.7: Ratio of Observed to Expected Number of Marriages (Revised Calculations) Between Ethnic Groups, New Haven, 1950**

| Ethnic group Grooms | | | | | Brides | | | | | | |
|---|---|---|---|---|---|---|---|---|---|---|---|
| | 1 | 2 | 3 | 4 | 5 | 6 | 7 | 8 | 9 | 10 | 11 |
| 1 British-American | 1.31 | 1.11 | 1.05 | 1.09 | 1.07 | 0.48 | 0.71 | 0.09 | — | 1.10 | 0.75 |
| 2 German | 1.13 | 1.18 | 1.04 | 1.05 | 1.00 | 0.42 | 1.00 | — | — | 1.16 | 0.75 |
| 3 Scandinavian | 1.09 | 1.09 | 1.20 | 1.07 | 0.60 | 0.35 | 0.68 | 0.19 | — | 1.21 | 0.67 |
| 4 Irish | 1.05 | 1.06 | 1.06 | 1.27 | 1.03 | 0.42 | 0.78 | 0.14 | — | 1.13 | 0.54 |
| 5 French | 0.98 | 1.11 | 1.05 | 1.07 | 1.08 | 0.68 | 0.58 | — | — | 1.21 | 0.86 |
| 6 Italian | 0.55 | 0.47 | 0.39 | 0.37 | 1.01 | 1.61 | 0.66 | 0.03 | — | 0.52 | 0.55 |
| 7 Polish | 1.00 | 0.73 | 0.49 | 0.77 | 0.95 | 0.61 | 1.38 | 1.95 | — | 0.91 | 0.66 |
| 8 Jewish | 0.14 | 0.25 | — | 0.21 | 0.16 | 0.05 | 0.12 | — | — | 0.16 | 0.10 |
| 9 Black | — | — | — | — | — | — | — | — | 2.00 | — | — |
| 10 Protestant Pool | 1.12 | 1.15 | 1.11 | 1.15 | 1.07 | 0.46 | 0.77 | 0.08 | — | — | — |
| 11 Catholic Pool | 0.77 | 0.79 | 0.72 | 0.52 | 1.10 | 0.53 | 0.57 | 0.05 | — | — | — |

Note: For column headings, see corresponding number row heading. For calculation of values above 1, see text.

the basis of total marriages.

In addition to giving ratios of observed to expected marriages within and between each ethnic group, ratios of observed to expected out-marriage to the combined Protestant and combined Catholic groups are also given.[3] These groups are referred to as the 'Protestant' and 'Catholic' pools in Tables 9.5, 9.6 and 9.7. They exclude ethnically endogamous marriages and indicate preferences in outmarriage within the combined 'religious' groups. Thus, for example Irish preferences for other Catholic nationalities would be measured by examining not only observed to expected ratios of Irish-French, Irish-Polish, Irish-Italian and Irish-'other Catholic' marriages but also the observed to expected ratios of Irish to French, Polish, Italian and other Catholics combined. This is to overcome one of the difficulties of Kennedy's evidence. She argues, for example, that in 1950 72.64 per cent of Irish, Italian and Polish marriages were with one another, showing a Catholic pot (Kennedy, 1952: 57). However, since we are not told the relative sizes of the marrying populations we are in no position to tell whether this figure is due largely to high rates of ethnic in-marriage or high rates of outmarriage to co-religionists. Clearly, the effect of adding together all Irish to Irish, French to French, Italian to Italian and Polish to Polish marriages would be to produce an equally large number of Catholic to Catholic marriages. It would not, however, represent a Catholic melting pot. The Protestant and Catholic pools in Tables 9.5, 9.6 and 9.7 thus represent outmarriages into the other ethnic groups, combined according to Kennedy's religious groupings.

From an analysis of Tables 9.5, 9.6 and 9.7 three main points emerge. First, ethnic endogamy is characteristic of New Haven marriages in all three years. Secondly, the amount of outmarriage of all the main groups represented in these tables has increased over time. Thirdly, there is no evidence for the existence of a separate Catholic melting pot.

In 1900, there was not a great deal of evidence for either the Catholic or the Protestant melting pot. Intermarriage rates for almost all ethnic groups, but particularly the larger ones, were below the randomly expected level. However, Irish grooms and brides, Polish grooms and brides and French brides all showed a similar preference for the Protestant pool, while German grooms showed a preference for brides from the Catholic pool in their outmarriages.

Kennedy explained the absence of a Catholic pool in 1900 on the grounds of the absence of Polish and Italian partners for the Irish,

'The fact that the intermarriage rate among Irish, Italians and Poles in 1870 and 1900 was lower than among the three non-Catholic groups was owing to the virtual absence of Italians and Poles in New Haven in those years' (Kennedy, 1944: 333). While this is true of 1870 and true of the Poles in 1900, it is not true of the Italians in 1900 who constituted the third largest group in the marrying population, after the British-Americans and Irish (see Table 9.2).

Perhaps the best way to conceptualise the marriage patterns predicted by Kennedy is by looking at Tables 9.6 and 9.7. According to the Kennedy thesis, there should be two diametrically opposed quadrants, rows one to three by columns one to three set against rows four to seven by columns four to seven. In each of these quadrants, if the Protestant and Catholic pots existed, all the values would be between one and two. Rows and columns beyond these boundaries should have values below one.

In 1930, apart from British-American grooms marrying Scandinavian brides (only 0.80), the Protestant pool is complete. The supposed Catholic pool, however, does not exist. Of the twelve cells (excluding those of the leading diagonal) in which values above one are predicted by Kennedy's thesis, only two conform (both Irish-French pairings). More significantly, instead of producing a diametrical opposition, the 'Protestant' pool laps over into the Irish and French, who for both grooms and brides show a preference for the 'Protestant' pool over the 'Catholic' pool. Thus, Kennedy's 'Protestant' pool was more extensive than its proposed 'Protestant' nationalities. The Irish and the French belonged more to the 'Protestant' pot than the 'Catholic'. Thus, the group is more realistically seen as one of 'old' immigrants rather than 'Protestants'. The Italians and Poles were distinct not only from this group, but from each other.

In 1950, the picture is even clearer. The 'old' quadrant, rows one to five by columns one to five, has values between one and two in every cell but one (0.98 for French grooms marrying British-American brides). The Irish and French grooms and brides overselect spouses from the Protestant pool. It is true, however, that the Irish and French overselect each other and that Italian grooms overselect French brides. Of the twelve cells in the Catholic quadrant three conform to the predicted Kennedy pattern.

The increasing degree of intermarriage over time is reflected, with a time lag, in the increasing complexity of mixed parental ethnicity in the later years. The simplification involved in assigning mixed parentage to the paternal ethnic group hides the nested system of mixed interaction within the whole. Within the endogamy of British-Americans marrying British-Americans, for instance, are subsystems of higher than random intermarriage of grooms and brides both having British-American fathers and German mothers or both having British-American fathers and Irish mothers. These subsystems contribute not only to the endogamous patterns reported in Tables 9.6 and 9.7, but also to apparent outmarriage too. Thus there is higher than random intermarriage between grooms having British-American fathers and Irish mothers and brides with Irish fathers and British-American mothers in 1950, for example. However, in order to demonstrate that the subsystems alone are not responsible for the interaction between the Protestant and Catholic groups, the intermarriages between the unmixed ethnic groups for 1950 were calculated, but are not published here. Although they differ in detail from the total tables for 1950, the general pattern confirms the wider analysis of inter-marriage between the groups.

Thus the cleavage of white society into Protestant, Catholic and Jewish national groups, which Kennedy foresaw as the American future, did not exist even in embryonic form at the beginning of the period for which she took her data and looked even more im-probable in the final year for which she took her material. The thesis was not true either for the time or the place.

The patterns which emerge from this survey are of overlapping and asymmetric choices of one group for another rather than distinct, independent parcels of reciprocated interaction within 'religious' divides.

## Ethnic Segregation and Intermarriage

While the analysis of intermarriage between groups was based on a 100 per cent count of individuals in the marrying population in the given year, segregation data were drawn largely from samples of the marrying populations. For 1900, for which all addresses had been collected, segregation was calculated on the basis of a 20 per cent sample of grooms' addresses for larger groups and by a full count for smaller groups. For 1930 and 1950 all addresses included in the 20 per cent sample were included plus a further sample in the case of groups for which the sample total came to less than 31 addresses. In the case of the French in 1950, for instance, all addresses were collected. For the French and Poles in 1900, the total numbers proved inadequate for analysis and they were omitted.

The areal frame employed was that of the 1977 ward map of New Haven to which were added the physically contiguous townships of East Haven, West Haven, North Haven and Hamden, which were treated as additional wards. New Haven contains 27 wards, so that there were in all a total of 31 areal units. The Registrar of Voters' Guide Book of March 1977, which classifies streets and house numbers, was used to assign addresses to wards. Where streets, extant at earlier periods, had been removed, they were located and ascribed to the appropriate contemporary wards. The analysis for 1900, 1930 and 1950 is therefore constructed on a strictly comparable areal base.

The use of wards as an areal frame is coarse in comparison with block or tract analysis. There are, however, several advantages in using such a frame. The first is that it is a neutral reference point. Wards have not, as far as could be ascertained, been constructed to emphasise or minimise a particular ethnic grouping. Secondly, the sampling basis of the population analysis makes too fine an areal basis unreal in view of the number of cases involved. Finally, the existence of the ward guide defining the appropriate ward for a given address greatly reduces the task of ascertaining the precise location of addresses that would be involved in quadrat areal allocations.

Tables 9.8, 9.9 and 9.10 show residential segregation between the specified ethnic groups in New Haven in 1900, 1930 and 1950. Segregation is measured by the index of dissimilarity (Duncan and Duncan, 1955). The pattern of ethnic segregation in New Haven which emerges from these longitudinal studies is similar to that found for similar periods in other cities in the United States. For example, for the 20 pairs of observations in 1950 for which roughly comparable categories are available in Chicago (Duncan and Lieberson, 1959), $r = 0.8$.

**Table 9.8: Ethnic Segregation by Wards, New Haven, 1900**

| Ethnic group | British-American | German | Scandinavian | Irish | Italian | Jewish |
|---|---|---|---|---|---|---|
| British-American | | | | | | |
| German | 46.23 | | | | | |
| Scandinavian | 44.65 | 48.36 | | | | |
| Irish | 43.96 | 27.81 | 38.61 | | | |
| Italian | 65.36 | 46.11 | 63.20 | 47.60 | | |
| Jewish | 71.23 | 57.39 | 70.43 | 58.69 | 50.19 | |
| Black | 56.41 | 68.91 | 71.52 | 66.43 | 80.15 | 78.44 |

Source: See text.

**Table 9.9: Ethnic Segregation by Wards, New Haven, 1930**

| Ethnic group | British-American | German | Scandinavian | Irish | French | Italian | Polish | Jewish |
|---|---|---|---|---|---|---|---|---|
| British-American | | | | | | | | |
| German | 40.48 | | | | | | | |
| Scandinavian | 41.72 | 51.11 | | | | | | |
| Irish | 48.28 | 39.32 | 51.54 | | | | | |
| French | 41.95 | 44.58 | 62.83 | 41.75 | | | | |
| Italian | 68.98 | 53.56 | 79.10 | 59.46 | 70.81 | | | |
| Polish | 55.92 | 39.30 | 76.93 | 47.44 | 55.40 | 44.37 | | |
| Jewish | 72.83 | 60.64 | 69.28 | 50.02 | 67.90 | 68.32 | 75.01 | |
| Black | 57.32 | 61.92 | 60.65 | 57.92 | 54.20 | 75.75 | 80.90 | 46.38 |

Source: See text.

**Table 9.10: Ethnic Segregation by Wards, New Haven, 1950**

| Ethnic group | British-American | German | Scandinavian | Irish | French | Italian | Polish | Jewish |
|---|---|---|---|---|---|---|---|---|
| British-American | | | | | | | | |
| German | 36.44 | | | | | | | |
| Scandinavian | 37.13 | 43.93 | | | | | | |
| Irish | 32.02 | 40.51 | 46.43 | | | | | |
| French | 30.16 | 53.21 | 49.71 | 33.07 | | | | |
| Italian | 45.64 | 56.99 | 59.16 | 41.78 | 44.97 | | | |
| Polish | 37.20 | 47.98 | 52.19 | 33.04 | 35.25 | 33.00 | | |
| Jewish | 52.78 | 49.14 | 68.73 | 55.42 | 48.89 | 57.58 | 52.88 | |
| Black | 67.96 | 72.06 | 81.34 | 72.31 | 62.60 | 69.38 | 66.36 | 66.34 |

Source: See text.

The hypothesis investigated is that there is an inverse relationship between the extent to which any pair of ethnic groups is residentially distinct and the extent to which intermarriage is transacted between them. Operationally, this may be tested by correlating the indices of residential dissimilarity of one ethnic group with each other ethnic group, with the corresponding set of values of observed to expected marriages taking place between them. For each reading of residential segregation in a given year, there are two corresponding values of intermarriage – one for grooms and one for brides. Thus, column one in Table 9.8 gives the indices of residential dissimilarity of British-American spouses from those of each other ethnic group. Column one of Table 9.5 gives the corresponding ratio of observed to expected selection of grooms from each ethnic group by British-American brides. Row one of Table 9.5 gives the corresponding values for British-American grooms. By correlating the corresponding values in the segregation and intermarriage tables one can correlate the ethnic choice of brides or grooms with their degree of residential dissimilarity. Correlating column one of Table 9.5 with column one of Table 9.8 gives $r = -0.8427$ (Pearson); correlating with row one of Table 9.5 instead of column one (i.e. grooms instead of brides) gives $r = -0.7163$. The correlation for segregation for both brides and grooms combined (i.e. column one of Table 9.5 with column one of Table 9.8 and row one of Table 9.8) gives $r = -0.7254$.

Tables 9.11, 9.12 and 9.13 show the degree of correlation for each

**Table 9.11: Correlation Coefficients (Pearson) of Ethnic Segregation with Ethnic Intermarriage (Ratio of Observed to Expected) New Haven, 1900**

| Ethnic group | Brides | Grooms | Brides and grooms |
|---|---|---|---|
| British-American | −0.8427 | −0.7163 | −0.7254 |
| German | −0.6006 | −0.6834 | −0.6433 |
| Scandinavian | −0.5891 | −0.6017 | −0.5824 |
| Irish | −0.7824 | −0.8613 | −0.7991 |
| Italian | −0.1337 | −0.3504 | −0.2531 |
| Jewish | − | +0.3153 | +0.2126 |
| Black | − | −0.7867 | −0.5304 |

Note: Overall 42 pairs of observations − 0.6387. Overall excluding black (30 pairs) − 0.6040.
Source: Correlation of Tables 9.5 and 9.8.

**Table 9.12: Correlation Coefficients (Pearson) of Ethnic Segregation with Ethnic Intermarriage (Ratio of Observed to Expected) New Haven, 1930**

| Ethnic group | Brides | Grooms | Brides and grooms |
|---|---|---|---|
| British-American | −0.8720 | −0.8712 | −0.8704 |
| German | −0.5581 | −0.7430 | −0.6448 |
| Scandinavian | −0.6109 | −0.8005 | −0.7049 |
| Irish | −0.6645 | −0.7400 | −0.6983 |
| French | −0.8517 | −0.5998 | −0.7213 |
| Italian | −0.5949 | −0.6233 | −0.5910 |
| Polish | −0.6120 | −0.0042 | −0.3488 |
| Jewish | +0.4306 | +0.5532 | +0.4552 |
| Black | − | − | − |

Note: Overall 72 pairs $r = -0.5597$. Excluding blacks $= -0.5948$ (56 pairs).
Source: Correlation of Tables 9.6 and 9.9.

ethnic group with all others, for grooms and for brides separately and combined for 1900, 1930 and 1950. They also show the overall correlation of the complete matrix of segregation indices with the complete matrix of intermarriage ratios for the corresponding year. In other words they show how the degree of segregation of each group from each other group correlates with the degree to which

**Table 9.13: Correlation Coefficients (Pearson) of Ethnic Segregation with Ethnic Intermarriage (Ratio of Observed to Expected) New Haven, 1950**

| Ethnic group | Brides | Grooms | Brides and grooms |
|---|---|---|---|
| British-American | −0.9319 | −0.9262 | −0.9278 |
| German | −0.7760 | −0.7708 | −0.7714 |
| Scandinavian | −0.9157 | −0.9449 | −0.9284 |
| Irish | −0.7981 | −0.8066 | −0.8023 |
| French | −0.8097 | −0.4757 | −0.6319 |
| Italian | −0.8531 | −0.6824 | −0.7399 |
| Polish | −0.6403 | −0.8297 | −0.7386 |
| Jewish | +0.4820 | −0.7700 | −0.1982 |
| Black | − | − | − |

Note: Overall correlation for 72 observations $r = -0.7949$. Overall correlation (without blacks) 56 pairs $r = -0.6646$.
Source: Correlation of Tables 9.7 and 9.10.

intermarriage takes place.

The general pattern of segregation thus correlates inversely and well with the general pattern of intermarriage. The North-west European groups have generally low or moderate levels of segregation from one another and high rates of intermarriage. The Poles, whose degree of segregation with this group had diminished greatly by 1950, also showed substantial increases in their degree of inter-marriage. On the other hand, the Italians maintained higher levels of segregation with most of the Western European groups and also manifested low rates of intermarriage with them. The Jewish population maintained both high rates of segregation and low inter-marriage with all groups. The blacks showed both the highest segregation and the least outmarriage.

Taking the ethnic groups individually, the highest inverse correlations are displayed by the British-Americans, Germans, Scandinavians, Irish and French. The Italians and Poles show rather low correlations until 1950, while for the Jewish group correlations are positive rather than negative; for the blacks, apart from 1900, no correlations are measurable. It may be that for groups which are highly segregated and highly endogamous that such minor degrees of outmarriage that occur follow different rules.

The degree of inverse correlation between the segregation of ethnic groups and their degree of intermarriage is arresting. For 1900, the overall correlation for the 42 pairs of observations is $-0.6387$; for 1930, the 72 pairs gave $-0.5597$; for 1950 the same 72 pairs gave $-0.7949$. These correlations were all significant at the 0.001 level.

The zero values in Tables 9.5, 9.6 and 9.7 and also in Tables 9.2, 9.3 and 9.4 give rise to some problems of interpretation. In particular, the high segregation indices of the black population and zero values for intermarriage influence the inverse correlations shown. The existence of some interaction in 1900 is evidence for the view that the zeroes should be considered as having a sampling rather than a structural origin (Bishop, Feinberg and Holland, 1975). The high segregation values fit in clearly with the main hypothesis. However, in order to demonstrate that the black-white figures do not influence the outcome unduly, correlations are given for intermarriage and segregation from which the figures for blacks have been excluded. Although in 1900 and 1950 the correlations decrease, they remain significant at the 0.001 level. For 1930 the removal of the black figures increases the correlation.

## Discussion

This study shows that the general hypothesis of Duncan and Lieberson, that spatial segregation and assimilation are inversely related, is borne out by more detailed investigation of ethnic intermarriage. The implication of the findings is that if rates of intermarriage correlate inversely with degrees of segregation, then rates of intermarriage may be predictable from trends in residential segregation. The causal direction of the correlation is not apparent from the analysis, but it may be that residential propinquity is an independent variable (Beshers, 1962).

The problem examined in this paper is one of simple intellectual curiosity. The conflicts between the spatial and non-spatial views of assimilation do not seem to be in the forefront of sociological investigation. The literature has swept past the two theories which have been examined. Yet the close correlation established between ethnic segregation and ethnic intermarriage may have a wider and more immediate significance than simply for the historical data examined here. The relationships examined held true for each of the dates examined. The presumption must be that it continues to operate at present. Even if the nature of marriage is changing, it gives us measurable data on the interaction between groups. Residential inter-mixture may well be the most significant factor in ethnic interaction in Western societies. If this is indeed the case, then the spatial allocation of housing may be one of the most fundamental variables in determining the outcome of ethnic assimilation.

## Notes

1. The attempt is made to replicate Kennedy's coding rules, as far as they are available from the 1944 and 1952 papers. Thus, although the German population is fairly evenly divided between Protestants and Catholics, Kennedy classed them as Protestants (which was largely the case in New Haven) and the same procedure is followed here. Similarly, although a significant minority of the Irish population is Protestant, the Irish are all classified as Catholic here. For the Jewish population, Judaism takes precedence over birth-place and nationality. Jews born in Poland, for example, are grouped with the Jewish population rather than with the Poles. Similarly, the black population is so grouped irrespective of country of birth.

2. 'Expected' figures in contingency tables are generated by taking the percentage that a row total forms of the grand total and applying it to the appropriate column total. Observed to expected ratios are calculated by dividing observed figures in a cell by the expected value. Where the expected and observed figures coincide, the value is one. For values below unity in standard tables, the size of the marginal values have no distorting effect,

but for values above unity, the maximum possible value is different for each cell and direct comparison is not possible. For example the ratio of observed to expected German—German marriages is 4.49 in 1900 and Polish—Polish marriages is 62.57. The maximum possible values, however, would have been 7.90 and 100.00 respectively.

In order to make direct comparison possible, values above unity are placed on a scale from 1 to 2 relative to their position between the 'expected' and the maximum possible value. The maximum is defined by the lower of the two marginal values. Thus, in 1900 with 111 German grooms and 114 German brides, the maximum number of German—German marriages would have been 111. Since German grooms formed 12.32 per cent of the total grooms, their 'expected' total of the 114 German brides would have been 14. The observed number was 63. This represents 49 more than the expected figure. The maximum is 97 more than the expected figure. 49 is 50.4 per cent of the value above unity. On the scale 1 to 2, therefore, German—German marriages in 1900 are 1.50.

3. The Protestant pool includes the British-Americans, Germans and Scandinavians only. The Catholic pool includes the Irish, French, Italians, Poles and 'other Catholic' groups. All figures are taken from Tables 9.2, 9.3 and 9.4. The Dutch are not included in either pool.

# Bibliography

Besanceney, P.H. (1965) 'On Reporting Rates of Intermarriage', *American Journal of Sociology*, 70, 717—21

Beshers, J.M. (1962) *Urban Social Structure*, Free Press, New York

Bishop, Y.M.M., Feinberg, S.E. and Holland, P.W. (1975) *Discrete Multivariate Analysis: Theory and Practice*, Massachusetts Institute of Technology Press, Cambridge

Duncan, O.D. and Duncan, B. (1955) 'A Methodological Analysis of Segregation Indexes', *American Sociological Review*, 20, 210—17

Duncan, O.D. and Lieberson, S. (1959) 'Ethnic Segregation and Assimilation', *American Journal of Sociology*, 64, 364—74

Glazer, N. and Moynihan, D.P. (1963) *Beyond the Melting Pot*, Massachusetts Institute of Technology Press, Cambridge

Goodman, L. (1965) 'On the Statistical Analaysis of Mobility Tables', *American Journal of Sociology*, 70, 564—85

Gordon, M.M. (1964) *Assimilation in American Life*, Oxford University Press, New York

Herberg, W. (1960) *Protestant, Catholic and Jew*, Doubleday, New York

Hollingshead, A.B. (1950) 'Cultural Factors in the Selection of Marriage Mates', *American Sociological Review*, 15, 619—27

Jones, F.L. (1967) 'Ethnic Concentration and Assimilation: an Australian Case Study', *Social Forces*, 45, 412—23

Kantrowitz, N. (1969) 'Ethnic and Racial Segregation in the New York Metropolis, 1960', *American Journal of Sociology*, 74, 685—95

Kennedy, R.J.R. (1944) 'Single or Triple Melting Pot? Intermarriage Trends in New Haven, 1870—1940', *American Journal of Sociology*, 49, 331—9

Kennedy, R.J.R. (1952) 'Single or Triple Melting Pot? Intermarriage in New Haven, 1870—1950', *American Journal of Sociology*, 58, 56—9

Lieberson, S. (1961) 'The Impact of Residential Segregation on Ethnic Assimilation', *Social Forces*, 40, 52—7

Lieberson, S. (1963) *Ethnic Patterns in American Cities*, Free Press, New York

Peach, G.C.K. (1974) 'Ethnic Segregation and Intermarriage Patterns in Sydney', *Australian Geographical Studies*, 12, 219–29

Ramsøy, N.R. (1966) 'Assortative Mating and the Structure of Cities', *American Sociological Review*, 31, 773–86

State of Connecticut (1871) Report of the State Librarian to the General Assembly relating to the Registration of Births, Marriages and Deaths for the year ending December 31st, 1870

State of Connecticut (1902) Annual Report of the Bureau of Vital Statistics for the year ending December 31st, 1900

State of Connecticut (1932) Eighty-third Registration Report of Births, Marriages, Divorces and Deaths, for the year ending December 31st, 1930

State of Connecticut (n.d.) Ninety-third Registration Report of Births, Marriages, Divorces and Deaths for the year ending December 31st, 1940

State of Connecticut (1951) One hundred and third Registration Report of Births, Marriages, Divorces and Deaths for the year ending December 31st, 1950

Thomas, J.L. (1951) 'The Factor of Religion in the Selection of Marriage Mates', *American Sociological Review*, 16, 487–91

Timms, D.W.G. (1969) 'The Dissimilarity between Overseas-born and Australian-born in Queensland: Dimensions of Assimilation', *Sociology and Social Research*, 53, 363–74

Tyree, A. (1973) 'Mobility Ratios and Associations in Mobility Tables', *Population Studies*, 27, 577–88

Yancey, W.L., Ericksen, E.P. and Juliani, R.N. (1976) 'Emergent Ethnicity: a Review and Reformulation', *American Sociological Review*, 41, 391–403

## Acknowledgement

The author gratefully acknowledges the award of the Social Science Fellowship by the Nuffield Foundation, London, which allowed him to undertake the present research. He also thanks the Sociology Department, Yale University, where he was Visiting Fellow while engaged on the work. The assistance of the Registrar of Vital Statistics, New Haven, is gratefully acknowledged. Most of this work appeared in two papers, one in *Ethnic and Racial Studies* (1980), 3, 1, 1–16 and in Annals, Association of American Geographers (1980), 70, 3, 371–81. Grateful acknowledgement is made to both journals.

# 10 SOCIAL STATUS, THE MARKET AND ETHNIC SEGREGATION

## Robin Ward and Ronald Sims

This paper sets out a framework for explaining the degree and pattern of ethnic residential segregation in urban areas. This is done by applying a Weberian approach to social stratification to the working of the local housing market. The models presented were devised in the course of a research programme examining the residential settlement of New Commonwealth minorities in Manchester and Birmingham. Before setting out the analytical models, there is a brief review of the form that ethnic settlement has taken since the Second World War in Birmingham, a city whose population of just over one million now includes something over 100,000 originating in the Indian subcontinent, the West Indies and other parts of the New Commonwealth (cf. Ward, 1978). This will provide an example against which the utility of the four models set out can be judged.

## The Development of Ethnic Residential Settlement in Birmingham

The local employment market in Birmingham benefited over the post-war years from the creation of many thousands of new jobs, many of them filled by local manual workers. The sustained demand for labour, which lasted until about 1960, was satisfied by inward migration from within Britain, from Ireland and, since the mid-fifties, from the West Indies, India and Pakistan. In the decade leading up to 1961 the number of those born in the New Commonwealth living in Birmingham rose from about 5,000 to about 30,000 and five years later was estimated to be about 50,000. By 1971, this estimate rose to 67,000 born in the New Commonwealth together with about 30,000 others born in Britain to New Commonwealth parents.

The housing market in the post-war period was tight, and many of those arriving to take up employment were obliged to find housing by sharing with other new arrivals in lodging-houses in inner areas. Rex and Moore (1967) stress the effects of such constraints on the housing chances of black people arriving in the city during the early sixties. The dense occupation of inner-area housing by those least able to find

217

any alternative was an inevitable consequence. Exploitative multi-racial lodging-houses spilled over into areas where local young married couples were still settling down in terraced housing. Black people were held responsible for this stigmatised form of multi-occupation which reinforced the desire of local people to join the flight to owner-occupied houses or council tenancies in suburbia. There was plenty of scope for such moves since, in addition to the development of suburban council estates, land was available on the periphery of the city and outside the boundary in Sutton Coldfield and Solihull for a large quantity of new private developments.

White owner-occupiers showed extreme reluctance to buy older properties in inner areas which were acquiring a substantial Asian and West Indian population. The inevitable result was the development of a ring of suburban wards of modern housing with an entirely white population of owner-occupiers and council tenants, many of them with manual jobs, circling the inner wards of Victorian terraced housing where Asians and West Indians were buying houses vacated by local white households. The speed of the transition in the population was at times rapid. Thus, the Asian electorate in Soho, an inner-city ward to the north-west of the city, increased from five in 1956 to 3,124 in 1971 and five years later was estimated at 4,593 (about one third of the total electorate). Sparkhill, a middle-ring ward to the south-east, had an estimated Asian adult population of 50 in 1956 but by 1971 this had risen to 2,028. Five years later, there were an estimated 4,559 adult Asians in the ward, as well as a substantial West Indian population. There is some very slight evidence of black suburbanisation by the 1970s: the number of Asians resident in suburban wards increased by several times in fact between 1971 and 1976. But they still remained a minute fraction of the total Asian population in the city. The overwhelming trend is still to concentration in areas of decaying housing in inner areas which they share with elderly white people who for economic or sentimental reasons have not joined the flight to the suburbs.

The local authority attempted to avoid a similar concentration of black families in council housing by enforcing a policy of dispersal over the public sector, but since the declaration of this policy as illegal under the terms of the Race Relations Act, the authority have been obliged to switch to a voluntary policy of scattering black families over the council stock which is unlikely to be effective. Since well under 10 per cent of Asians in Birmingham are in council housing, this affects West Indians much more than Asians.

**Models of Ethnic Residential Segregation**

It is not the aim of this paper to document the concentration of Asian families in old and decaying housing in inner areas of Birmingham. We are concerned rather to show how models incorporating a Weberian understanding of social stratification may be useful in interpreting patterns of segregation. First, we set out the *market* model, in which the movement of the white working class to the suburbs is put in the context of changes in the working of the local housing market during the post-war period. In Birmingham this suburban migration has been facilitated by market processes resulting from the arrival of immigrants, particularly from the New Commonwealth, looking for cheap, bought housing. Secondly, the *status* model interprets white flight to suburbia as a response to the declining style of life in inner and middle-ring areas. Of particular relevance in Birmingham is the notion of status threats experienced by the white working class consequent on the settlement of New Commonwealth households in inner areas. Thirdly, in the *market-discrimination* model, competition for access to desirable housing leads to white competitors using their influence to restrict the opportunities to black families to gain access to such housing. It is argued that in Birmingham this has been of particular relevance in the sphere of public housing. Finally, in the *status-discrimination* model, status threats to the life-style in white suburban areas associated with the arrival of New Commonwealth immigrants lead to restrictions being placed on their entry into such property. The potential importance of this phenomenon is stressed for the maintenance of ethnic residential segregation in Birmingham.

*The Market Model*

Any account of the residential segregation of ethnic minorities in British cities must benefit from this being put in the context of significant trends in the housing market in London and major provincial cities in Britain.

(a) Slum clearance has decimated the large swathe of inner-area, privately-rented, unfurnished property and much cheap owner-occupied housing too. Families displaced have been rehoused in central and to some extent suburban new council developments.
(b) Where pressure on housing has significantly increased, a common response has been, in the short run, the spread of housing in multi-occupation in transitional areas of housing formerly occupied by

the middle class. In the longer term the response has been more numerous speculative suburban estates of housing, bought not by those crowded into multi-occupied houses, but by middle-class and skilled working-class families. Parallel with this process has been a huge increase in mortgage finance from building societies and other financial institutions. This filtering process has provided residential space for immigrants to acquire cheap housing in middle-ring areas, much of it bought with the aid of council mortgages. Arguably, increasing overall pressure on local housing by working-class families has been one factor influencing the rate of new council building, though this has also been a consequence of broader economic and political considerations.

(c)  Council housing, much of it suburban, some in central areas, has, particularly since the decline of slum clearance, accommodated large numbers of mainly working-class families formerly living in privately-rented housing in inner and intermediate areas. The overall trend has been for access to council housing via the waiting list to be based more on criteria of need than on rights and qualifications.

(d)  The rate of return on capital invested in domestic property, in part a consequence of legislation on rents and the security of tenure, has been sufficiently low to induce large numbers of private and institutional landlords to sell investment property to sitting tenants, to put it on the open market, or on occasion to transfer it to local authority control. This has been a counterbalance to the reduction in cheap housing for purchase in inner areas consequent on slum-clearance programmes. In some areas such investment property has been bought up by the local authority well in advance of slum clearance to use as temporary council housing.

(e)  With the overall reduction in pressure on housing over the 1970s, there has been a sharp decrease in the quantity of old housing in trans-itional areas used as lodging-houses. Over the same period, however, the expansion in higher and further education, occupational mobility and household fragmentation have led to a greater demand for rooms and flats by students, young clerical and professional workers and other small domestic units. As a result while the quantity of residential property in multi-occupation may not have changed significantly, its function and its location have done so.

(f)  In the last few years comprehensive slum-clearance programmes have been largely replaced by area improvement policies involving much more limited demolition and more upgrading of decaying housing in inner and intermediate areas. As a result much Victorian terraced property which otherwise would have been demolished is likely to remain for some time. Given the contraction in overall demand for housing and raising of housing standards, those owning such property are likely to find difficulty filtering into better property for lack of purchasers except where housing associations or the local authority intervene to buy up property coming on the market.

(g)  The scope for council intervention in the local housing market, whether through clearance, improvement, the purchase of inner-area property or the allocation of mortgages on property not favoured by building societies, is likely to be reduced by a series of cuts in central government funds for local housing investment programmes. Offset against this is income from the sale of council houses, which on a large enough scale would significantly alter the balance between the section of the working class accumulating and inheriting wealth in the form of domestic property and the section remaining within what would increasingly become a 'welfare sector'.

Thus the market for domestic property has been very significantly affected by non-economic considerations. The local authority, through central government finance, has had an enormous influence on the nature, distribution and tenure structure of housing through slum clearance, new building, improvement policies and mortgage allocation (in addition to the control it has exercised on multi-occupied housing in the private sector). Political interventions in housing have also taken the form of direct central government subsidy of owner-occupation, through tax relief on mortgages and the exclusion of most residential property from capital gains tax. This has greatly increased the economic advantages of owner-occupation and the extent of inequality based on wealth inherited in the form of domestic property.

Further, as is discussed below, those controlling access to housing may restrict the opportunities of some of those competing for it. However, despite this, despite the political interventions in housing allocation and finance, and despite the varying housing demand of different sections of the population, the economic interests of government, national and local, construction and finance capital and those in the market to buy or rent housing remain of major significance. Thus, in so far as ethnic minorities, together with the rest of the population, have distinctive economic interests in housing, we should expect these interests to be a major influence on the pattern of residential segregation or integration. Market interests, given the structure of subsidies for housing in Britain, can be expected to lead to a high degree of socio-economic segregation. In particular, a high, regular income, a middle-class occupation and increasingly the inheritance of capital deriving from parental owner-occupation will not only maintain but reinforce inequalities between those owning modern domestic property and those confined either to renting or to purchasing cheap and inferior inner-area housing.

Secondly, the greater the rate of economic expansion in an urban area, the greater the demand for housing and so the greater the potential for speculative new suburban building. On the one hand, this allows those more economically successful in mixed-income residential areas to move out to areas of good quality owner-occupation, while inner areas come to be monopolised by low-income households whether owning or renting. On the other hand, this movement towards a dual residential market is likely to be paralleled by dualism in the labour market with those occupying newer suburban housing working in modern plants in the periphery of the city, while established firms in the inner city find it difficult to recruit skilled labour, given trends in the residential market. In so far as those with distinctive economic interests in housing recognise this and act collectively in terms of them, a sociological analysis in terms of the concept of 'housing class' drawn by Rex from Weber may be useful (Rex and Moore, 1967; Rex and Tomlinson, 1979).

### The Status Model

It is commonplace to note the importance of life-style variables in housing behaviour. The decline of inner areas and demand for a style of life based on a modern house in suburbia has been a feature of urban areas in Britain for many years, though this was given an enormous boost by the mushrooming of suburban developments backed by cheap loan finance in the inter-war years (Ward, 1975). Positive features of this have been the attractions of suburban life: modern housing, incorporating modern domestic technology and fashion, and a social and physical environment considered particularly suitable for bringing up children. Educational considerations have also been a major force underlying the preference for a suburban life-style.

Those remaining in declining inner areas marked by old, decaying housing and schools, a dirty environment and a lack of open spaces have found their position in the status order under threat. This may be a consequence of trends in the residential structure of inner areas, such as the change in use of former middle-class residences which under the pressure of immigration become lodging-houses catering for a recently arrived or transient population. It may follow the entry of a stigmatised group, which is held to be responsible for the area deteriorating. British community studies show that such processes have had a quite varied impact on local residents: the middle class have mostly already abandoned such areas; working-class families aspiring to middle-class standards and way of life react with particular hostility, though the traditional, solidary working class may be equally hostile to their familiar patch being taken over; those looked down on as 'roughs' by the 'respectables' do not display the sort of prestigious style of life which is punctured by the advent of unapproved residents or ways of using the residential space (Ward, 1975). Those with high income and regular employment are most likely to react by abandoning the area for suburbia. If they were renting, they are not held back by the need to dispose of a house. Where there is a potential replacement population seeking more residential space, often recently arrived members of an ethnic minority, the sale of an inner-area house may be on terms which are economically advantageous to the vendor. As noted above, the greater the degree of economic expansion and the greater the consequent pressure on housing by those drawn in through opportunities for employment, the more likely this is.

So, suburban migration in Britain has normally preceded black immigration into inner areas, though the process of status threat leading to white flight is easily reinforced by the social and economic conditions surrounding black immigration. Black settlement in the context of economic expansion is likely to make white flight seem both desirable and feasible.

A similar variety of life-styles occurs within the heterogeneous public sector of housing. In some areas first priority for new council property goes to those rehoused from slum clearance, which is likely to contain low-status residents in inner areas. Here the initial pattern of allocation may represent an inversion of the status order. But it seems clear that the process of status sorting described above for the private sector is replicated in public housing where there is the same range in the reputational status of estates. While some estates have stabilised with a substantial minority of black tenants, in others the same process of white flight is in evidence, though the bureaucratic nature of council house allocation restricts the range of alternatives available to those who seek to escape from an estate with an increasing proportion of black people.

We have argued that residential distributions, including those involving ethnic minorities, are based on status stratification and market processes. In particular we have pointed to the increasing segregation of the middle class, together with skilled working-class families in the primary sector of the labour market, in modern bought housing in suburbia. This is achieved through a section of the population using their economic resources to obtain access to a desired style of life and to maintain status differentials based on the residential area. At the same time such moves are likely not only to maintain but to reinforce inequalities between those in modern bought housing and those left in the inner city, whether in owned or rented housing.

But it should not be assumed that black people are looking for housing only in those areas being abandoned by whites. Where black families aspire to good quality, modern housing, they are in competition with whites looking for similar property. Such demand is likely to threaten the status order in areas not being abandoned by whites. The first of these possibilities is considered in the *market-discrimination* model to which we now turn; the second is dealt with in the subsequent section on the *status-discrimination* model.

### The Market-discrimination Model

The third model briefly outlined above, labelled the market-discrimination model, would apply where a section of those involved in the market for a good concluded that it was in their *economic* interests to restrict the opportunities of another section; in the field of housing this would occur where some of those wanting housing were able to restrict the access of others competing for the same housing. The normal process of market competition would lead to an economic good being available to whoever offered the highest price or was the first to offer the price designated by the seller. Where some of those competing for a good wish to restrict the opportunities of others in the market for it, they face structural difficulties. Whether they can do this depends on the influence they can exert over those offering housing. To be effective, collective action is required, which is the more unlikely since those who would need to act collectively are themselves in competition for the same good.

In the case of bought housing, it would require, say, white households looking for housing to buy to persuade estate agents (and other vendors) to sell at a lower price to whites than to blacks, thus improving their chances in the market. There is evidence, in fact, that black families have been required to pay more than white families to buy equivalent houses (Fenton, 1977; Karn, 1969). But it seems more reasonable to see this as a result of processes within the symbolic order.

There are various reasons why the agent may discriminate against black potential purchasers. He may take instructions to this effect from the vendor (despite this being against the law). He may be racially prejudiced and allow this to affect the way he sells the property. He may take the view that if he sells a particular house to a black family, this will prejudice the future flow of instructions to sell properties in the area, on which his livelihood depends. He may require a higher price from a black purchaser (or the full price instead of accepting an offer) since he realises that black people trying to buy houses are at a disadvantage and in consequence may be prepared to trade off accepting a higher purchase price for a reduction in the higher search costs of house-buying (Fenton, 1978). But none of these considerations imply that white buyers can use their influence to persuade the agent to sell to whites at a lower price or to refuse to sell to blacks. If, as a result of an agent selling properties to black families, white families decided to avoid other property in the area and as a result the agent found difficulty disposing of property there on the terms he would have expected, conceivably this would lead him to define his interest in terms of discriminating against blacks to avoid a reduction in white demand for housing in particular districts. However, it is likely that the basis underlying any fall-off in white demand would reflect status considerations by those searching for housing rather than an assessment of their economic interests.

The one situation where it is more reasonable to suppose that whites competing with blacks for housing may, because of their economic interests, successfully influence those allocating housing to restrict its availability to blacks is in the public sector. Since in Britain council housing is quite heavily subsidised, it is, following the decline in controlled tenancies in the private sector, more advantageous for those who cannot afford to buy a property to get into council housing, rather than renting from a private landlord. Since council housing allocation policy in a particular area is decided by the local authority, and since local councillors are particularly dependent on housing as an area in which they can demonstrate their value and thus retain their electoral support, councillors in wards where many white families are still renting from private landlords have a strong interest in trying to ensure that eligibility and allocation policies are more favourable to the main body of their constituents than to black households.

In many circumstances, this could be (and has been) achieved: by requiring a long period of residence before immigrants were deemed eligible to go on to the waiting list; by weighting the criteria for eligibility to favour long-established local people rather than those whose case for rehousing rested solely on housing need; and by influencing allocation policy so that locals were offered better properties. Such policies have not been used exclusively against black immigrants. In both Birmingham and Manchester, for example, the period of residence required before newly arriving families could register for council housing was lengthened at a time when New Commonwealth immigrants comprised a minute proportion of new arrivals. Most immigrants at the time were in fact Irish (cf. Sutcliffe and Smith, 1974). It is probable, however, that over the past thirty years local whites have gained substantial economic benefits over black families by the way that council housing eligibility and allocation policies were framed and applied. Such effects may be more likely where there is a fragile political balance between the two main parties at the ward level or in the balance of representation on the local council. But it has to be recognised that eligibility criteria have increasingly been based on need (which is likely to favour those disadvantaged in the private sector, including black people) rather than factors such as length of residence or war service which tend to favour local people. This does not imply, of course, that council housing allocations are not made in a racially biased manner even when the policy being implemented is non-discriminatory (Flett, 1979).

## The Status-discrimination Model

The fourth model for understanding the basis of ethnic residential segregation to which we have referred was labelled the *status-discrimination* model. This applies where status considerations are the basis of intervention in the housing market to discriminate against ethnic minorities seeking housing. In the private sector of the British housing market this has taken three main forms: first, restricted access to rooms to rent (and houses to buy) in *transitional areas* built for the middle classes in the Victorian period; secondly, restricted access to houses to buy in *residual areas* of terraced housing built for the proletariat, also dating back to the nineteenth century; thirdly, restricted access to owner-occupation in more modern *suburban areas.*

The first New Commonwealth settlers in British cities found lodgings in *transitional areas* which became the nuclei of more established ethnic colonies where an increasing proportion of ethnics have bought houses. In the early days they found their way to such districts through a combination of self-selection, direction and exclusion from other areas. Such districts have for years housed a variety of settlers at a cost related to the degree of difficulty they would experience obtaining housing anywhere else (those finding rooms with a landlord from the same ethnic group normally paid a lower rent or lived rent free but were frequently involved as a result in other obligations to the landlord). Even within such areas there is internal stratification: some parts are recognised as containing 'housing of the last resort' and black settlement may soon be accepted as merely one of a variety of residential features which would give rise to status fears elsewhere; in other parts such concerns are still very real, though typically they have been undergoing a phase of population turnover for some time before the arrival of black people. The greater the pressure on accommodation, the harder it has been for Asians and West Indians to find housing and the higher the costs they have faced housing themselves in transitional areas, whether by renting or buying (Rex and Moore, 1967; Fenton and Collard, 1977).

For historical reasons British cities have varied greatly in the amount of housing built for the upper middle class, or for clerks and artisans and their families in the second half of the nineteenth century. These were the districts which were abandoned, often with great rapidity, by their former occupants in the inter-war period when speculative suburban developments of housing to buy first became typical. In cities where a great deal of such housing remains but has not been subject to gentrification, New Commonwealth families have typically moved from lodgings in the larger houses to buy the smaller properties which, having been built to a much higher standard than the working-class terraces, when modernised can form reasonably satisfactory housing. But where the size of the New Commonwealth population has exceeded the amount of housing available in such districts, black settlement has extended into areas still largely occupied by a residual element of the local working class.

Secondly, housing in *residual areas* has become available to black families to buy as former occupants have died or moved out to council housing or owner-occupation in suburbia. Where employment opportunities expanded sharply in the post-war period and drew in large quantities of extra labour from outside, former residents typically obtained better-paid employment in modern suburban plants and moved out to suburbia to live. The greater the quantity of this movement, the more pressing the need for a replacement residential population, such as has been provided by Irish immigrants and, more recently, West Indians, Indians and Pakistanis. In the early stages of such residential turnover, black newcomers are likely to face considerable discrimination. As the transition proceeds, however, the amount of vacated housing together with reduced white demand for accommodation in such areas has made New Commonwealth people a valuable replacement population, to buy property either from departing owners or from landlords trying to transfer their capital into a more profitable sector of the economy. In some cities this has resulted in very high rates of ethnic residential segregation. The racial discrimination which is likely in the early stages of the transition tends to disappear, since market conditions do not easily permit it — there is little demand for housing to buy in such districts except from black families.

It is outside the scope of this paper to describe in detail the nature of black demand for housing in British cities (see Dahya, 1974). Clearly, their economic circumstances and status interests have been influential factors in their pattern of residential settlement. An account of the housing demand of black people in Britain would stress their socio-economic position, their motives for migrating to Britain and their intentions with regard to returning to their home country. It would demonstrate that for large sections of the New Commonwealth population the status arena within which they have taken decisions about housing has been the home village (or in the later stages of settlement in Britain, the ethnic community centred on a particular inner area). They have been less concerned to become incorporated into the life-style of the respectable local working class — this would be evidenced, for example, in the move to a more modern suburban residential area. While they undoubtedly face the prospect of discrimination if they attempt to achieve this, in most cases — and this may be greatly to their long-term economic disadvantage — they have not made the attempt or even considered making it.

The main reason for not enlarging on this topic is that, regardless of the nature of the housing for which New Commonwealth families have been looking (and there is much evidence of their housing interests being defined in a way that has led to *voluntary* ethnic residential segregation), decisions over access to housing (which are the basis of segregation) have been taken by white individuals and institutions and it is their economic and symbolic interests which have therefore been crucial. We have argued above that in some circumstances it has been in the economic interests of white vendors to sell to black families. The main point being made in regard to the status-discrimination model, however, is that discrimination against black people trying to buy housing may reflect symbolic interests.

Unpublished survey evidence has shown, for example, that white owners have been reluctant to sell to blacks even in circumstances where it was in their economic interests to do so. For example, the steadfast refusal of white families who are desperate to move out to suburbia, to consider offers of the asking price from black families because they will only consider moving out if they can find a white family to sell to, shows with particular clarity the effect of status considerations on the tendency to racial discrimination.

Housing in *suburban areas* represents the third situation available to New Commonwealth families. Except among the middle-class section of ethnic minority populations there may be little demand for suburban residence. Certainly studies have shown the suburban Asian population (and very few West Indians live in modern suburban property) to consist largely of business and professional people (Fenton, 1977). It is here that white opposition to black settlement is likely to be greatest but least often tested; and this is so despite the likely objective economic advantages of buying property in suburbia. But where the black population has expanded from transitional areas of primary settlement through residual areas to the fringe of suburbia, such opposition is put to the test. The outcome in such cases is likely to depend on the circumstances determining the path of black suburbanisation in American cities (Johnston, 1971; Rose, 1976). American studies have emphasised the characteristics of the white population in suburbia, differentiating, for example, those with a local orientation from those with a more cosmopolitan outlook (see Berry, Goodwin, Lake and Smith, 1976). Berry stresses the significance of the status order in white suburbia in structuring the pattern of black entry into white suburban neighbourhoods.

In Britain it may be equally important to examine the impact of black settlement on inner and intermediate districts in assessing the likely reactions of whites to black demand for suburban housing. Ward (1975) has shown great variation between British cities in this respect. In some cities the residential settlement pattern of black people (itself in part a consequence of racial discrimination) has given an objective basis to white fears, however mistaken, that entry of black households into a neighbourhood will lead to a deterioration in the style of life. In other cases black settlement has had little effect on the way housing has been used and given rise to fewer fears on this score.

We have referred to various circumstances in which white estate agents or vendors may feel that as a consequence of status threats their economic interests are jeopardised by selling to blacks, though there is little evidence that this is justified. Fenton (1977) has shown, for example, that controlling for quality of housing, house prices in areas with a higher level of New Commonwealth population were no lower than in areas with few New Commonwealth households. The notion that property values fall with black entry into residential neighbourhoods is widespread. But this is unlikely to be the only (or even the main) consideration in the decisions taken by white estate agents and vendors over sales to black people. For example, the convenience of having a purchaser to complete a chain of sales may easily outweigh other factors; an offer of the full asking price is unlikely to be refused where there is no sign of additional interest in the property. Agents (and vendors) may in fact put a price on their prejudice, or the prejudice they attribute to other people whose views influence their behaviour (Banton, 1979), with the result that black families may succeed in purchasing suburban property, but at the cost of some price discrimination. Finally, even in suburbia, housing is not homogeneous: there are streets where housing tends to 'stick' when it is for sale, or where a lower rate of appreciation is found. Here black people are less likely to face restrictions on account of their skin colour. But, despite all this, we may expect discrimination (or the fear of it) to continue to be a normal feature of the suburban property market. This is likely to be based on status considerations but there are a variety of circumstances in which these may be overridden by economic factors.

## Interpreting Ethnic Residential Segregation

It is in our view crucial to see that discrimination is not an inevitable response to the entry of blacks into a white housing market. Its extent, location and significance is contingent on market processes and the varied demand for residentially-based life-styles. In interpreting the pattern of ethnic residential segregation in Birmingham, therefore (or any other city), it is of great importance to analyse the working of the local housing market and the spatial distribution of residentially-based life-styles. We conclude this paper by listing some of the factors which need to be emphasised in accounting for ethnic segregation in Birmingham.

It is our working hypothesis that, at least in the private sector, market and status factors have frequently not led to overt discrimination against black people in their search for housing. Central to the process of residential succession has been, in our view, the heavy demand for suburban owner-occupation by high-income, white, working-class families. Given the overall pressure on housing in the city, this demand has been satisfied for many thousands of such families over the past thirty years. The desire to get away from areas being taken over by black people has intensified the pre-existing desire to escape to the suburbs. Suburban migration has thus become for many an alternative to discriminating against black people trying to secure housing in middle-ring, white, working-class residential areas.

Within the *middle ring* of the city there has been a heavy black demand for housing to buy. As a result in both transitional and residual areas of the city the population has come to consist of Asian and West Indian owner-occupiers together with white families, many of them renting from private landlords, who cannot or will not move out. Those whites, mainly elderly, who remain, harbour fierce resentment about their districts being taken over by black people, but they have little opportunity for discriminating against them. They bitterly regret that white families have largely stopped buying houses in their districts.

By way of contrast *suburban areas* continue to be populated almost entirely by white people, though increasingly they are in manual employment (many of the former middle-class residents have moved out of the city altogether into peripheral districts where they view the life-style and in particular the educational provision as preferable). Suburban whites too show a high level of prejudice towards black people but may have little occasion to discriminate against them, because there is little demand for suburban property by Asian and West Indian families. The resulting segregation is likely to be reinforced by the economic differentials which are forming and again this can be expected to intensify, whatever the level of racial discrimination. At the risk of some oversimplification, it can be argued that there is, as a result of market processes and housing demand, less discrimination but more inequality and racial prejudice than would be found in an area where fewer black people had settled and where the rate of economic expansion had been lower. In the latter case more white resistance could be predicted to black attempts to buy into white working-class areas. Where a high level of segregation between whites in good quality modern property and blacks in poor, and often substandard, old housing is based not so much on the practice of discrimination (for whatever reason) as on the nature of demand for housing and the mechanisms of the housing market, this gives rise to particular concern. In such a situation a remedy cannot be sought in the intensive application of anti-discrimination legislation. Some, especially among the Asians, will be in a position to buy suburban property by using the surplus created by their business activities but this solution will only be open to comparatively few.

It might be argued that this presents an unjustifiably gloomy picture of the likely overall pattern of ethnic residential segregation, since it is concerned exclusively with the private sector of housing. In the public sector, it might be asserted, West Indians, who comprise a large fraction of the black population of Birmingham, are much more evenly distributed. Recent figures from the National Dwelling and Housing Survey carried out in 1977/78 certainly show that a higher proportion of West Indians than of whites were resident in council property in Birmingham by the late seventies. Further, they had been subject to an enforced policy of dispersal which could have been expected to reverse the trend shown above in the private sector. It might further be argued that, to the extent that this was the case, the long-term consequences of the degree of ethnic segregation overall were less serious, since among those renting council housing there was no process of capital accumulation to create economic differentials as in the private sector.

Such arguments are largely fallacious. In the first place, despite the large quantity of council housing allocations to West Indians and the operation of the dispersal policy, it still remained in 1978 that in inner areas of the city on average 15–20 per cent of the population in council property were West Indian whereas in suburban districts figures were mostly 1 to 2 per cent. Thus their heavy concentration in inner wards mirrors the uneven distribution found in the private sector. Furthermore, the preferences shown by black households are overwhelmingly for inner districts while white households with equal consistency opt for suburban estates. In the second place, the planned expansion in council house sales will reinforce the economic polarisation in the private sector. White tenants who have a virtual monopoly of good-quality, council-built houses in popular suburban estates are being offered a very attractive investment. For a heavy demand can be anticipated for such houses by white working-class families wanting to move out to suburbia once this property is within the private sector. But West Indians are concentrated with poor whites in inner-area developments of flats and poor quality old housing taken over by the council and there would appear to be relatively little potential here for substantial capital accumulation through purchase of a council tenancy.

The overall result therefore is likely to be a continuing high rate of ethnic residential segregation over a long period, with blacks (and poor whites) in decaying terraces of middle-ring housing and inner-area council flats, while respectable white families continue to monopolise housing opportunities in suburbia. This divide can be expected to continue until houses in inner areas are made sufficiently attractive to draw in younger white households. In a period of economic recession when central government has allocated a sharply reduced amount of money to local housing investment programmes, the need to pay for an expansion of political intervention in inner-area housing on a scale which would significantly affect the basic pattern outlined in this paper is likely to go unheeded. It has to be concluded that the damaging long-term consequences of ethnic polarisation along the lines outlined will have to become a reality before the process of economic inequality based on ethnic residential segregation is disturbed.

## Bibliography

Banton, M. (1979) 'Two Theories of Racial Discrimination in Housing', *Ethnic and Racial Studies*, 2, 416–27

Berry, B.J.L., Goodwin, C.A., Lake, R.W. and Smith, K.B. (1976) 'Attitudes Toward Integration: The Role of Status in Community Response to Racial Change', in B. Schwartz (ed.), *The Changing Face of the Suburbs*, University of Chicago Press, Chicago, pp. 221–64

Dahya, B. (1974) 'The Nature of Pakistani Ethnicity in Industrial Cities in Britain', in A. Cohen (ed.), *Urban Ethnicity*, Tavistock, Association of Social Anthropologists Monograph No. 12, London, pp. 77–117

Fenton, M. (1977) *Asian Households in Owner Occupation: A Study of the Pattern, Costs, and Experiences of Households in Greater Manchester*, SSRC Research Unit on Ethnic Relations Working Paper on Ethnic Relations No. 2, Bristol

Fenton, M. (1978) 'Costs of Discrimination in the Owner-occupied Sector', *New Community*, 6, 279–82

Fenton, M. and Collard, D. (1977) *Do Coloured Tenants Pay More? Some Evidence*, SSRC Research Unit on Ethnic Relations Working Paper on Ethnic Relations No. 1, Bristol

Flett, H. (1979) *Black Council Tenants in Birmingham*, SSRC Research Unit on Ethnic Relations Working Paper on Ethnic Relations No. 12, Aston

Johnston, R.J. (1971) *Urban Residential Patterns*, Bell, London

Karn, V. (1969) 'Property Values Amongst Indians and Pakistanis in a Yorkshire Town', *Race*, 10, 269–84

Rex, J. and Moore, R. (1967) *Race, Community and Conflict: A Study of Sparkbrook*, Oxford University Press for the Institute of Race Relations, London

Rex, J. and Tomlinson, S. (1979) *Colonial Immigrants in a British City: A Class*

*Analysis*, Routledge and Kegan Paul, London

Rose, H. (1976) *Black Suburbanization: Access to Improved Quality of Life or Maintenance of the Status Quo?*, Ballinger, Cambridge, Mass.

Sutcliffe, A. and Smith, R. (1974) *The History of Birmingham, Volume 3: Birmingham 1939–1970*, Oxford University Press, London

Ward, R.H. (1975) 'Residential Succession and Race Relations in Moss Side, Manchester', unpublished PhD Thesis, University of Manchester

Ward, R.H. (1978) 'Race Relations in Britain', *British Journal of Sociology*, 29, 464–80

# 11 ETHNIC RESIDENTIAL SEGREGATION, ETHNIC MIXING AND RESOURCE CONFLICT: A STUDY IN BELFAST, NORTHERN IRELAND

F.W. Boal

## Functions of Ethnic Segregation

Ethnic residential segregation and ethnically segregated areas can be considered as resources in situations of ethnic conflict. The underlying themes are those of resource conservation and resource enlargement. Four basic functions for ethnic segregation can be outlined (Boal, 1972; 1976). First we can consider the physical defensive role of the cluster. By joining the ethnic cluster, members of a particular group reduce their isolation, and the existence of the group itself within a clearly defined area enables an organised defence to be developed. Secondly it is possible to find considerable evidence for the avoidance function of ethnic residential segregation. For instance Kramer (1970: 67) indicates that the ethnic 'minority' community may be the only place in which its members feel at ease. According to her, they opt for ethnic enclosure in an alien world, finding it a 'haven of refuge in unfriendly surroundings'. It is psychologically supportive to have neighbours from a familiar background (Hiro, 1973: 26). Porter (1975: 30) refers to the psychic shelter of ethnic affiliation.

A third function for ethnic segregation is that of preservation and promotion of an ethnic group's own cultural heritage. This, of course, may be part of an avoidance mechanism, but it also appears for many groups to be something more positive. Dahya, in his discussion of Pakistani ethnicity in industrial cities in Britain notes that 'the immigrant community's ecological base serves several important functions which are related to the community's need to create, manifest and defend its ethnic identity' (Dahya, 1974: 95). This preservation function is enhanced by the development of ethnic institutions (schools, religious establishments, clubs, etc.). The development is facilitated by concentrated residence by the ethnic group. Finally it may be noted that spatial concentration can provide an ethnic group with a secure base for action in the struggle of its members with society in general. This struggle may take a peaceful political form or it may become violent. In the former instance spatial concentration may facilitate the election of ethnic group members to political office through which they may attempt to achieve gains for their supporters. In the latter the urban ethnic concentration provides a potential base for insurrectionary activity, where the urban guerrilla is the fish and the people are the sea in which the fish swims (Kitson, 1971).

Most analyses of the functions of ethnic residential segregation emphasise these in terms of minority groups, many of whom are relatively recent immigrants into the urban environments concerned. However, majority or host communities should also be viewed in ethnic terms and consequently the functions of ethnic segregation apply to them as well. They may have concerns about safety, about avoiding contact with 'strange' people and about preserving cultural purity. They may also have an interest in the attack function in that by attempting to manipulate the residential patterns of minority ethnic groups, electoral positions may be strengthened, bases for the operation of majority group paramilitary forces may be ensured, and minority groups may be corralled in such ways that they can be more readily controlled.

As suggested at the beginning, ethnic concentration should be viewed in terms of resource conservation and enlargement. The concentration locks into the ethnic group local resources of housing, territorial space and even employment. Conversely it locks out members of other groups. Parkin has developed the concept of closure which he subdivides into exclusionary closure and usurpationary closure. He quotes Weber as defining social closure as 'the process by which social collectivities seek to maximize rewards by restricting access to resources and opportunities to a limited circle of eligibles' (Parkin, 1979: 44), and extends the notion 'to encompass other forms of collective social action designed to maximize claims to rewards and opportunities. Closure strategies would then include not only those of an exclusionary kind, but also those adopted by the excluded themselves as a direct response to their status as outsiders' (Parkin, 1979: 44–5). Thus the ethnic residential concentration will be the result not only of exclusionary closure by others, but exclusionary closure by the ethnically concentrated group or groups themselves as a means of forging a common political entity and some measure of collective consciousness. This, in turn, becomes the basis for the operation of usurpation, which is 'that type of social closure mounted by a group in response to its outsider status and the collective experience of exclusion . . . the aim of biting into the resources and benefits accruing to dominant groups in society' (Parkin, 1979: 74). It is at this point that the attack functions of the ethnic residential cluster come into play.

## The Belfast Context

Examination of urban residential segregation in a particular context requires as a preliminary that historical and social circumstances be made specific. The critical introduction of ethnic differentiation into the Irish scene is usually associated with the Ulster Plantation in the early seventeenth century (Robinson, forthcoming). However, predating this, a new Scottish colony was established in Antrim and Down. Stewart (1977: 37) notes that this colony was permanent, and decisive in terms of population; it not only securely buttressed the wider plantation that was to follow, but gave much of Antrim and Down a marked predominance of inhabitants of Scottish origin, most of whom were Protestant. It has been suggested (Workers' Association, 1973) that the system of production organised was an example of capitalism in its infancy in that a surplus was sold on the market and small amounts of capital were accumulated, to be invested in handicraft industries (Boserup, 1972). This provided a springboard for the large-scale industrialisation of north-east Ulster in the nineteenth century, creating an industrial enclave in Ireland not unlike developments in south Wales and central Scotland (Hechter, 1975). Belfast developed as the core of this industrialisation, basically forming part of the great industrial triangle of the valleys of the Mersey, the Clyde and the Lagan. Indeed one might develop this notion by suggesting that Belfast in the nineteenth century was a British industrial city that happened to be in the island of Ireland. Like similar British industrial cities (Glasgow, Liverpool, Manchester), Belfast received a substantial flow of Irish Catholic immigrants, and basically like them there was a series of riots in the early and middle parts of the nineteenth century, generated by the native workers' response to the perceived threat of this immigration (Boal, 1980).

The relations of Catholic and Protestant were exacerbated during the latter part of the nineteenth century and the early decades of the twentieth by the development of Irish nationalism on the one hand, which saw its objectives best met by political separation from the rest of the United Kingdom, and by the development on the other hand of Ulster Unionism which saw its interests being best maintained by continued membership of the UK. The partition of the UK in 1920, which resulted in a political division of Ireland, reflected this national split. Unfortunately within the new unit of Northern Ireland a large proportion of the Catholic population were unaccepting of this division. Thus the national split between Northern and Southern Ireland became encapsulated within the north itself, and this was as marked in Belfast as anywhere else (Boal, Murray and Poole, 1976).

**Figure 11.1: The Structure of Northern Ireland Society**

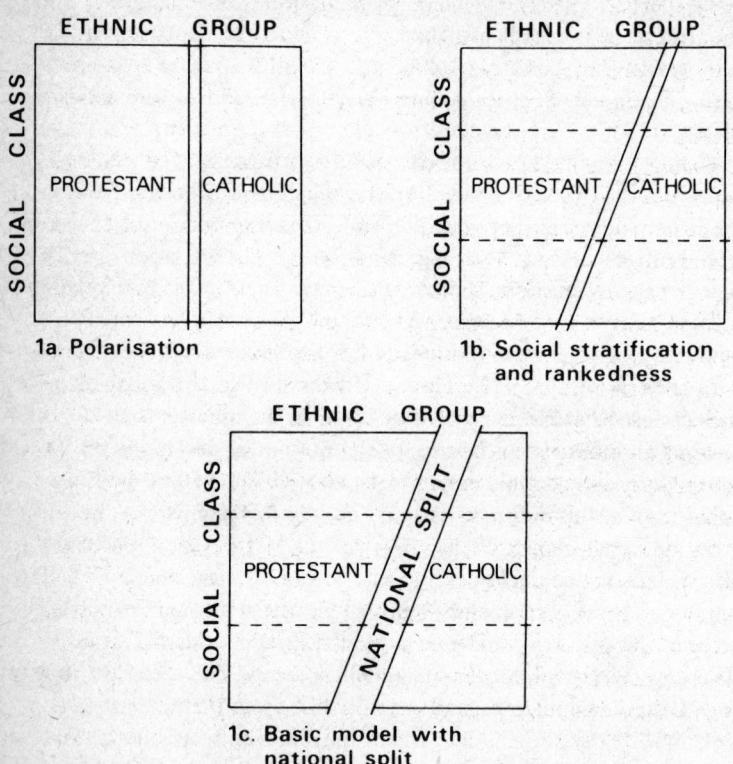

1a. Polarisation

1b. Social stratification and rankedness

1c. Basic model with national split

The basic structural attributes of ethnic relations in Northern Ireland can be expressed diagrammatically (Figure 11.1) and this provides a framework for the examination of ethnic residential segregation and mixing in Belfast. First, the two ethnic groups can be visualised as composing two distinct societies with limited interaction between them, both of them essentially normal societies except that the presence of the other group provides an external enemy, increasing group consciousness and enhancing ideological conformity within the groups and ideological distance between them. Boserup and Iversen (1967) refer to such a structure as polarisation (Figure 11.1a). Secondly, as in all societies characterised by capitalist economic organisation, social stratification exists. This cross-cuts the ethnic structure. However, as Boserup and Iversen suggest, there is also what they call a degree of rankedness present. While Protestants and Catholics are widely represented in all the main social class strata, Protestants are to a degree disproportionately represented in the non-manual and professional categories, and Catholics in the unskilled manual (Aunger, 1975) (Figure 11.1b). Finally we can impose a national split approximately along the line of ethnic cleavage (Figure 11.1c).

Figure 11.1c has also been constructed to emphasise the numerical majority-minority relationship of Protestants and Catholics, with Protestants forming approximately 63 per cent of the total population (Compton, 1978: 80). The majority-minority relationship is even more marked within the Belfast Urban Area, where in 1972 Protestants formed 75 per cent of *households* (Boal, Poole and Murray, 1976). However, the majority-minority relationship must also be viewed in a wider context in that if there was a constitutional change involving the formation of a politically united island of Ireland, Protestants would become a one-in-three minority. This creates what Jackson (1971) has referred to as the double-minority situation. It means that Protestant and Catholic behaviour and attitudes cannot be fully understood in terms of Northern Ireland majority-minority relationships alone. It also means that the struggle over resources is not confined to the bounds of urban territoriality but extends to questions of territoriality at an inter-state level. Solutions to problems of ethnic relations where a national split does not exist will have only limited relevance to Northern Ireland in general and to Belfast in particular.

### Segregation and Mixing in Belfast

Given the functions suggested earlier for ethnic segregation and given the conflict environment within which Belfast has developed as an urban centre (Boal and Murray, 1977) it is not surprising that there are high levels of segregation in the city, as shown by data derived from a household survey carried out in the Belfast Urban Area in the latter part of 1972 and into 1973 (Boal, Poole and Murray, 1976).[1] At that time 71 per cent of Protestant households resided in streets that were almost entirely Protestant; 66 per cent of Catholic households resided in streets that were almost entirely Catholic. Ethnic residential mixing does exist, however, and in an environment of conflict it is the existence of this mixing that is so unexpected, and perhaps, so difficult to explain.

To achieve an examination of the extent and character of ethnic residential mixing a two-fold classification system is imposed on the data. First, households are classified according to the ethnic composition of the street in which they reside. Households living in streets where 10 per cent or less of the households are of the opposite ethnic-religious persuasion to themselves are considered to be living in segregated situations (in practice the 0–9 per cent Catholic and the 91–100 per cent Catholic streets have very few 'minority' households present indeed). The broad band of streets 10–90 per cent Catholic is broken down into three subcategories. The first split is at 50 per cent, which provides an indicator as to whether a particular household is in an ethnic majority or ethnic minority situation. The second split is at 30 per cent. This is for two reasons — the fact that 30 per cent is reasonably close to the Catholic-Protestant household balance in the urban area as a whole, and the fact that 90 per cent of all households in ethnically mixed streets reside in Protestant majority situations. Consequently it will be useful to disaggregate the Protestant majority mixed streets into those that have a marked majority and those where the Protestant numerical predominance is less clear.

The second household classification imposed is that of 'house-category'. This attempts to absorb in one variable the separate variables of social class and tenure. Gordon (1964), through his concept of the Ethclass, indicates that social class divisions within ethnic groups may have considerable importance. Additionally, since segregation is the consequence of a very large number of individual location decisions within the framework of a housing system that is differentiated in terms of means of entry, it is important to bring the house tenure classification into consideration. An analysis of the distribution of occupationally differentiated households within the housing stock in Belfast (Poole, 1975) shows that two basic 'house-categories' can be distinguished. The first consists of all households in the private sector, whether owner-occupied or rented, with the exception of small terraced houses.[2] Throughout this category, non-manual households are overrepresented; this category is labelled *Upper*. The second consists of all households in the public sector, together with small terraced houses in the private sector. This category is throughout characterised by an overrepresentation of manual households, and is here labelled *Lower*. The *Lower* category was further subdivided into private and public sector housing as it was known that the specific procedures involved in acquiring housing in the two subcategories were quite different. We thus emerge with a trichotomous classification of households in terms of the type of dwelling occupied — *Upper*, *Lower Private* and *Lower Public*.

## Occurrence of Ethnic Residential Mixing

Table 11.1 provides the data for an examination of the degree and distribution of ethnic residential mixing in Belfast at the end of 1972.

**Table 11.1: Ethnic Residential Mixing, Belfast Urban Area 1972**

| Ethnic house-category group | Per cent in all mixed streets | Per cent in mixed streets that are (Per cent Catholic) | | | Per cent in mixed streets in majority situations |
|---|---|---|---|---|---|
| | | 10–29 | 30–49 | 50–90 | |
| Protestant Upper | 38 | 31 | 6 | 1 | 97 |
| Protestant Lower (Private) | 18 | 14 | 2 | 2 | 89 |
| Protestant Lower (Public) | 35 | 32 | 2 | 1 | 98 |
| Catholic Upper | 55 | 28 | 15 | 12 | 22 |
| Catholic Lower (Private) | 30 | 10 | 6 | 14 | 47 |
| Catholic Lower (Public) | 14 | 11 | 2 | 1 | 7 |

Households in the *Upper* category are the most likely to reside in mixed streets. This is most markedly the case with Catholic households (55 per cent in mixed streets). Next come Protestant households in the *Lower Public* category and Catholic households in the *Lower Private*. The least mixed households are the Protestant *Lower Private* and the Catholic *Lower Public* (18 and 14 per cent respectively in mixed streets). The greatest contrast exists between Catholic *Upper* and Catholic *Lower Public* households, the former being the most mixed, the latter the least.

We can go a step further and examine the situation, within the mixed streets, of households in the various ethnic house-category groups. It will be seen that Protestant households residing in mixed streets overwhelmingly experience majority situations while Catholic households markedly experience minority situations. However, the latter conclusion must be qualified by noting that Catholic *Lower Private* households are about equally divided between majority and minority mixing. Finally we can note not only that Protestants experience majority mixing whilst Catholics experience minority mixing, but also that a great deal of the mixing occurs in streets where Protestants form large majorities (streets 70–90 per cent Protestant).

A number of important contrasts between Protestant and Catholic households in mixed streets are evident. Catholics will tend to be younger than Protestants, and they are likely to have larger numbers of children. Within the *Upper* and *Lower Private* house-categories, Catholics are likely to have moved into their present dwelling more recently than Protestants and they are more likely to be owner-occupiers. Protestant-Catholic contrasts are most marked where Catholics form a majority, these contrasts being at their sharpest in the *Lower Private* house-category, where the Protestant population seems to form a small residual group: relatively elderly folk who have resided in their present dwelling for a long time.

### Perceived Ethnic Composition Change

Crucial to an understanding of ethnic residential mixing will be information on the extent to which the various mixed states are relatively unchanging or the extent to which they display change. One approach to this is through an examination of residents' perception of the degree of ethnic change in their local environs. Our survey (Boal, Poole and Murray, 1976) provides data on this. Respondents were asked to assess 'the religious composition of their neighbourhood' on a seven-point scale running from 'all Protestant', through 'same number Protestant and Catholic' to 'all Catholic'. They were asked to make the assessment for the time when they first took up residence in their present dwelling and for the time of interview.

The observations made *in situ* on neighbourhood ethnic environmental change suggest a division of the housing situations as follows:

1. streets 10 to 29 per cent Catholic: little change observed in the *Upper* house-category, some change towards more Protestant in the *Lower Private* category, and a more marked change towards

more Protestant in public sector housing;
2. streets 30 to 49 per cent Catholic: generally display a perceived shift towards a more Catholic environment;
3. streets 50 to 90 per cent Catholic: major shifts towards more Catholic environments observed for all three housing categories, the greatest shift of all being in the *Lower Private* situation.

Thus it is evident that, in the *Upper* house-category, the mixed streets with relatively small Catholic minorities display either considerable ethnic stability or only slow change. In the *Lower Private* and *Lower Public* categories these mixed streets display shifts towards more Protestant environments (that is, they are Catholic 'retreat' situations). Once the proportion Catholic in streets rises to over 30 per cent, however, the neighbourhood ethnic change pattern becomes quite different. Here the shift is towards more Catholic environments (in other words they are Protestant 'retreat' situations). The most marked of these retreat situations occurs within the *Lower Private* house-category where not only is there a greater degree of observed ethnic shift, but the actual numbers of households involved are considerably larger than is the case with the public sector.

## Discussion of Residential Mixing

In a situation of considerable ethnic conflict and ethnic residential segregation, ethnic residential mixing may occur where conflict is less severe, where substitutes for residential segregation are employed, or where the mixed areas are, in fact, transitional states. In the light of our examination of some of the characteristics of mixed area households and of their perception of the degree of ethnic change in their neigh-bourhoods, we can comment on these suggestions.

The first observation is that middle-class (*Upper* house-category) areas tend to be less ethnically segregated than working-class areas, or, in other words, a middle-class household is less likely to be located in a segregated street than a working-class household. Three reasons for this can be suggested. First, it has been observed, at least in cities in Western Europe and North America, that people like to live with others who belong to the same culture, share values, ideals and norms; understand and respond to the same symbols; and agree about child-rearing, interaction, density and life-style (Rapoport, 1977: 251). This can be associated with a further set of observations — that working-class areas have tighter-knit networks of social interaction within local areas and that the neighbourhood may be viewed as an extension of the home. Marc Fried has noted that with the middle class there is a relatively impermeable boundary between the walls of the dwelling and the street, whilst with the working class there is high permeability between the dwelling unit and the immediately environing area (Fried, 1973; Fried and Gleicher, 1961). The neighbourhood is an extension of the house (Willmott and Young, 1960). In these circumstances interaction within the local area will be intense and difficult to avoid. Thus ethnically incompatible neighbours will be undesirable. In the more privatised, lower-density middle-class areas, however, local interaction is less intense, contact with ethnic incompatibles may be minimised, and social networks developed that are much less dependent on the residents of one's own street. Thus, in the middle-class context, provided basic middle-class behavioural norms are adhered to, the presence of members of the 'other' ethnic group should not present too great difficulties. In the working-class context this presence becomes much more significant and the desired level of ethnic homogeneity will be raised significantly; and thus the levels of segregation increased over those   pertaining in the middle-class areas.

Greater degrees of ethnic residential mixing in the middle-class situation may also be a function of the lesser degree of inter-ethnic conflict within the middle-class (*Upper* house-category) group. The greater degree of conflict in the working-class context is generated by resource scarcity and competition: scarcity of reasonably good-quality working-class housing and competition for jobs.

A further factor that may contribute to more ethnic mixing in the middle-class context derives from the 'reservoir' hypothesis. This suggests that an ethnic group's reaction to the in-movement of a member of a different group will partly be conditioned by how large they perceive the reservoir of potential followers of that inmover. If the inmoving group is perceived as growing numerically as well as being large to start with, it will be seen as a much greater threat than a small or numerically stable group. In Belfast, Catholics are perceived as a growing group. More significantly in this context the class structure of the Catholic ethnic group is such that working-class Catholics compose a larger proportion of the working class than middle-class Catholics compose of the middle class. Thus it will be in working-class situations that Catholic in-movement will be perceived as having a considerable potential for accelerated growth, and where, consequently, it will be more strongly resisted, or alternatively, reacted to by accelerated out-movement by Protestants. Either way segregation will be increased in everything but the very short term. In the American context, 'future expectations about the fate of a neighborhood have appeared to play an important role in determining the rate at which neighborhoods may [racially] change' (Goering, 1978: 76).

A number of ethnic street situations have been pinpointed as being mixed but in a transitional state, in the process of which they become more ethnically segregated. The first point to be made here is that in most mixed streets Protestant households form substantial majorities. This is not surprising given the Protestant-Catholic balance of households in the Belfast Urban Area. For instance, in 1969, within the area of the old Belfast County Borough, about 25 per cent of households were Catholic. If all households were allocated randomly amongst the streets a distribution is generated whereby over three-quarters of all households are located in streets between 20 and 39 per cent Catholic (Poole and Boal, 1973: 25). This random distribution would, therefore, be one with the overwhelming majority of households living in mixed but Protestant majority streets. In fact only a minority of households live in mixed streets, but these streets are indeed over-whelmingly Protestant majority situations. A further observation follows, however. That is based on the evidence derived from residents' perceptions of neighbourhood ethnic change. This evidence suggests that where Catholic proportions of households at street-scale level exceed something of the order of 30 per cent, change in neighbourhood ethnic composition appears to be in the direction of more Catholic. On the other hand where Protestants are in excess of 70 per cent (with the exception of the *Upper* house-category), change seems to be towards more Protestant. This suggests that Protestants are not par-ticularly tolerant of situations where there is a large Catholic minority or where there is a Catholic majority, and Catholics do not favour situations where they are a small minority. The former interpretation is given some reinforcement by Fairleigh in a study of personality and social factors in what he calls 'religious' prejudice:

> The main finding was that the Protestants felt significantly more social distance from Catholics than did Catholics from Protestants. And religion was the most important factor associated with the Protestant decision — high social status was relatively unimportant if the religion was different. For the Catholic group, religion was

also an important consideration in the level of friendship envisaged, but slightly less than the other person's interests or jobs. (Fairleigh, 1976: 11)

Basically the nature of inter-ethnic relations and the insecurities and fears associated with local minority status create instability in many ethnically mixed contexts. This means that such contexts are ethnically transitional. This may well be reinforced by what Schelling (1974: 49) calls 'unravelling'. He suggests, as a general behavioural process, that many people may not want complete segregation, but they fear the prospect of becoming a small minority in a particular street or neighbourhood. Because of this they move house. This move changes the ethnic residential environment for others of their own group who find themselves becoming more isolated. They, in turn, respond to the new situation by moving. Thus over time the neighbourhood becomes completely segregated.

Our survey data indicate that the situations where the greatest number of households experience transitional mixing are those in the *Lower Private* house-category. These areas are basically working class and 'economically open' to the relatively large Catholic portion of that class. However, only limited spatial segments of the *Lower Private* housing stock display features of ethnic transition. These segments are in close proximity to inner Catholic areas and tend to lie outwards along the same sectors as these inner areas. 'Invasion' occurs within specific sectors – cross-sector movement is rare (Boal, 1969; 1978). An additional factor contributing to the ethnic transitivity of parts of the *Lower Private* stock is the spatially restricted pattern of the opportunity structure for Catholics, creating concentrated outward pressure.

Public sector mixed housing also indicates transition as a dominant theme. However, in this case transition has either already gone a long way or mixing was at a low level even before the latest outburst of open conflict starting in 1969. It seems likely that the segregating processes are at their most severe in the public sector. First, a considerable amount of new public sector stock is replacement housing for those displaced by inner-city redevelopment and the old areas that were redeveloped tended to be highly segregated to start with. The operation of the public sector system may present possibilities for manipulated ethnic residential mixing, particularly in periods of relatively subdued conflict. However, when conflict is severe, then the ease with which household transfers can be organised through the central authority is likely to facilitate segregating household moves (Murray and Osborne, 1977). In addition the obligation on the public authority to rehouse persons displaced by ethnic conflict means that the public sector has to provide for those households most likely to seek the security of an area dominated by their own group. Finally the very fact that the public sector stock is rental means that tenure is much less restricting on moves than is the case with owner-occupation. Basically, then, the public sector displays some ethnic transitional mixing, but in a context of very high degrees of segregation. The public sector housing resource has been divided into two fairly self-contained subsystems. Public sector stock rarely shifts from one ethnic group to another. Instead the resource conflict is focused on attempts to get as much as possible of new public housing located in areas that will be territorially pre-empted for one's own ethnic group.

## Conclusion

Ethnic residential segregation can clearly be seen as a resource preserving/conserving mechanism. It can also be viewed as a base for attempts to increase the resources available to a group. Exclusionary closure is a dominant theme. Ethnic residential mixing, on this basis, would appear to be a threat to ethnic group reproduction and resource conservation. However, it appears from our Belfast data that ethnic residential mixing occurs in two contexts: one where specifically ethnic resource conservation is seen to be less necessary, and where other mechanisms are substituted for ethnic residential segregation itself; and the other where instability exists in the ethnic residential spatial pattern, and where, in consequence, mixing represents a transitional state between two situations of exclusionary closure.

Instability can be created by localised conflict outbursts, by differential change in ethnic group numbers and by redevelopment and rehousing processes instigated by the public planning and housing sectors. Transition is likely to occur when there is a shift from the use of 'voice' to the use of 'exit' (Hirschman, 1970). Voice operates where an attempt is made to end an objectionable state of affairs (in this case the threat of residential invasion) without leaving the situation (that is by repelling the invaders). Exit occurs where escape from the objectionable state of affairs is the strategy adopted (that is, the group threatened with invasion begins to retreat). As Hirschman (1970: 83) says, 'the willingness to develop and use the voice mechanism is reduced by exit'. Thus if few housing alternatives are open, a group will hold its ground and mixing will be limited. If alternative (and relatively attractive) locations are available, the group may start to relocate, opening up entry opportunities for an incoming group. In this situation ethnic residential mixing will develop, but probably only in its transitional form. It seems reasonable to suggest that transitional mixing represents exclusionary closure adjustments, as one group retreats to re-establish its enclosure. Additionally the incoming group may be merely extending its exclusionary hold on territory and housing stock. It needs to be emphasised in the Belfast context that the recurrent outbursts of open ethnic conflict are crucial destabilising elements. The fact that Northern Ireland has, in Lord Hailsham's words, been 'indulging terrorism' for the whole of the 1970s decade, gives the current outburst an added significance.

Our evidence suggests that in the early 1970s not all ethnically mixed areas were transitional. It seems likely that in periods when ethnic conflict is less severe, many mixed residential areas will display much less transitivity than they have recently. In such circumstances inertia will not only retain existing segregation, it will also tend to retain mixing as well. An analogy with sand dunes suggests itself here — severe environmental conditions may damage or remove stabilising vegetation cover, leading to considerable instability in the sand dune systems; conversely a period of less severe environmental stress may lead to the establishment of stabilising vegetation cover and consequent stabilisation of the dunes themselves.

Earlier it has been claimed that ethnic residential segregation provides a base for usurpatory activity. To what extent can mixing be associated with this? The data on perception of ethnic change indicate that those mixed areas with a large Protestant majority (with the exception of *Upper* house-category) tend to be Catholic retreat situations. Equally Catholic majority areas tend to be situations of Protestant retreat. However, areas with relatively small Protestant majorities (streets 30—49 per cent Protestant) also seem to be ones of Protestant retreat. The large Protestant majority mixed areas seem to indicate the operation of exclusionary closure; that may also be true for the Catholic majority mixed areas. However, the perceived Catholic in-movement in the small Protestant majority areas appears to be a consequence of the joint operation of Protestants retreating to re-established exclusionary closure elsewhere on the one hand, and on the other of Catholics advancing in usurpatory moves to obtain more territory and an increment of housing stock. Additionally some of the majority Catholic mixed areas may represent the near terminal phase of similar exclusionary/usurpationary moves. Thus the application of Parkin's model to situations of ethnic residential segregation and ethnic residential mixing requires a subtle approach, and this no more so than in Belfast where the double-minority factor operates — that is, where Catholics are seen as the usurpationary group, Protestants as the exclusionary, but where the wider Irish context suggests to both groups a possible reversal of this relationship. Thus overriding the whole situation is the national split whereby one group (the Protestants) hopes to retain some degree of dominance within the existing constitutional frame, and whereby the other (the Catholics) hopes to reverse the dominance in an alternative 'all-Ireland' frame.

The nature and dynamics of ethnic residential segregation tell us a great deal about ethnic relations; the present study indicates that the same can be said of the nature and dynamics of ethnic residential mixing.

## Notes

1. The Belfast Urban Area is coextensive with the continuously built-up area. Belfast County Borough was the inner part of the built-up area (in American parlance, the 'central city'), and was governed by Belfast Corporation. The County Borough as a political unit was abolished in 1973.

2. Small terraced houses are distinguished by being either two-storey with a frontage of up to 7.5 metres or three-storey with a frontage of up to 5.0 metres.

## Bibliography

Aunger, E.A. (1975) 'Religion and Occupational Class in Northern Ireland', *Economic and Social Review*, 7, 1–18

Boal, F.W. (1969) 'Territoriality on the Shankill-Falls Divide, Belfast', *Irish Geography*, 6, 30–50

Boal, F.W. (1972) 'The Urban Residential Sub-community — A Conflict Interpretation', *Area*, 4, 161–8

Boal, F.W. (1976) 'Ethnic Residential Segregation', in D.T. Herbert and R.J. Johnston (eds.), *Social Areas in Cities, Volume 1: Spatial Processes and Form*, John Wiley, London, pp. 41–79

Boal, F.W. (1978) 'Territoriality on the Shankill-Falls Divide, Belfast: The Perspective from 1976', in D.A. Lanegran and R. Palm (eds.), *An Invitation to Geography* (Second Edition), McGraw-Hill, New York, pp. 58–77

Boal, F.W. (1980) 'Two Nations in Ireland', *Antipode*, 12, 38–44

Boal, F.W. and Murray, R.C. (1977) 'Belfast — City in Conflict', *Geographical Magazine*, 49, 364–71

Boal, F.W., Murray, R.C. and Poole, M.A. (1976) 'Belfast: The Urban

Encapsulation of a National Conflict', in S.E. Clarke and J.L. Obler (eds.), *Urban Ethnic Conflict: A Comparative Perspective*, Comparative Urban Studies Monograph No. 3, Institute of Research in Social Science, University of North Carolina, Chapel Hill, pp. 77–131

Boal, F.W., Poole, M.A. and Murray, R.C. (1976) 'Religious Residential Segregation and Residential Decision Making in the Belfast Urban Area', Report to Social Science Research Council, available from National Lending Library, Boston Spa, Yorkshire, England

Boserup, A. (1972) 'Contradictions and Struggles in Northern Ireland', *Socialist Register*, pp. 157–92

Boserup, A. and Iversen, C. (1967) 'Rank Analysis of a Polarized Community: A Case Study from Northern Ireland', *Papers, Peace Research Society (International)*, 8, 59–76

Compton, P.A. (1978) *Northern Ireland: A Census Atlas*, Gill and MacMillan, Dublin

Dahya, B. (1974) 'The Nature of Pakistani Ethnicity in Industrial Cities in Britain', in A. Cohen (ed.), *Urban Ethnicity*, Tavistock, London, pp. 77–118

Fairleigh, J. (1976) 'Personality and Social Factors in Religious Prejudice', in *Sectarianism – Roads to Reconciliation*, papers presented at the 22nd Annual Summer School of the Social Study Conference, Dungarvan, 1974, pp. 3–13

Fried, M. (1973) *The World of the Urban Working Class*, Harvard University Press, Cambridge, Massachusetts

Fried, M. and Gleicher, P. (1961) 'Some Sources of Residential Satisfaction in an Urban Slum', *Journal of the American Institute of Planners*, 28, 305–15

Goering, J.M. (1978) 'Neighborhood Tipping and Racial Transition: A Review of Social Science Evidence', *Journal of the American Institute of Planners*, 44, 68–78

Gordon, M.M. (1964) *Assimilation in American Life*, Oxford University Press, New York

Hechter, M. (1975) *Internal Colonialism: The Celtic Fringe in British National Development, 1536–1966*, University of California Press, Berkeley

Hiro, D. (1973) *Black British, White British*, Penguin Books, Harmondsworth, Middlesex

Hirschman, A.O. (1970) *Exit, Voice and Loyalty*, Harvard University Press, Cambridge, Massachusetts

Jackson, H. (1971) *The Two Irelands – A Dual Study of Intergroup Tensions*, Minority Rights Group, London

Kitson, F. (1971) *Low Intensity Operations*, Faber and Faber, London

Kramer, J.R. (1970) *The American Minority Community*, Thomas Y. Crowell, New York

Murray, R. and Osborne, R. (1977) 'Segregation on Horn Drive – A Cautionary Tale', *New Society*, 40, 106–8

Parkin, F. (1979) *Marxism and Class Theory: A Bourgeois Critique*, Tavistock Publications, London

Poole, M.A. (1975) 'Social Class and Housing Class', paper presented at the Institute of British Geographers Annual Conference, Oxford

Poole, M.A. and Boal, F.W. (1973) 'Religious Residential Segregation in Belfast in Mid-1969: A Multi-Level Analysis', in B.D. Clark and M.B. Gleave (eds.), *Social Patterns in Cities*, Institute of British Geographers Special Publication No. 5, London, pp. 1–40

Porter, J. (1975) 'Ethnic Pluralism in Canada', in N. Glazer and D.P. Moynihan (eds.), *Ethnicity: Theory and Experience*, Harvard University Press, Cambridge, Massachusetts, pp. 267–304

Rapoport, A. (1977) *Human Aspects of Urban Form*, Pergamon, Oxford
Robinson, P. (forthcoming) 'Plantation and Colonisation: The Historical
    Background', in F.W. Boal and J.N.H. Douglas (eds.), *Integration and
    Division: Geographical Perspectives on the Northern Ireland Problem*,
    Academic Press, London
Schelling, T. (1974) 'On the Ecology of Micromotives', in R. Marris (ed.),
    *The Corporate Society*, Macmillan, London, pp. 19–64
Stewart, A.T.Q. (1977) *The Narrow Ground: Aspects of Ulster, 1609–1969*,
    Faber, London
Willmott, P. and Young, M. (1960) *Family and Class in a London Suburb*,
    Routledge and Kegan Paul, London
Workers' Association (1973) *One Island: Two Nations*, Workers' Association,
    Belfast

## Acknowledgement

The financial support of the Social Science Research Council is gratefully
acknowledged.

# NOTES ON CONTRIBUTORS

HOWARD E. ALDRICH is Professor of Organizational Behaviour at the New York State School of Industrial and Labor Relations, Cornell University, Ithaca, USA. He is Associate Editor of *Administrative Science Quarterly* and author of *Organizations and Environments* (Prentice Hall, 1979) as well as numerous articles on organisational theory, the police, civil disorders and on ethnic minorities and business in the USA and UK.

F.W. BOAL is Reader in Geography, Department of Geography, Queen's University, Belfast, Northern Ireland. He is editor, together with J.N.H. Douglas, of *Integration and Division: Aspects of the Northern Ireland Problem* (Academic Press, forthcoming).

JOHN C. CATER is Lecturer in Geography at Edge Hill College of Higher Education, Ormskirk. He was previously Research Fellow on studies of ethnic residence and business at Liverpool Polytechnic. He is currently studying the interaction of institutional actors and immigrants in the housing and property markets.

PETER JACKSON is Lecturer in Geography, Department of Geography, University College London. A former Fulbright Visiting Fellow in the United States, he is co-editor, with Susan Smith, of *Social Interaction and Ethnic Segregation* (Academic Press, 1981).

DAVID R. JAMES is a sociologist at the University of Kansas. He was formerly a postdoctoral fellow at the Center for Demography and Ecology, University of Wisconsin.

TREVOR P. JONES is Senior Lecturer in Geography, Department of Social Studies, Liverpool Polytechnic. He is currently working on problem housing areas for the Borough of Knowsley.

NATHAN KANTROWITZ is Professor of the Department of Sociology and Anthropology, Kent State University, Kent, Ohio, USA. He is the author of *Ethnic and Racial Segregation in the New York Metropolis* (Praeger, 1973).

STANLEY LIEBERSON is Professor of Sociology, University of Arizona and was the Claude Bissell Distinguished Visiting Professor, University of Toronto, 1979–80. Among his many publications are *Ethnic Patterns in American Cities* (Free Press, 1963) and *A Piece of the Pie* (University of California Press, 1980).

DAVID McEVOY is Principal Lecturer in Geography, Department of Social Studies, Liverpool Polytechnic. With Aldrich, Cater and Jones he is extending their Social Science Research Council survey of Asian business in Bradford, Leicester and Ealing into a longitudinal study.

CERI PEACH is Lecturer in Geography at Oxford University and Fellow of St Catherine's College, Oxford. He is the author of *West Indian Migration to Britain: A Social Geography* (Institute of Race Relations and Oxford University Press, 1968) and is the editor of *Urban Social Segregation* (Longman, 1975).

JOHN REX is Director of the Social Science Research Council's Research Unit on Ethnic Relations and Professor of Sociology, University of Aston, Birmingham, England. He wrote, with Robert Moore, *Race Community and Conflict* (Institute of Race Relations and Oxford University Press, 1967) and, with Sally Tomlinson, *Colonial Immigrants in a British City: A Class Analysis* (Routledge and Kegan Paul, 1979).

VAUGHAN ROBINSON holds the Heyworth Prize Fellowship at Nuffield College, Oxford. He was awarded Oxford University's Frere Exhibition for Indian Studies in 1980. He is the author of numerous papers and monographs on Asian immigrants in Britain.

HAROLD M. ROSE is Professor of Urban Affairs and Geography at the University of Wisconsin-Milwaukee. He is the author of *The Black Ghetto: A Spatial Behavioral Perspective* (McGraw Hill, 1971), *Geography of the Ghetto: Perceptions, Problems and Alternatives* (Northern Illinois University Press, 1972) and *Black Suburbanization: Access to Improved Quality of Life or Maintenance of the Status Quo?* (Ballinger, 1976).

RONALD SIMS is Research Associate of the SSRC Research Unit on Ethnic Relations. He is a geographer working in the field of Asian residential settlement.

SUSAN SMITH is a Junior Reseach Fellow at St Peter's College Oxford. She is co-editor, with Peter Jackson, of *Social Interaction and Ethnic Segregation* (Academic Press, 1981).

ALMA F. TAEUBER served as Research Associate on the project, Demographic Effects of School Desegregation, at the Institute for Research on Poverty, University of Wisconsin. She is the author, with Karl E. Taeuber, of *Negroes in Cities* (Aldine, 1965).

KARL E. TAEUBER is Director of the Center for Demography and Ecology and Fellow at the Institute for Research on Poverty, University of Wisconsin. His research on housing and school segregation has been the basis for testimony as an expert witness in many school segregation trials.

ROBIN WARD is Deputy Director of the Social Sciences Research Council Research Unit on Ethnic Relations and Visiting Reader in Sociology at the University of Aston in Birmingham.

FRANKLIN D. WILSON, a sociologist and demographer at the University of Wisconsin, is the author of *Residential Consumption, Economic Opportunities and Race* (Academic Press, 1979). He was codirector, with Karl E. Taeuber, of the project, Demographic Effects of School Desegregation.

# INDEX